EVERYMAN CLASSICS

ALEXIS DE TOCQUEVILLE

The Ancien Regime

Translated by John Bonner

Introduction by Norman Hampson
Professor of History, University of York

J. M. Dent & Sons: London
EVERYMAN'S LIBRARY

Printed and bound in Great Britain by
Cox & Wyman Ltd, Reading
for
J.M. Dent & Sons Ltd
91 Clapham High Street, London SW4 7TA

First published as an Everyman Classic, 1988

No. 1438 Paperback ISBN 0 460 01438 2

Contents

Contents

Introduction

When the late Alfred Cobban once said to a group of historians of the French Revolution that one of their nineteenth-century predecessors stood out above all the rest, he did not need to mention any names. Everyone understood that he was referring to Alexis de Tocqueville. Why Tocqueville, who wrote only one comparatively short book about the origins of the revolution, should enjoy such an outstanding reputation, is not immediately obvious. Although he had originally intended to analyse both the revolution and its Napoleonic sequel, when he died, Tocqueville had not got beyond 1789. His book is about the way in which the Ancien Régime destroyed itself and it has virtually nothing to say about what happened afterwards.

Tocqueville's admirers have had no inhibitions about drawing attention to the defects of his work. His argument does not conform to any clear logical pattern. He first divided his book into two parts, then into three, but the different sections are not distinct and neither division is really satisfactory. When he returned to a subject that he had already treated, his emphasis was so different that he virtually contradicted himself. The most obvious and perhaps the most fundamental cause of the revolution was the monarchy's inability to solve its financial problems, but Tocqueville ignored this almost entirely. His method of argument was to substantiate broad generalisations by a few convenient illustrations that were not necessarily typical of the situations he was purporting to explain. Subsequent research has called the accuracy of his evidence into question: he presented the reign of Louis XVI as a period of prosperity when it is now regarded as one of relative recession. His treatment of specific subjects, such as the opposition to the revolution in the Vendée, could be extraordinarily superficial. If his book were to be submitted today for a PhD it would be unlikely to get one.

What he set out to do was to write 'philosophical' history. This was an eighteenth-century genre which, even in his own day, was beginning to look old-fashioned. In this kind of history, what matters is less the discovery of new evidence that the thinking of new thoughts. The historian is a man with a message for the society of his own times and the value of the message is not to be equated with the range and reliability of its documentation. If he is to convince his readers, the historian must not fly in the face of the evidence, but his main concern is to draw conclusions rather than to reveal complexities or to probe minutiae. Writers of this stamp took scholarship seriously – Tocqueville himself was a pioneer in the exploration of administrative history from archival sources – but they expected to be judged for their insight rather than their erudition. If we are to understand the nature of Tocqueville's book and the extraordinary extent of its influence we therefore have to start by finding out the kind of man he was and the way in which his own experience had led him to a particular vision of France's past and the problems that it posed.

Alexis de Tocqueville came from the old Norman nobility. Although his father, Hervé, was imprisoned during the Terror and most of his grandmother's family were guillotined, the Tocquevilles, in the nineteenth century, were neither cavalier royalists nor aristocratic die-hards. The history of the reign of Louis XVI that Hervé published in 1850 was curiously similar to the more famous book that his son brought out six years later, in its understanding of the point of view of both the revolutionaries and their opponents. There may have been some disappointment in the family when Alexis married an English commoner, but it did not do any lasting damage to his relationship with his father. It was not surprising that such a man should have combined an innate sympathy and respect for the aristocratic values of pre-revolutionary French society with an understanding of their limitations and an acceptance of the inevitability of change. His wife's nationality sharpened his awareness of what was specifically French, in contrast to the significantly different society that lay just across the Channel from his ancestral home.

Born in 1805, Alexis grew up during the Bourbon restoration and had begun to follow a legal career when the Bourbons were overthrown in 1830. Unlike many of his class, he accepted the

1830 revolution, although with some embarrassment, and in the following year he arranged to be sent on a mission to the United States, ostensibly to study American prisons. His year in America left him with ideas that were to colour the rest of his life. Whereas previous French commentators had tended to see America in terms of noble savages, primitive settlers and the adolescence of humanity, for Tocqueville it represented the future. He saw the United States as the embodiment of a kind of 'democratic' society that would spread irresistibly throughout the rest of the world. When he called it 'democratic' he was thinking as a sociologist rather than a political theorist, in terms of social equality rather than universal suffrage. Frenchmen, especially those of Tocqueville's own class, were inclined to equate democracy with Jacobins and the Terror. He saw its dangers as less dramatic and more insidious. What he valued most was individual liberty and he particularly admired the way in which Americans practised self-government and self-help. He conceived of liberty in a way that probably owed something to the aristocratic past of his family; it implied an assertion of the individual's independence of the state, his resistance to social pressures to conform, and his recognition of the obligation to public service. All of these were liable to be threatened by egalitarianism. Thanks to the Puritan origins of new England, the size of the country, its lack of any aristocratic past and the weakness of the central government, Tocqueville believed that the United States had escaped from the worst consequences of egalitarianism, both in terms of political centralisation and the temptation to put private comfort before collective endeavour.

Tocqueville's concern, however, was with France, rather than America and when he looked back across the Atlantic he became alarmed. The accidental factors that had preserved the United States from the worst dangers of democracy would not be there to exercise their beneficent influence when the irresistible egalitarian tide reached the French coast. In France, a tradition of bureaucratic centralisation – accepted by revolutionaries, Bonapartists and royalists alike – left to central government most of the decisions that the Americans had to take for themselves. When the spread of social equality had eliminated a leisured class with its tradition of public service, the leaderless masses would be content to practise the private virtues in their homes, public life would wither and, whatever the form of their constitution, Frenchmen would no longer be in control of their own destinies, unless purposeful political action could protect the values that circumstances would otherwise endanger.

When Tocqueville set all this down, in *Democracy in America*, he became an instant celebrity. In 1839 he was elected to the National Assembly and two years later he was made a member of the French Academy. His political career soon gave him practical experience of the problems of democracy in France. When the Orleanist monarchy was overthrown in February 1848, Tocqueville accepted this revolution, as he had accepted the previous one, and he was elected to the new republican Assembly. From the outset, however, he was preoccupied with what he saw as the danger of mob violence and social revolution. He foresaw and thoroughly approved of the bloody repression of June 1848. Foreign Minister for several months in 1849, he suspected the ambition of the new President, Louis Napoleon, but could see no way of thwarting him, except by popular insurrection that seemed to him even worse. When Louis Napoleon seized power in 1851, the coup d'état put an end to Tocqueville's political career and returned him to private life until his death in 1859.

In his enforced retirement, Tocqueville turned back to the problem that he had been facing, on and off, since the 1830s – the implicit subject of *Democracy in America* : why was it so difficult to establish political liberty in France? Formerly he had diagnosed the disease; after the coup d'état all that remained was to prepare a post-morten on the victim. His first instinct was to attribute the responsibility to that other Bonaparte who had seized power in 1799, and Tocqueville had written a couple of chapters on the Consulate before he realised that he was beginning his story in the middle. Always more concerned with the functioning of institutions than with the gladiatorial contests of politicians, he dismissed the French Revolution as 'a transitory and fairly uninteresting period separating the administrative Ancien Régime from the administrative system created by the

Consulate'. His problem was therefore to explain how the former had given rise to the latter. The place to look for the answer, from his point of view, was not in the political records of the old royal government or the revolutionary Assemblies, but in the archives of the provincial administration, which showed what actually happened in practice. It was from this background, with these preoccupations and sustained by this evidence, that the *Ancien Régime* emerged.

In his foreword, Tocqueville claimed never to have shared the common belief that 1789 had constituted a new start in French history. This followed logically from the importance he attached to *moeurs*, the national characteristics which determined how institutions would actually work and how a people would respond to the accidents of its political history. Tocqueville set himself three problems: why the revolution took place in France when the decay of the old aristocratic order was common to the whole of Europe; why a movement produced by the Ancien Régime should have been so intent on destroying it; why a process that was to culminate in the establishment of an empire should have begun by overthrowing a monarchy. He then repeated the message of *Democracy in America* that the demise of aristocratic society was inevitable. This process was particularly liable to lead to despotism in the case of countries like France, unlike England which had retained its aristocracy, and America which had never had one to lose. Democracy brought individualism, in the sense of each man thinking primarily of his own personal comfort and the pursuit of wealth. Like his contemporary, Mazzini, Tocqueville believed that, in an egalitarian society, liberty alone could lead men to concert with each other and to transcend their individual limitations in the pursuit of a collective purpose. Despotism had no such rewards to offer but it demanded fewer material sacrifices and, once established, it was likely to prove self-perpetuating. The real subject of his book was therefore democracy in France.

He began his first volume by trying to define the nature of the French Revolution. In opposition to the conventional royalist

view, he said that it was not so much an anti-religious movement as a new religion in its own right, which aspired to the
regeneration of the human race. As such, it was part of a
European trend, and it was not the first of its kind. What made it
different from all the others was not the nature of the message
but the receptivity of the society to which it was addressed. This
was not confined to France. The whole of Europe had shared
similar feudal institutions, which had gradually been superseded
by absolute monarchies. Although feudal institutions were
everywhere in decay by 1789, feudal attitudes still survived and
with them some vestiges of aristocractic liberties that had long
lost their original social justification. The achievement of the
revolution was therefore to complete the work of the monarchy
by sweeping away not merely the surviving ruins of feudal
institutions, but the mental attitudes that had outlived them. Its
destruction of privilege meant that the entire population had
either to attain to a new dignity as citizens or succumb to a new
degradation as subjects. The revolutionary crisis itself was
merely the logical outcome of a movement that had been under
way for generations, 'Chance played no part whatever in the
outbreak of the revolution.'

The first dozen chapters of Book II, which he grouped as a
separate book in his second edition, addressed his first question:
why did the crisis occur in France? He argued that 'feudalism'
was more bitterly hated in France than in Central and Eastern
Europe, not because it was more oppressive but because a free
peasantry was better able to resist and more disposed to
challenge seigneurs who had retained their privileges when they
had been deprived of the local power and responsibility that
had formerly legitimised them. This was Tocqueville's cue for a
long examination of the ways in which the monarchy had
stripped all classes – nobles, bourgeois and peasants – of the
right to manage their own affairs, the kind of local self-
government that had so much impressed him in America. Even
the sovereign law courts, or parlements, which from time to time
challenged the monarchy on political issues, found their jurisdiction more and more curtailed as the government created special
courts to punish the infringement of its own regulations. The

result of all this was a mechanical state in which every form of local and individual initiative had been suppressed. Even reformers took it for granted that any improvements must be planned and executed by the central government.

Tocqueville then went on to describe the social consequences of bureaucratic centralisation. With the destruction of all centres of local power, and of all intermediate authorities, Frenchmen had become more like each other, in the sense that the state treated them all equally, as subjects. The distinctive character-istics of the provinces were similarly eroded by the central government. Tocqueville believed that because the nobility had lost much of their wealth, along with their power, in this respect too, they had become more like the middle class. The growing homogeneity of the population made for more tension rather than less. What had once been a meaningful social hierarchy, accepted by both its upper and its lower elements, survived merely as privilege without responsibility, which set one section of society against another. The nobility had become an exclusive caste and as the burden of taxation increased, their fiscal privileges became more obvious and more offensive to the rest of the population. Wealthy commoners fled to the towns, not to enjoy the benefits of self-government, but to avoid having to collect taxes, and to compete for such personal advantages as municipal office afforded. Everywhere, privilege had become an exemption from common obligations rather than a reward for the discharge of local duties. It was challenged all the more vigorously since its beneficiaries no longer inspired any fear.

As if conscious that he had gone too far and left the revolutionaries without much to do, Tocqueville then back-tracked. With all its faults, the Ancien Régime had to be better than the society that had taken its place. He therefore conceded that the holders of venal offices had enjoyed the kind of independence that came from security in their jobs. Privileges and social prejudices, however unjustified and divisive, had encouraged a minority of the population to assert what it claimed as its rights. Some provinces had retained their local estates, with the limited autonomy that this implied. The clergy in particular were a self-financing and self-governing body, with the self-confidence that came from their education and their practice of the kind of political action that, for Tocqueville, was both the manifestation of liberty and the means of preserving it. In their attitude towards the peasantry, the middle classes had developed some of the attitudes of an aristocracy. The law courts had retained their independence of the state and they had given all sections of society the habit of prosecuting claims by law, rather than by force. The population as a whole was free from the enervating obsession with material well-being that he believed to be the particular curse of his own century.

Putting it all together, Tocqueville arrived at the predictable conclusion that there had been more liberty in the eighteenth century than there was in his own day; not enough to provide the basis for a free society, but sufficient to produce the memorable protagonists of 1789. Alexis, like his father, had a good deal of admiration for the energy and dedication of the revolutionaries, whatever his views about the consequences of their actions.

He then reverted to his previous argument, devoting an especially sympathetic chapter to the plight of the peasantry, isolated from their natural leaders in the other classes, increasingly exploited, as he thought, by a rural squirearchy that no longer felt responsible for them, and deserted by their priests. This was Tocqueville at his most impressionistic, waving aside objections with the bland assurance that 'I am speaking of classes; they alone should concern the historian'. Whatever the validity of his conclusions, they were at least proof that he had no romantic illusions about the merits of the 'good old days'.

He next transferred his attention to the intellectual side of the Ancien Régime, in a transition so abrupt that he later decided to make it the beginning of a third book. As always, his concern was to explain a movement in terms of the social factors that he believed to have determined it, rather than to treat it as a subject in its own right, full of particularities and internal contradictions. For him, the Enlightenment was a social product and he was not interested in exploring the individual contributions of particular men. This meant lumping together writers who had bitterly opposed each other's ideas. It also involved him in some rather tendentious assumptions. Excluded, like everyone else, from experience of political life, the French philosophers had taken refuge in abstractions. They saw everything in terms of universal principles and their confidence in human perfectibility was unclouded by the sobering experience of actual government. At the same time, unlike their German contemporaries, who were in the same boat, they had *chosen* to direct their attention to human rights and natural law, rather than to metaphysics. This had made them the only politicans in a depoliticised society. True to form, Tocqueville argued that the ideas themselves were not new; what gave them a new force was their enthusiastic reception throughout an entire population that had lost its bearings, its social cohesion and the sense of political reality that comes from responsibility for finding workable solutions to practical problems. What made France unique in Europe was the extent to which the Enlightenment had penetrated all levels of society. What it had done was to substitute a new religion of Man for a Church that was rejected as traditional, hierarchical and dedicated to the service of an authority that transcended human reason. Tocqueville would not have been the complicated man he was if he had remained wholly unmoved by the spectacle of this collective crusade for the redemption of humanity. He believed that only the French were capable of such a unique rejection of both the temporal and the spiritual status quo and he could not wholly condemn a movement that 'tore men away from their individual egoism', even if he found something Satanic in their revolt.

Where the Enlightenment showed its cloven hoof, in his opinion, was in putting public utility and social engineering before liberty. If this was indeed the case, it seemed to sever its link with the revolution, and Tocqueville, who had previously argued that the French Revolution was inevitable, now said that if France had had a ruler like Frederick II of Prussia, the Ancien Régime could have been given a new lease of life by reform from above. This brought him to look at the reign of Louis XVI. Since he was never much concerned about economic history, he was able to convince himself that this had been a period of prosperity in which the evils of the Ancien Régime that he had analysed at such length had been substantially reduced. Taxes had been raised with more humanity; the upper classes had begun to call attention to the sufferings of their inferiors, and the government itself had initiated a policy of reform. In the process, it publicised the existence of injustices that it then found itself unable to eliminate. Well-intentioned ministers, by the arbitrary way in which they sought to improve on ancient institutions, destroyed all respect for tradition and the rights of individuals, and gave future revolutionaries a lesson in the unrestricted use of state power.

This ushered in Tocqueville's conclusion. The Ancien Régime had by now become thoroughly unstable. 'Feudalism' had retained only its oppressive aspects, while the monarchy had done away with its *raison d'être*. The nobility had been isolated from the rest of the community, increasingly hated for its ever more visible privileges, as it lost the authority that had once been accepted as justifying them. Centralisation, with its concentration of power and population in Paris, had made the government vulnerable to insurrection. The Church had lost its moral authority since it had come to be regarded as part of a morally discredited order. A depoliticised society responded to the siren voices of the philosophers offering instant solutions to every problem. Tocqueville believed that the outbreak of revolution had been the occasion when the 'people' had taken command of a state apparatus that had been busily engaged in bringing about its own destruction. The revolution had seen the brief fusion of the passions for liberty and for equality, but while the former was fleeting and fragile, the latter was more robust and abiding. If the objective was essentially equality, the quickest way to achieve it was by taking over the power of the state and developing it for new purposes. He ended with a final paradox that drastically modified, if it did not contradict, much of his previous argument: the revolution could only have occurred in France, because of unspecified national characteristics of the French people which had remained basically unchanged over two or three millennia.

There is scarcely an assertion in all this involved argument that present-day historians would not feel inclined to challenge. Some of it is blatantly self-contradictory. Tocqueville claimed, for example, in his conclusion, that eighteenth-century French government had been exceptionally mild – and then went on to attribute the extreme violence of the revolution to the fact that the 'people' had been brutalised by their recent sufferings. A contemporary critic accused him of arriving at his conclusions before he began to examine the evidence. This was going rather too far, but his conception of history meant that all the evidence had to point in the same direction – which it never does – and involved him in some unconvincing mental gymnastics. We are therefore left with no answer to our original question: why is his book universally accepted as a classic and why has it so successfully withstood the erosion of time?

Part of the answer lies in the fact that there are so many insights in the *Ancien Régime* that it can serve as grist for almost any mill. The Marxist historian, Georges Lefebvre, interpreted Tocqueville's search for a means of preserving the virtues of aristocratic society within a world that was becoming increasingly egalitarian, in economic terms. Tocqueville, as Lefebvre understood him, was looking for 'a government where the old nobility and the upper-middle class would unite in defence of their ownership of the means of production, which constituted the basis for their pre-eminence'. Lefebvre, without quite recruiting Tocqueville to the Marxist cause, praised him for writing analytical rather than descriptive history, for putting the emphasis on social and economic forces rather than on individuals, for his determinism and for recognising the existence of sudden mutations like that of 1789, within the continuous historical process.

More recently, François Furet has extracted a very different ore from the same seams. For Furet, Tocqueville's great merit was that, instead of treating the revolution as a kind of gigantic hiatus, he reintegrated it within the continuous unfolding of French history, as the acceleration of an age-old process rather than a new start. As a historian of ideas, Furet maintained that the *Ancien Régime* differed from *Democracy in America* in the sense that Tocqueville liberated intellectual and political forces from what he had previously believed to be their dependence on social ones, and gave them their autonomy. His revolution was not so much a product of social determinism as a transformation of values and mental attitudes, even a matter of national temperament. It was, in fact, 'the realisation of an ideological eschatology'. Tocqueville's main contribution to the theory of revolutions was his appreciation of their obscurity, since those who participated in them were blinded at every turn by their own ideology. Furet's Tocqueville, in other words, contradicts Lefebvre's in just about every conceivable way.

There is more to this than trailing Tocqueville as a reluctant captive behind one's own triumphant chariot. It is almost impossible for anyone to put forward a view of the nature and significance of the French Revolution that has not been anticipated, in one form or another, by Tocqueville. For him, as for Marx, it was a decisive stage in the creation of modern society, a particularly dramatic episode in a universal process, rather than a unique event to be studied outside its temporal context. This was the way in which contemporaries saw it, not merely in France, but in the England of Blake and Wordsworth and the Germany of Kant and Goethe. Inseparable from this view of the revolution is the feeling that it was also, in some sense, a missed opportunity. The day that ensued did not live up to the promise of that dawn when it was bliss to be alive. Any account of the French revolution that ignores these two dimensions, however great its erudition, is not aiming at the heart of the matter.

Tocqueville put first things first. He was trying to explain why and how the revolution mattered. He may have been mistaken about some of his evidence or bullied it into seeming to support his conclusions, but his was an honest and profound mind expounding the truth as he understood it and his insights may still be meaningful even when the evidence that originally supported them is no longer acceptable. Concern for accuracy is a very proper preoccupation of the historian. When he neglects it he becomes a mere propagandist, a peddler of quack medicines. But there is more to truth than the avoidance of error, and accuracy alone never made great history. There will always be something to learn from Tocqueville and those who are unable to subscribe to the gospel will still benefit from the sermon.

Tocqueville's truths were different from those of Marx. They would have been more comprehensible to the revolutionaries themselves, whose actions, after all, determined what the historian's material was going to be. His central propositions are hard to deny. The kind of aristocratic society that he described as 'feudal' has been in continuous retreat throughout the world, until it has virtually disappeared. In that sense, we are all democrats now, from Leningrad to Los Angeles. One of the main causes of this process has been the growth of political and administrative centralisation. To an extent that would have exceeded Tocqueville's most pessimistic forecasts, the omnipotence of governments, and their readiness to coerce and manipulate their subjects, have been characteristic of the twentieth century, whether the governments in question have been fascist, communist or 'liberal'. In part the demise of aristocratic society has also been due to pressure from below, whether exercised peacefully or through revolution. Few would dare to claim that the result of all this has been an extension of human liberty, whether this is defined in the negative sense, as the non-infringement of human rights, or conceived more positively as the assertion of human dignity by active participation in the self-government of a free community.

Freedom in the aristocratic sense was a matter of liberties rather than of liberty, of the exemption of some from the obligations imposed on others. Exclusiveness was of its essence, since to generalise it would have destroyed its meaning. It may have been vicious in principle but it did engender habits of independence that imposed limits on the oppressive power of the state, from which the population as a whole may, in some instances, have benefited. It has gone for good and if Tocqueville, in certain moods, was half-inclined to regret it, he had no illusions about its limitations or about the possibility of ever restoring it. The all-important question for him was whether a 'democratic' society could generate the energy and will itself to accept the self-restraint that alone would be able to sustain

xviii INTRODUCTION

political liberty in the future. Jacksonian America suggested that it might be possible, but most of the cards in the American hand were trumps. Tocqueville had hoped that intelligence, foresight and will might win for France what circumstances had given to the United States. When he wrote the *Ancien Régime* it looked as though he had been too optimistic. Three revolutions and two empires suggested that Frenchmen would never be able to resist the temptation to snatch up the bureaucratic wand that had fallen from the hands of the monarchy and play at sorcerer's apprentices with it. Whatever their motives, Jacobins and Bonapartists were both intent on bringing the people into conformity with the institutions that were thought to be good for them. The restored Bourbons, in their turn, had been content to leave ill alone and to make few structural changes to their flawed inheritance.

For all its pessimism, the tone of the *Ancien Régime* is nevertheless not one of despair, perhaps not even one of resignation. The revolution of 1789 had inspired men to transcend their individual limitations in their dedication to a common purpose. Everything had gone wrong, and not by accident, but if Tocqueville had really believed that understanding why they had lost their way would do nothing to help his fellow-countrymen to find it again, he would presumably not have laboured so hard and so long for the melancholy satisfaction of proving to them that their predicament was beyond hope.

Tocqueville's two cheers for democracy are very much our own concern. He himself regarded England as in most respects, and notably in the surviving strength of its aristocracy, an exception to the European rule. America was another world. Both countries have changed a good deal since then, and not always for the better. They have become more 'European' in the sense that in neither can the cause of individual liberty be left to the providential operation of exceptional social or geographical circumstances. As their distinctiveness fades, Tocqueville's analysis of how France failed to solve its own problems becomes more relevant to them too. Its universal message has become more urgent as its ostensible subject sinks back into history. As an explanation of the origins of the French Revolution, the

Ancien Régime has become less and less acceptable; as a primer for democrats it is more important than ever.

February 1988   N. Hampson

Select Bibliography

A. DE TOCQUEVILLE
Oeuvres complètes (ed. J.P. Mayer).
Democracy in America, Eng. trans. New York, 1969.
The Ancien Régime and the Revolution (introduction by Georges Lefebvre), Eng. trans. New York, 1955 (vol. II contains Tocqueville's drafts for the sequel that he did not live to complete).
Souvenirs (introduction by F. Braudel), Eng. trans. New York, 1970.
G. LEFEBVRE
'A propos de Tocqueville' (*Annales historiques de la Révolution française* XXVII, 1955).
M. REINHARD
'Tocqueville, Historien de la Révolution Française' (*Annales historiques de la Révolution française* XXXII, 1960).
J. LIVELY
The Social and Political Thought of Alexis de Tocqueville, Oxford, 1962.
R. HERR
Tocqueville and the Old Regime, Princeton, 1962.
F. FURET
'Tocqueville and the Problem of the French Revolution' in *Interpreting the French Revolution*, Eng. trans. Cambridge, 1981.
A. JARDIN
Alexis de Tocqueville , Paris, 1984.
R. R. PALMER
The Two Tocquevilles: Father and Son, Princeton, 1987.

Biographical Notes

ALEXIS DE TOCQUEVILLE was born in Paris on 29 July 1805. His father was a royalist prefect who was made a peer of France by Charles X. Although Tocqueville was of a delicate disposition, he chose to pursue the demanding career of a politician. After the July Revolution of 1830 when Tocqueville's position became precarious because of his father's royalist connections, he obtained permission to visit America in order to study prison reform. Among the various publications which followed was the first part of Tocqueville's best known work, *Democracy in America*, which focused on social equality and liberty. The work was acclaimed in America as well as throughout Europe, and particularly in England where, during his visit in 1835, Tocqueville established many lifelong friendships, including that of John Stuart Mill. His ties were reinforced by his marriage in 1836 to an Englishwoman, Mary Mottely. Tocqueville was elected to the Chamber of Deputies in 1839, but it was not until after the February Revolution of 1848, when he was elected to the Constituent Assembly, that he began to exert his influence. He also served as minister of foreign affairs from June to October 1849 but was dismissed by Louis Napoleon who then briefly imprisoned him for opposing the coup d'etat in December 1851. He was subsequently deprived of all political offices for refusing allegiance to the new regime. He then began years of research which culminated in the publication of *L'ancien régime et la Révolution* in 1856, which again brought him public acclaim. He died at Cannes on 16 April 1859.

NORMAN HAMPSON was born in Lancashire in 1922. His education, at Manchester Grammar School and University College, Oxford, was interrupted by four years' service in the navy, including two with the Free French. After graduation he joined the staff of Manchester University, working first in the extra-mural and then in the French and History departments. In 1967 he became Professor of Modern History at Newcastle upon Tyne, moving to York in 1974. His books include *A Social History of the French Revolution* (1963), *The Enlightenment* (1968), *The Life and Opinions of Maximilien Robespierre* (1974), *Will and Circumstance* (1983) and *Prelude to Terror* (1988).

Preface

The book I now publish is not a history of the Revolution. That history has been too brilliantly written for me to think of writing it afresh. This is a mere essay on the Revolution.

The French made, in 1789, the greatest effort that has ever been made by any people to sever their history into two parts so to speak, and to tear open a gulf between their past and their future. In this design, they took the greatest care to leave every trace of their past condition behind them; they imposed all kinds of restraints upon themselves in order to be different from their ancestry; they omitted nothing which could disguise them.

I have always fancied that they were less successful in this enterprise than has been generally believed abroad, or even supposed at home. I have always suspected that they unconsciously retained most of the sentiments, habits, and ideas which the old regime had taught them, and by whose aid they achieved the Revolution; and that, without intending it, they used its ruins as materials for the construction of their new society. Hence it seemed that the proper way of studying the Revolution was to forget, for a time, the France we see before us, and to examine, in its grave, the France that is gone. That is the task which I have here endeavoured to perform; it has been more arduous than I had imagined.

The early ages of the monarchy, the Middle Ages, and the period of revival have been thoroughly studied; the labours of the authors who have chosen them for their theme have acquainted us not only with the events of history, but also with the laws, the customs, the spirit of the government and of the nation in those days. No one has yet thought of examining the eighteenth century in the same close, careful manner. We fancy that we are familiar with French Society of that age because we see clearly what glittered on its surface, and possess detailed biographies of the illustrious characters, and ingenious or eloquent criticisms on the works of the great writers who flourished at the time. But of the manner in which public business was transacted, of the real working of institutions, of the true relative position of the various classes of society, of the condition and feelings of those classes which were neither heard nor seen, of the actual opinions and customs of the day, we have only confused and frequently erroneous notions.

I have undertaken to grope into the heart of this old regime. It is not far distant from us in years, but the Revolution hides it.

To succeed in the task, I have not only read the celebrated books which the eighteenth century produced; I have studied many works which are comparatively unknown, and deservedly so, but which, as their composition betrays but little art, afford perhaps a still truer index to the instincts of the age. I have endeavoured to make myself acquainted with all the public documents in which the French expressed their opinions and their views at the approach of the Revolution. I have derived much information on this head from the reports of the States, and, at a later period, from those of the Provincial Assemblies. I have freely used the *cahiers,* which were presented by the three orders in 1789. These *cahiers,* whose originals form a large series of folio volumes, will ever remain as the testament of the old French society, the final expression of its wishes, the authentic statement of its last will. They are a historical document that is unique.

Nor have I confined my studies to these. In countries where the supreme power is predominant, very few ideas, or desires, or grievances can exist without coming before it in some shape or other. But few interests can be created or passions aroused that are not at some time laid bare before it. Its archives reveal not merely its own proceedings, but the movement of the whole nation. Free access to the files of the Department of the Interior and the various prefectures would soon enable a foreigner to know more about France than we do ourselves. In the eighteenth century, as a perusal of this work will show, the government was already highly centralized, very powerful, prodigiously active. It was constantly at work aiding, prohibiting, permitting this or that. It had much to promise, much to give. It exercised paramount influence not only over the transaction of business, but over the prospects of families and the private life of individuals. None of its business was made public; hence people did not shrink from confiding to it their most secret infirmities. I have devoted much time to the study of its remains at Paris and in the provinces.*

I have found in them, as I anticipated, the actual life of the old regime, its ideas, its passions, its prejudices, its practices. I have found men speaking freely their inmost thoughts in their own language. I have thus obtained much information upon the old regime which was unknown even to the men who lived under it, for I had access to sources which were closed to them.

As I progressed in my labours, I was surprised to find in the France of that day many features which are conspicuous in the France we have before us. I met with a host of feelings and ideas which I have always credited to the Revolution, and many habits which it is supposed to have engendered; I found on every side the roots of our modern society deeply imbedded in the old soil. The nearer I drew to 1789, the more distinctly I noticed the spirit which brought about the Revolution. The actual physiognomy of the Revolution was gradually disclosed before me. Its temper, its genius were apparent; it was all there. I saw there not only the secret of its earliest efforts, but the promise also of its ultimate results – for the Revolution had two distinct phases: one during which the French seemed to want to destroy every remnant of the past, another during which they tried to regain a portion of what they had thrown off. Many of the laws and political usages of the old regime which disappeared in 1789 reappeared some years afterward, just as some rivers bury themselves in the earth and rise to the surface at a distance, washing new shores with the old waters.

The especial objects of the work I now present to the public are to explain why the Revolution, which was impending over

---

* I have made especial use of the archives of some of the greater intendants' offices, such as those of Tours, which are very complete; they refer to a very large district (*généralité*), placed in the centre of France, and containing a million of souls. My thanks are due to the young and able keeper of the archives, M. Grandmaison. Other intendants' offices, such as that of Ile de France, have satisfied me that business was conducted on the same plan throughout most of the kingdom

every European country, burst forth in France rather than elsewhere; why it issued spontaneously from the society which it was to destroy; and how the old monarchy contrived to fall so completely and so suddenly.

My design is to pursue the work beyond these limits. I intend, if I have time and my strength does not fail me, to follow through the vicissitudes of their long revolution these Frenchmen with whom I have lived on such familiar terms under the old regime; to see them throwing off the shape they had borrowed from this old regime, and assuming new shapes to suit events, yet never changing their nature, or wholly disguising the old familiar features by changes of expression.

I shall first go over the period of 1789, when their affections were divided between the love of freedom and the love of equality; when they desired to established free as well as democratic institutions, and to acknowledge and confirm rights as well as to destroy privileges. This was an era of youth, of enthusiasm, of pride, of generous and heartfelt passions; despite its errors, men will remember it long, and for many a day to come it will disturb the slumbers of those who seek to corrupt or to enslave the French.

In the course of a hasty sketch of the Revolution, I shall endeavour to show what errors, what faults, what disappointments led the French to abandon their first aim, to forget liberty, and to aspire to become the equal servants of the master of the world; how a far stronger and more absolute government than the one the Revolution overthrew then seized and monopolized all political power, suppressed all the liberties which had been so dearly bought, and set up in their stead empty shams; deprived electors of all means of obtaining information, of the right of assemblage, and of the faculty of exercising a choice, yet talked of popular sovereignty; said the taxes were freely voted, when mute or enslaved assemblies assented to their imposition; and, while stripping the nation of every vestige of self-government, of constitutional guarantees, and of liberty of thought, speech, and the press – that is to say, of the most precious and the noblest conquest of 1789 – still dared to claim descent from that great era.

I shall stop at the period at which the work of the Revolution appears complete, and the new society created. I shall the.. examine that new society. I shall try to discover wherein it resembles and wherein it differs from the society which preceded it; to ascertain what we have gained and what we have lost by the universal earthquake; and shall lastly attempt to foresee our future prospects.

A portion of this second work I have roughly sketched, but it is not yet fit for the public eye. Shall I be permitted to finish it? Who knows? The fate of individuals is even more obsure than that of nations.

I trust I have written this work without prejudice; but I do not claim to have written dispassionately. It would be hardly decent for a Frenchman to be calm when he speaks of his country, and thinks of the times. I admit that, in studying every feature of the society of other times, I have never lost sight of that which we see before us. I have tried not only to detect the disease of which the patient died, but to discover the remedy that might have saved him. I have acted like those physicians who try to surprise the vital principle in each paralysed organ. My object has been to draw a perfectly accurate, and, at the same time, an instructive picture. Whenever I have found among our ancestors any of those masculine virtues which we need so much and possess so little – a true spirit of independence, a taste for true greatness, faith in ourselves and in our cause – I have brought them boldly forward; and, in like manner, whenever I have discovered in the laws, or ideas, or manners of olden time, any trace of those vices which destroyed the old regime and weaken us today, I have taken pains to throw light on them, so that the sight of their mischievous effects in the past might prove a warning for the future.

In pursuing this object, I have not, I confess, allowed myself to be influenced by fears of wounding either individuals or classes, or shocking opinions or recollections, however respectable they may be. I have often felt regret in pursuing this course, but remorse, never. Those whom I may have offended must forgive me, in consideration of the honesty and disinterestedness of my aim.

I may perhaps be charged with evincing in this work a most inopportune love for freedom, about which I am assured that Frenchmen have ceased to care.

I can only reply to those who urge this charge that in me the feeling is of ancient date. More than twenty years have elapsed since I wrote, in reference to another society, almost these very words.

In the darkness of the future three truths may be plainly discerned. The first is, that all the men of our day are driven, sometimes slowly, sometimes violently, by an unknown force – which may possibly be regulated or moderated, but can not be overcome – toward the destruction of aristocracies. The second is, that, among all human societies, those in which there exists and can exist no aristocracy are precisely those in which it will be most difficult to resist, for any length of time, the establishment of despotism. And the third is, that despotisms can never be so injurious as in societies of this nature; for despotism is the form of government which is best adapted to facilitate the development of the vices to which these societies are prone, and naturally encourages the very propensities that are indigenous in their disposition.

When men are no longer bound together by caste, class, corporate or family ties, they are only too prone to give their whole thoughts to their private interest, and to wrap themselves up in a narrow individuality in which public virtue is stifled. Despostism does not combat this tendency; on the contrary, it renders it irresistible for it deprives citizens of all common passions, mutual necessities, need of a common understanding, opportunity for combined action: it ripens them, so to speak, in private life. They had a tendency to hold themselves aloof from each other: it isolates them. They looked coldly on each other: it freezes their souls.

In societies of this stamp, in which there are no fixed landmarks, every man is constantly spurred on by a desire to rise and a fear of falling. And as money, which is the chief mark by which men are classified and divided one from the other, fluctuates incessantly, passes from hand to hand, alters the rank of individuals, raises families here, lowers them there, every one is forced to make constant and desperate efforts to acquire or retain it. Hence the ruling passions become a desire for wealth at all cost, a taste for business, a love of gain, and a liking for comfort and material pleasures. These passions pervade all classes, not excepting those which have hitherto been strangers to them. If they are not checked they will soon enervate and degrade them all. Now, it is essential to despotism to encourage and foster them. Debilitating passions are its natural allies; they serve to divert attention from public affairs, and render the very name of revolution terrible. Despotism alone can supply the secrecy and darkness which cupidity requires to be at ease, and which embolden men to brave dishonour for the sake of fraudulent gain. These passions would have been strong in the absence of despotism: with its aid they are paramount.

On the other hand, liberty alone can combat the vices which are natural to this class of societies, and arrest their downward progress. Nothing but liberty can draw men forth from the isolation into which their independence naturally drives them – can compel them to associate together, in order to come to a common understanding, to debate, and to compromise together on their joint concerns. Liberty alone can free them from money-worship, and divert them from their petty, everyday business cares, to teach them and make them feel that there is a country above and beside them. It alone awakens more energetic and higher passions than the love of ease, provides ambition with nobler aims than the acquisition of wealth, and yields the light which reveals, in clear outline, the virtues and the vices of mankind.

Democratic societies which are not free may be rich, refined, ornate, even magnificent, and powerful in proportion to the weight of their homogeneous mass; they may develop private virtues, produce good famly-men, honest merchants, respectable landowners, and even good Christians – for their country is not of this world, and it is the glory of their religion that it produces them in the most corrupt societies and under the worst governments – the Roman empire during its decline was full of such as these; but there are things which such societies as those I speak of can never produce, and these are great citizens, and, above all, a great people. I will go farther; I do not hesitate to affirm that the common level of hearts and minds will never cease to sink so long as equality and despotism are combined.

This is what I thought and wrote twenty years ago. I acknowledge that nothing has since happened that could lead me to think or write otherwise. As I made known my good opinion of liberty when it was in favour, I cannot be blamed for adhering to that opinion now that it is in disgrace.

I must, moreover, beg to assure my opponents that I do not differ from them as widely as they perhaps imagine. Where is the man whose soul is naturally so base that he would rather be subject to the caprices of one of his fellow-men than obey laws which he had helped to make himself, if he thought his nation sufficiently virtuous to make a good use of liberty? I do not think such a man exists. Despots acknowledge that liberty is an excellent thing; but they want it all for themselves, and maintain that the rest of the world is unworthy of it. Thus there is no difference of opinion in reference to liberty; we differ only in our appreciation of men; and thus it may be strictly said that one's love for despotism is in exact proportion to one's contempt for one's country. I must beg to be allowed to wait a little longer before I embrace that sentiment.

I may say, I think, without undue self-laudation, that this book is the fruit of great labour. I could point to more than one short chapter that has cost me over a year's work. I could have loaded my pages with footnotes, but I have preferred inserting a few only, and placing them at the end of the volume, with a reference to the pages to which they apply. They contain examples and proofs of the facts stated in the text. I could furnish many more if this book induced anyone to take the trouble of asking for them.

BOOK FIRST

Chapter 1

Contradictory Opinions formed upon the Revolution when it broke out.

Philosophers and statesmen may learn a valuable lesson of modesty from the history of our Revolution, for there never were events greater, better prepared, longer matured, and yet so little foreseen.

With all his genius, Frederick the Great had no perception of what was at hand. He touched the Revolution, so to speak, but he did not see it. More than this, while he seemed to be acting according to his own impulse, he was, in fact, its forerunner and agent. Yet he did not recognize its approach; and when at length it appeared full in view, the new and extraordinary characteristics which distinguished it from the common run of revolutions escaped his notice.

Abroad, it excited universal curiosity. It gave birth to a vague notion that a new era was at hand. Nations entertained indistinct hopes of changes and reforms, but no one suspected what they were to be. Princes and ministers did not even feel the confused presentiment which it stirred in the minds of their subjects. They viewed it simply as one of those chronic diseases to which every national constitution is subject, and whose only effect is to pave the way for political enterprises on the part of neighbours. When they spoke truly about it, it was unconsciously. When the principal sovereigns of Germany proclaimed at Pilnitz, in 1791, that all the powers of Europe were menaced by the danger which threatened royalty in France, they said what was true, but at bottom they were far from thinking so. Secret dispatches of the time prove that these expressions were only intended as clever pretexts to mask their real purposes, and disguise them from the public eye. They knew perfectly well – or thought they knew – that the French Revolution was a mere local and ephemeral accident, which might be turned to account. In this faith they formed plans, made preparations, contracted secret alliances; quarrelled among themselves about the booty they saw before them; were reconciled, and again divided; were ready, in short, for everything except that which was going to happen.

Englishmen, enlightened by the experience of their own history, and trained by a long enjoyment of political liberty, saw, through a thick mist, the steady advances of a great revolution; but they could not discern its form, or foresee the influence it was destined to exercise over the world and over their own interests. Arthur Young, who travelled through France just before the outbreak of the Revolution, was so far from suspecting its real consequences that he rather feared it might increase the power of the privileged classes. 'As for the nobility and the clergy,' says he, 'if this revolution enhances their preponderance, I fear it will do more harm than good.'

Burke's mind was illumined by the hatred he bore to the Revolution from the first; still he doubted for a time. His first inference was that France would be weakened, if not annihilated. 'France is at this time,' he said, 'in a political light, to be considered as expunged out of the system of Europe. Whether she can ever appear in it again as a leading power is not easy to determine; but at present I consider France as not politically existing, and most assuredly it would take up much time to restore her to her former active existence. *Gallos quoque in bellis floruisse audivimus* – "We have heard that the Gauls too were once noted in war," may be the remark of the present generation, as it was of an ancient one.'

Men judged as loosely on the spot. On the eve of the outbreak, no one in France knew what would be the result. Among all the contemporaneous *cahiers*, I have only found two which seem to mark any apprehension of the people. Fears are expressed that royalty, or the court, as it was still called, will retain undue preponderance. The States-General are said to be too feeble, too short-lived. Alarm is felt lest they should suffer violence. The nobility is very uneasy on this head. Several *cahiers* affirm that 'the Swiss troops will swear never to attack the citizens, even in case of affray or revolt'. If the States-General are free, all the abuses may be corrected; the necessary reform is extensive, but easy.

Meanwhile the Revolution pursued its course. It was not till the strange and terrible physiognomy of the monster's head was visible; till it destroyed civil as well as political institutions, manners, customs, laws, and even the mother tongue; till, having dashed in pieces the machine of government, it shook the foundations of society, and seemed anxious to assail even God himself; till it overflowed the frontier, and, by dint of methods unknown before, by new systems of tactics, by murderous maxims, and 'armed opinions' (to use the language of Pitt), overthrew the landmarks of empires, broke crowns, and crushed subjects, while, strange to say, it won them over to its side: it was not till then that a change came over men's minds. Then sovereigns and statesmen began to see that what they had taken for a mere everyday accident in history was an event so new, so contrary to all former experience, so widespread, so monstrous and incomprehensible, that the human mind was lost in endeavouring to examine it. Some supposed that this unknown power, whose strength nothing could enhance and nothing diminish, which could not be checked, and which could not check itself, was destined to lead human society to complete and final dissolution. M. de Maistre, in 1797, observed that 'the French Revolution has a satanic character'. On the other hand, others discerned the hand of God in the Revolution, and inferred a gracious design of Providence to people France and the world with a new and better species. Several writers of that day seem to have been exercised by a sort of religious terror, such as Salvian felt at the sight of the barbarians. Burke, pursuing his idea, exclaims, 'Deprived of the old government, deprived in a manner of all government, France, fallen as a monarchy to common speculators, appears more likely to be an object of pity or insult, according to the disposition of the circumjacent powers, than to be the scourge and terror of them all; but out of the tomb of the murdered monarchy in France has arisen a vast, tremendous, unformed spectre, in a far more terrific guise than any which ever yet have overpowered the imagination and subdued the fortitude of man. Going straight forward to its end, unappalled by peril, unchecked by remorse, despising all common maxims and all common means, that hideous phantom has overpowered those who could not believe it was possible she could at all exist except on the principles which habit rather than nature has persuaded them are necessary to their own particular welfare and to their own ordinary modes of action.'

Now, was the Revolution, in reality, as extraordinary as it seemed to its contemporaries? Was it as unexampled, as deeply subversive as they supposed? What was the real meaning, what the true character of this strange and terrible revolution? What did it actually destroy? What did it create?

It appears that the proper time has come to put these questions and to answer them. This is the most opportune moment for an inquiry and a judgment upon the vast topic they embrace. Time has cleared from our eyes the film of passion which blinded those who took part in the movement, and time has not yet impaired our capacity to appreciate the spirit which animated them. A short while hence the task will have become arduous, for successful revolutions obliterate their causes, and thus, by their own act, become inexplicable.

Chapter 2

That the fundamental and final Object of the Revolution was not, as some have supposed, to destroy religious and to weaken political Authority.

One of the first measures of the French Revolution was an attack upon the Church. Of all the passions to which that Revolution gave birth, that of irreligion was the first kindled, as it was the last extinguished. Even when the first enthusiasm of liberty had worn off, and peace had been purchased by the sacrifice of freedom, hostility to religion survived. Napoleon subdued the liberal spirit of the Revolution, but he could not conquer its anti-Christian tendencies. Even in the times in which we live, men have fancied they were redeeming their servility to the most slender officials of the state by their insolence to God, and have renounced all that was free, noble, and exalted in the doctrines of the Revolution, in the belief that they were still faithful to its spirit so long as they were infidels.

Yet nothing is easier than to satisfy one's self that the anti-religious war was a mere incident of the great Revolution; a striking, but fleeting expression of its physiognomy; a temporary result of ideas, and passions, and accidents which preceded it – anything but its own proper fruit.

It is generally understood – and justly so – that the philosophy of the eighteenth century was one of the chief causes of the Revolution; and it is not to be denied that that philosophy was deeply irreligious; but it was twofold, and the two divisions are widely distinct.

One division or system contained all the new or revived opinions with reference to the conditions of society, and the principles of civil and political law. Such were, for example, the doctrines of the natural equality of man, and the consequent abolition of all caste, class, or professional privileges, popular sovereignty, the paramount authority of the social body, the uniformity of rules. . . . These doctrines are not only the cause of the French Revolution; they are, so to speak, its substance; they constitute the most fundamental, the most durable, the truest portion of its work.

The other system was widely different. Its leaders attacked the Church with absolute fury. They assailed its clergy, its hierarchy, its institutions, its doctrines; to overthrow these, they tried to tear up Christianity by the roots. But this portion of the philosophy of the eighteenth century derived its origin from objects which the Revolution destroyed: it naturally disappeared with its cause, and was, so to speak, buried in its triumph. I purpose returning to this great topic hereafter, and will add but one word here in order to explain myself more fully. Christianity was hated by these philosophers less as a religious doctrine than as a political institution; not because the priests assumed to regulate the concerns of the other world, but because they were landlords, seigniors, tithe-holders, administrators in this; not because the Church could not find a place in the new society which was being established, but because she then occupied the place of honour, privilege, and might in the society which was to be overthrown.

See how time has confirmed this view, and is still confirming it under our own eyes! Simultaneously with the consolidation of the political work of the Revolution, its religious work has been undone. The more thoroughly the political institutions it assailed have been destroyed; the more completely the powers, influences, and classes which were peculiarly obnoxious to it have been conquered, and have ceased in their ruin to be objects of hatred; in fine, the more the clergy have held themselves aloof from the institutions which formerly fell by their side, the higher has the power of the Church risen, and deeper has it taken root in men's minds.

This phenomenon is not peculiar to France; every Christian Church in Europe has gained ground since the French Revolution.

Nothing can be more erroneous than to suppose that democracy is naturally hostile to religion. Neither Christianity nor even Catholicism involves any contradiction to the democratic principle; both are, in some respects, decidedly favourable to it. All experience, indeed, shows that the religious instinct has invariably taken deepest root in the popular heart. All the religions which have disappeared found a last refuge there. Strange, indeed, it would be if the tendency of institutions based on the predominance of the popular will and popular passions were necessarily and absolutely to impel the human mind toward impiety.

All that I have said of religions I may repeat with additional emphasis in regard to political authority.

When the Revolution overthrew simultaneously all the institutions and all the usages which had governed society and restrained mankind within bounds, it was, perhaps, only natural to suppose that its result would be the destruction, not of one particular frame of society, but of all social order; not of this or that government, but of all public authority. There was a degree of plausibility in assuming that it aimed essentially at anarchy; yet I will venture to say that this also was an illusion.

Less than a year after the Revolution had begun, Mirabeau wrote secretly to the king, 'Compare the present state of things with the old regime, and console yourself and take hope. A part – the greater part of the acts of the national assembly are decidedly favourable to a monarchical government. Is it nothing to have got rid of Parliament, separate states, the clerical body, the privileged classes, and the nobility? Richelieu would have liked the idea of forming but one class of citizens; so level a surface assists the exercise of power. A series of absolute reigns would have done less for royal authority than this one year of Revolution.' He understood the Revolution like a man who was competent to lead it.

The French Revolution did not aim merely at a change in an old government; it designed to abolish the old form of society. It was bound to assail all forms of established authority together; to destroy acknowledged influences; to efface traditions; to substitute new manners and usages for the old ones; in a word, to sweep out of men's minds all the notions which had hitherto commanded respect and obedience. Hence its singular anarchical aspect.

But a close inspection brings to light from under the ruins an immense central power, which has gathered together and grasped all the several particles of authority and influence formerly scattered among a host of secondary powers, orders, classes, professions, families, and individuals, sown broadcast, so to speak, over the whole social body. No such power had been seen in the world since the fall of the Roman empire. This new power was created by the Revolution, or, rather, it grew spontaneously out of the ruins the Revolution made. If the governments it created were fragile, they were still far stronger than any that had preceded them, and their very fragility, as will be shown hereafter, sprang from the same cause as their strength.

It was the simple, regular, grand form of this central power which Mirabeau discerned through the dust of the crumbling institutions of olden time. The masses did not see it, great as it was. Time gradually disclosed it to all; and now, princes can see nothing else. Admiration and envy of its work fill the mind, not only of the sovereigns it created, but of those who were strangers or inimical to its progress. All are busy destroying immunities, abolishing privileges throughout their dominions; mingling ranks, leveling, substituting hired officials in the room of an aristocracy, a uniform set of laws in the place of local franchises, a single strong government instead of a system of diversified authorities. Their industry in this revolutionary work is unceasing; when they meet an obstacle, they will sometimes even borrow a hint or a maxim from the Revolution. They have been noticed inciting the poor against the rich, the commoner against the noble, the peasant against his lord. The French Revolution was both their scourge and their tutor.

Chapter 3

That the French Revolution, though political, pursued the same Course as a religious Revolution, and why.

All political and civil revolutions have been confined to a single country. The French Revolution had no country; one of its leading effects appeared to be to efface national boundaries from the map. It united and divided men, in spite of law, traditions, characters, language; converted enemies into fellow-countrymen, and brothers into foes; or, rather, to speak more precisely, it created, far above particular nationalities, an intellectual country that was common to all, and in which every human creature could obtain rights of citizenship.

No similar feature can be discovered in any other political revolution recorded in history. But it occurs in certain religious revolutions. Therefore those who wish to examine the French Revolution by the light of analogy must compare it with religious revolutions.

Schiller observes with truth, in his History of the Thirty Years' War, that one striking effect of the Reformation was that it led to sudden alliances and warm friendships among nations which hardly knew each other. Frenchmen were seen, for instance, fighting against Frenchmen, with Englishmen in their ranks. Men born on distant Baltic shores marched down into the heart of Germany to protect Germans of whom they had never heard before. All the foreign wars of the time partook of the nature of civil wars; in all the civil wars foreigners bore arms. Old interests were forgotten in the clash of new ones; questions of territory gave way to questions of principle. All the old rules of politics and diplomacy were at fault, to the great surprise and grief of the politicians of the day. Precisely similar were the events which followed 1789 in Europe.

The French Revolution, though political, assumed the guise and tactics of a religious revolution. Some further points of resemblance between the two may be noticed. The former not only spread beyond the limits of France, but, like religious revolutions, spread by preaching and propagandism. A political revolution, which inspired proselytism, and whose doctrines were preached abroad with as much warmth as they were practised at home, was certainly a new spectacle, the most strikingly original of all the novelties which were presented to the world by the French Revolution. But we must not stop here. Let us go further, and try to discover whether these parallel results did not flow from parallel causes.

Religions commonly affect mankind in the abstract, without allowance for additions or changes effected by laws, customs, or national traditions. Their chief aim is to regulate the concerns of man with God, and the reciprocal duties of men toward each other, independently of social institutions. They deal, not with men of any particular nation or any particular age, but with men as sons, fathers, servants, masters, neighbours. Based on principles essential to human nature, they are applicable and suited to all races of men. Hence it is that religious revolutions have swept over such extensive areas, and have rarely been confined, as political revolutions have, to the territory of one people, or even one race; and the more abstract their character, the wider they have spread, in spite of differences of laws, climate, and race.

The old forms of paganism, which were all more or less interwoven with political and social systems, and whose dogmas wore a national and sometimes a sort of municipal aspect, rarely travelled beyond the frontiers of a single country. They gave rise to occasional outbursts of intolerance and persecution, but never to proselytism. Hence, the first religious revolution felt in

Western Europe was caused by the establishment of Christianity. That faith easily overstepped the boundaries which had checked the outgrowth of pagan systems, and rapidly conquered a large portion of the human race. I hope I shall exhibit no disrespect for that holy faith if I suggest that it owed its successes, in some degree, to its unusual disentanglement from all national peculiarities, forms of government, social institutions, and local or temporary considerations.

The French Revolution acted, with regard to things of this world, precisely as religious revolutions have acted with regard to things of the other. It dealt with the citizen in the abstract, independent of particular social organizations, just as religions deal with mankind in general, independent of time and place. It inquired, not what were the particular rights of French citizens, but what were the general rights and duties of mankind in reference to political concerns.

It was by thus divesting itself of all that was peculiar to one race or time, and by reverting to natural principles of social order and goverment, that it became intelligible to all, and susceptible of simultaneous imitation in a hundred different places.

By seeming to tend rather to the regeneration of the human race than to the reform of France alone, it roused passions such as the most violent political revolutions had been incapable of awakening. It inspired proselytism, and gave birth to propagandism; and hence assumed that quasi religious character which so terrified those who saw it, or, rather, became a sort of new religion, imperfect, it is true, without God, worship, or future life, but still able, like Islamism, to cover the earth with its soldiers, its apostles, and its martyrs.

It must not be supposed that all its methods were unprecedented, or all the ideas it brought forward absolutely original. On many former occasions, even in the heart of the Middle Ages, agitators had invoked the general principles on which human societies rest for the purpose of overthrowing particular customs, and had assailed the constitution of their country with arguments drawn from the natural rights of man; but all these experiments had been failures. The torch which set Europe on fire in the eighteenth century was easily extinguished in the fifteenth. Arguments of this kind can not succeed till certain changes in the condition, customs, and minds of men have prepared a way for their reception.

There are times when men differ so widely that the bare idea of a common law for all appears unintelligible. There are others, again, when they will recognize at a glance the least approach toward such a law, and embrace it eagerly.

The great wonder is not that the French Revolution employed the methods it did, and conceived the ideas it brought forth; what is wonderful and startling is that mankind had reached a point at which these methods could be usefully employed, and these ideas readily admitted.

Chapter 4

How the same Institutions had been established over nearly all Europe, and were everywhere falling to pieces.

The tribes which overthrew the Roman empire, and eventually constituted modern nations, differed in race, origin, and language; they were alike in barbarism only. They found the empire in hopeless confusion, which they aggravated; and thus, when they settled, each was isolated from the others by the ruins it had made. Civilization was almost extinct. Social order had ceased to exist. International communication was difficult and dangerous. Safety dictated the division of the great European family into a thousand little states, which soon became exclusive and hostile to each other.

Yet out of this chaos uniform laws suddenly issued.

They were not borrowed from Roman legislation. They were, indeed, so much opposed to it that the old Roman law was the instrument afterward used to transform and abolish them. [1] Their principles were original, and wholly different from any that had ever been broached before. Composed of symmetrical parts, knit together as closely as the articles of any modern code, they constituted a body of really learned laws for the use of a semi-barbarous people.

It is not my design to inquire how such a system was formed and spread over Europe. I merely note the fact that, during the Middle Ages, it existed to some extent in every country; and in many, to the total exclusion of all other systems.

I have had occasion to study the political institutions which flourished in England, France, and Germany during the Middle Ages. As I advanced in the work, I have been filled with amazement at the wonderful similarity of the laws established by races so far apart and so widely different. They vary constantly and infinitely, it is true, in matters of detail, but in the main they are identical everywhere. Whenever I discovered in the old legislation of Germany a political institution, a rule, or a power, I knew that a thorough search would bring something similar to light in France and England; and I never failed to find it so. Each of the three nations enabled me to understand the other two.

In all three the government was carried on in accordance with the same principles: the political assemblies were constituted from the same materials, and armed with the same powers; society was divided into the same classes, on the same sliding-scale; the nobles occupied the same rank, enjoyed the same privileges, were marked by the same natural characteristics – in short, the men were, properly speaking, identically the same in all.

The city constitutions resembled each other; the rural districts were governed on one uniform plan. There was no material difference in the condition of the peasantry; land was held, occupied, cultivated on the same plan, and the farmer paid the same taxes. From the confines of Poland to the Irish Sea we can trace the same seigniories, seigniors' court, feuds, rents, feudal services, feudal rights, corporate bodies. Sometimes the names are the same, and, what is still more remarkable, the same idea pervades all these analogous institutions. I think it is safe to say that in the fourteenth century the various social, political, administrative, judicial, economical, and literary institutions of Europe were more nearly alike than they are now, though civilization has done so much to facilitate intercourse and efface national barriers.

The task I have undertaken does not require me to relate how this old constitution of Europe gradually gave way and broke down; I merely state that in the eighteenth century it was in proximate ruin everywhere. [2] Decay was least conspicuous in the eastern half of the continent, and most in the west; but old age and decrepitude were prominent on all sides.

The records of the old Middle-Age institutions contain the history of their decline. It is well known that land registers (*terriers*) were kept in each seigniory, in which, century after century, were entered the boundaries of the feuds and seigniories, the rents due, the services to be rendered, the local customs. I have seen registers of the fourteenth and thirteenth centuries, which are masterpieces of method, perspicuity, and intellect. The more modern ones grow more obscure, more incomplete, more confused as they approach our own day. It would seem as though the civilization of society had involved the relapse of the political system into barbarism.

The old European constitution was better preserved in Germany than in France; but there, too, a portion of the institutions to which it had given life were already destroyed. One can judge of the ravages of time, however, better from the portion which survived than from that which had perished.

Of the municipal franchises which, in the thirteenth and fourteenth centuries, had converted the chief cities of Germany into rich and enlightened republics, [3] a mere empty shadow remained. Their enactments were unrepealed; their magistrates bore the old titles, and appeared to perform the old duties; but the activity, the energy, the civic patriotism, the manly and fruitful virtues of olden time had vanished. These venerable institutions seemed to have sunk down without distortion.

All the surviving medieval sources of authority had suffered from the same disease; all alike were decayed and languishing. Nor was this all: everything which, without actually growing out of the medieval system, had been connected with it and marked by its stamp, seemed equally lifeless. Aristocracy wore an air of servile debility. Even political freedom, which had filled the Middle Ages with its works, became sterile in the dress in which they had clothed it. Those provincial assemblies which had preserved their old constitution in its integrity were rather a hindrance than a help to civilization. They presented a stolid, impenetrable front to the march of intellect, and drove the people into the arms of monarchs. There was nothing venerable in the age of these institutions; the older they grew, the smaller their claims to respect; and somehow, the more harmless they became, the more hatred they seemed to inspire. A German writer, whose sympathies were all on the side of the old regime under which he lived, says, 'The present state of things is shameful for all of us, and even contemptible. It is strange how unfavourably men look upon everything that is old. Novelty penetrates even the family circle, and overturns its peace. Our very housekeepers want to get rid of their old furniture.' Yet in Germany, as in France, society was then thrilling with activity, and highly prosperous; but (mark this well! it is the finishing touch to the picture) every living, acting, producing agent was new, and not only new, but contrary to the old.

Royalty had nothing in common with medieval royalty; its prerogatives were different, its rank had changed, its spirit was new, the homage it received was unusual. The central power encroached on every side upon decaying local franchises. A hierarchy of public functionaries usurped the authority of the nobles. All these new powers employed methods and took for their guide principles which the Middle Ages either never knew or rejected, and which, indeed, were only suitable for a state of society they never conceived.

At first blush it would appear that the old constitution of Europe is still in force in England; but, on a closer view, this illusion is dispelled. Forget old names, pass over old forms, and you will find the feudal system substantially abolished there as early as the seventeenth century: all classes freely intermingled, an eclipsed nobility, an aristocracy open to all, wealth installed as the supreme power, all men equal before the law, equal taxes, a free press, public debates – phenomena which were all unknown to medieval society. It was the skilful infusion of this young blood into the old feudal body which preserved its life, and imbued it with fresh vitality, without divesting it of its ancient shape. England was a modern nation in the seventeenth century, though it preserved, as it were embalmed, some relics of the Middle Ages.

This hasty glance at foreign nations was essential to a right comprehension of the following pages. No one can understand the French Revolution without having seen and studied something more than France.

Chapter 5

What did the French Revolution really achieve?

The object of the preceding inquiries was to clear the way for the solution of the question I originally put: What was the real object of the Revolution? what was its peculiar character? why was it brought about? what did it achieve?

It is an error to suppose, as some have done, that the object of the Revolution was to overthrow the sovereignty of religious creeds. Despite appearances, it was essentially a social and political revolution. It did not tend to perpetuate or consolidate disorder, to 'methodize anarchy' (as one of its leading opponents remarked), but rather to augment the power and the rights of public authority. It was not calculated to change the character of our civilization, as others imagined, or to arrest its progress, or even to alter, essentially, any of the fundamental laws upon which our Western societies rest. When it is disengaged from the extraneous incidents which imparted a temporary colouring to its complexion, and is examined on its own proper merits, it will be seen that its sole effect was to abolish those institutions which had held undivided sway over Europe for several centuries, and which are usually known as the feudal system; in order to substitute therefor a social and political organization marked by more uniformity and more simplicity, and resting on the basis of the equality of all ranks.

That alone required a stupendous revolution; for these old institutions were not only connected and interwoven with all the religious and political laws of Europe, but had, besides, created a host of ideas, and feelings and habits, and customs, which had grown up around them. To destroy and cut out of the social body a part which clung to so many organs involved a frightful operation. This made the Revolution appear even greater than it was. It appeared the universal destroyer; for what it did destroy was linked, and, in some degree, incorporated with almost everything else.

Radical as it was, the Revolution introduced fewer innovations than has been generally supposed, as I shall have occasion to show hereafter. What it really achieved was the destruction – total, or partial, for the work is still in progress – of everything which proceeded from the old aristocratical and feudal institutions, and of everything which clung to them or bore in any way their distinguishing mark. It respected no legacy of the past but such as had been foreign to these institutions, and could exist without them.

It was, least of all, a casual accident. True, it took the world by surprise; yet it was the mere natural result of very long labours, the sudden and violent termination of a task which had successively engaged ten generations of men. Had it never taken place, the old social edifice would none the less have fallen, though it would have given way piecemeal instead of breaking down with a crash. The Revolution effected suddenly, by a convulsive and sudden effort, without transition, precautions, or pity, what would have been gradually effected by time had it never occurred. That was its achievement.

It is surprising that this fact, which we discern so plainly today, should have once been hidden from the eyes of the shrewdest observers. Burke appeals to the French: 'Had you but made it to be understood that, in the delusion of your amiable error, you had gone farther than your wise ancestors; that you were resolved to assume your ancient privileges while you preserved the spirit of your ancient and your recent loyalty and honour; or, if diffident of yourselves, and not clearly discerning the almost obliterated constitution of your ancestors, you had but looked to your neighbours in this land, who had kept alive the ancient principles and the models of the old common law of Europe. . . .'

Burke can not see that the real object of the Revolution is to abolish that very common law in Europe; he does not perceive that that, and nothing else, is the gist of the movement.

But, as society was everywhere prepared for this Revolution, why did it break out in France rather than abroad? Why did it present features here which were either wholly dropped or only partially reproduced in other countries? This secondary inquiry is worth resolving: it will form the subject of the following Book.

BOOK SECOND

Chapter 1

Why the feudal Rights were more odious to the People in France than anywhere else.

A paradox meets us at the threshold of the inquiry. The Revolution was designed to abolish the remains of the institutions of the Middle Ages: yet it did not break out in countries where those institutions were in full vitality and practically oppressive, but, on the contrary, in a country where they were hardly felt at all; whence it would follow that their yoke was the most intolerable where it was in fact lightest.

At the close of the eighteenth century there was hardly any part of Germany in which serfdom was completely abolished. [4/5] Generally speaking, peasants still formed part of the stock on lands, as they had done during the Middle Ages. Nearly all the soldiers in the armies of Maria Theresa and Frederick were absolute serfs.

In 1788, the general rule with regard to German peasants was that they should not leave the seigniory, and if they did that they should be brought back by force. They were subject to dominical courts, and by them punished for intemperance and idleness. They could not rise in their calling, or change it, or marry without leave from their master. A great proportion of their time was given up to his service. Seigniorial *corvées* were rigorously exacted, and absorbed, in some places, three days of the week. The peasant rebuilt and kept in repair his seignior's house, took his produce to market, served him as coachman and messenger. Many years of his youth were spent in domestic service on the manor. A serf might obtain a farm, but his rights of property always remained inchoate. He was bound to farm his land under his seignior's eye, according to his seignior's directions; he could neither alienate nor mortgage it without leave. He was sometimes bound to sell the produce of his farm, sometimes forbidden to sell; he was always bound to keep his land under cultivation. His estate did not wholly pass to his children; a portion went to the seignior.

I have not groped through antiquated laws to find these rules; they are to be found in the code drawn up by Frederick the Great, and promulgated by his successor just before the French Revolution broke out.[6]

Nothing of the kind had existed for many, many years in France. Peasants came and went, bought and sold, wrought and contracted without let or hindrance. In one or two eastern provinces, acquired by conquest, some stray relics of serfdom survived; but it had disappeared everywhere else; and that so long ago, that even the period of its disappearance had been forgotten. Elaborate researches of recent date establish that it had ceased to exist in Normandy as early as the thirteenth century.

But of all the changes that had taken place in the condition of the French peasantry, the most important was that which had enabled them to become freeholders. As this fact is not universally understood, though it is so important, I shall dwell upon it briefly.

It has been commonly believed that the subdivision of farms began with and was caused by the Revolution. All kinds of evidence establish the very reverse.

Twenty years before the outbreak, agricultural societies deplored the subdivision of farm lands. About the same period Turgot declared that 'the division of estates was so general that a property barely sufficient to maintain a family was often parcelled out among five or six children, who were consequently unable to support themselves by agriculture alone'. A few years later, Necker observed that the number of small rural estates had become *immense*.

A few years before the Revolution a steward of a seigniory informed his employer, in a secret report, that 'estates are being subdivided so equally that the fact is growing alarming: everybody wants to have a piece of this and a piece of that, and farms are incessantly split into shreds'. What more could be said of our own time?

I have myself taken infinite pains to reconstruct the *cadastres*, so to speak, of the old regime, and I have occasionally succeeded. The law of 1790, imposing a land tax, devolved upon each parish the duty of preparing a schedule of the estates within its limits. Most of these schedules have disappeared. I have, however, discovered them in some villages, and I find, on comparing them with our modern rolls, that the number of landed proprietors was formerly one half and sometimes two thirds of what it is now; a surprising fact, as the total population of France has, since that time, increased more than twenty-five per cent.

Then, as now, a sort of mania for the acquisition of land pervaded the rural population. A judicious contemporary observer notes that 'land is selling above its value, owing to the rage of the peasantry to become landowners. All the savings of the lower classes, which in other countries are lodged in private hands or invested in public securities, are used for the purchase of land in France.'

None of the novelties which astonished Arthur Young on his first visit to France appeared to him so striking as the infinite subdivision of land among the peasantry, who, he estimated, held among them one half the landed property in the kingdom. 'I had no idea of such a state of things,' he writes more than once; nor, indeed, could he have, for no such phenomenon existed beyond the frontiers of France or their immediate neighbourhood.

There had been peasant proprietors in England, but they were, even then, growing rare. In Germany, too, there had been, from time to time, in every section of the country, free farmers owning portions of the soil.[7] The oldest German customs recognized a freehold peasantry, and embraced curious regulations regarding land held by them; but the number of such landholders was always small, and their case an exceptional one.

The only portions of Germany where, at the close of the eighteenth century, the peasantry were landholders, and comparatively free, were those which bordered on the Rhine;[8] and it was in the Rhenish provinces that the French revolutionary fever developed itself first and raged most fiercely. Those portions of Germany which resisted the Revolution the longest were those where neither freeholds nor rural liberty had made their appearance; a significant fact.

It is, then, a vulgar error to suppose that the subdivision of property in France dates from the Revolution. It began much farther back. It is true that the Revolution was the means of bringing into market the Church property and many of the estates of the nobility; but it will be found, on examination of the sales (a task which I have occasionally had patience to perform), that the bulk of these lands passed into the hands of persons who held land already, so that no great increase in the number of landowners can have taken place. They were already, to use the ambitious but accurate expression of M. Necker, *immensely* numerous.[9]

The Revolution did not divide, it freed land. All these small landowners were bound to render various feudal services, of which they could not get rid, and which gravely impeded a proper development of their property.

That these services were onerous cannot be questioned. Still, the very circumstance which it would seem ought to have lightened their burden rendered it intolerable. A revolution scarcely less radical than that which had enabled them to become freeholders had released the peasantry of France, alone out of all Europe, from the government of their rural lords.

Brief as is the interval which divides us from the old regime, and often as we see persons who were born under it, it seems already lost in the night of time. So radical was the revolution which has intervened, that it appears to have perished ages ago, and to be now buried in obscurity. Hence there are but few persons who can give a correct answer to the simple question – How were the rural districts governed before 1789? Nor, indeed, can any precise and comprehensive answer be found in books, or elsewhere than in the official records of the time.

I have often heard it remarked that, long after the nobility had ceased to participate in the government of the kingdom, the rural administration remained in their hands, and the seigniors still governed the peasantry. This too looks like a misconception.

In the eighteenth century, all parochial business was transacted by functionaries who were not seigniorial agents, and who, instead of being chosen by the seigniors, were either appointed by the intendant of the province or elected by the peasantry. It devolved upon these officers to distribute the taxes, to repair the churches, to build schools, to convene and preside over parish meetings; to administer and superintend the expenditure of the funds of the *commune*; to institute or answer, on behalf of the community, all necessary legal proceedings. The seignior had lost not only the management, but even the supervision of these petty local matters. All parish officers were subject to the government or the central power, as I shall show in the following chapter. Nor did the seignior figure any longer as the king's deputy in the parish. The execution of the laws, the assembling of the militia, the levying of the taxes, the promulgation of the king's commands, the distribution of his alms, were no longer intrusted to the seignior. They devolved upon new functionaries. The seignior was in fact nothing more than a simple individual, isolated from his fellows by the enjoyment of peculiar immunities and privileges; his rank was different – his power no greater than theirs. The intendants were careful to remind their sub-agents that 'the seignior is nothing more than the first peasant in the parish'.

The *cantons* exhibit the same spectacle as the parishes. Nowhere do the nobles, either collectively or separately, administer public affairs.

This was peculiar to France. Everywhere else, that striking feature of the old feudal system, the connection between the ownership of land and the government of its inhabitants, had been partially preserved. England was administered as well as governed by its chief land-holders. In parts of Germany, such as Prussia and Austria, the sovereigns had contrived to shake off the control of the nobility in state affairs; but they still abandoned the government of the rural districts to the seigniors, and even where they assumed to control, did not venture to supersede them.

In France, the only public department in which the nobles still had a hand was the administration of justice. Leading noblemen still preserved a right of jurisdiction over certain cases (which were decided by judges in their name), and occasionally issued police regulations for the use of their seigniories; but their jurisdiction had been so curtailed, and limited, and overridden by the royal courts, that the seigniors who still enjoyed it viewed it rather as a source of income than as a source of power.

The other rights of the nobility had shared the same fate. They had lost their political significance, but their pecuniary value had been retained and occasionally augmented.

I am alluding now only to those tangible privileges which were known as feudal rights proper, as they alone affected the people.

It is no easy matter to point out what they actually were in 1789, for their number had been immense, and their diversity prodigious. Many had disappeared altogether. Others had undergone modifications, so that the words used to describe them were not easily understood even by contemporaries; they are necessarily full of obscurities for us. Still, a careful study of the writers on feudal law in the eighteenth century, and a searching inquiry into the various local customs, permits us to range the then existing feudal rights in a few leading classes, all others being mere isolated cases.

Seigniorial *corvées* were almost wholly disused. Many of the tolls on highways were either substantially reduced or abolished, though they were still met with in a majority of the provinces. The seigniors still levied a toll upon fairs and markets. It is well known that they enjoyed an exclusive privilege of hunting. Generally speaking, none but they could keep pigeons or own dove-cotes. The farmers were everywhere bound to carry their grain to the seignior's mill, their grapes to his wine-press. Mutation fines – a tax paid to the seignior on every purchase or sale of lands within the seigniory – were universally in force. On all land, moreover, ground-rents (*cens et rentes foncières*) and returns in money or kind were exacted from the proprietor by the seignior, and were essentially irredeemable. One single feature is common to all these various rules: all bear upon the soil or its produce; all are levelled at the farmer.

Clerical seigniors enjoyed the same advantages as their lay brethren; for, though there was no similitude between the Church and the feudal system in point of origin, destiny, or character, and though they were never actually incorporated into one, they clung together so closely that they seemed incrusted one upon the other.[10ab]

Bishops, canons, *abbés* held feuds and seigniories in virtue of their ecclesiastical rank; convents were usually the seigniors of the village in which they stood.[11] They owned serfs at a time when no other seignior in France did. They exacted *corvées*, levied toll upon fairs and markets, owned the only oven, the only mill, the only wine-press, the only bull in the seigniory. Besides these rights as seigniors, the French clergy, like the clergy elsewhere, levied tithes.

The main point, however, to which I wish to draw attention just now, is the fact that analogous feudal rights were in force all over Europe at that time, and that in France they were far less burdensome than in other parts of the Continent. As an illustration of the difference I may cite *corvées*, which in France were rarely claimed and slight, in Germany universally and rigorously exacted.

More than this, the feudal rights which roused most indignation among our ancestors, as being not only unjust, but inimical to civilization — such, for instance, as tithes, inalienable ground-rents (*rentes foncières*), interminable rent-charges, and mutation fines, which, in the somewhat forcible idiom of the eighteenth century, were said to constitute the 'slavery of the land', were all more or less in force in England. Many of them are still in full vigour, and yet English agriculture is the most perfect and richest in the world. The English people hardly notice their existence.

How did it happen, then, that these usages roused in France a hatred so fierce that it survived its cause, and seems as though it would never be extinguished? The phenomenon is due partly to the fact that the French peasant was a landholder, and partly to his emancipation from the government of his seignior. Other causes co-operated, no doubt; but, I take it, these were the main reasons.

Had the peasantry not been landholders, they would have paid no attention to many of the burdens laid by the feudal system on real estate. Tithes, which are levied on produce, interest no one but farmers. Rent-charges are immaterial to those who do not own land. Legal hindrances to the development of property are no serious inconvenience to those who are hired to develop it for others. And, on the other hand, if the French peasantry had still been governed by their seigniors, they would have borne with the feudal rights more patiently, for they would have viewed them in the light of a natural consequence of the constitution of the country.

Aristocracies, which possess not merely privileges, but actual power, which govern and administer public affairs, may exercise private rights of great magnitude without attracting much attention. In the old feudal times people looked upon the nobility as they now look on government: they bore its impositions for the sake of the protection it afforded. If the nobility possessed inconvenient privileges and exacted onerous duties, it secured public order, administered justice, executed the laws, succoured the weak, managed public affairs. It was when it ceased to do these things that the burden of its privileges began to be felt, and its very existence became inexplicable.

Picture to yourself, I beg, the French peasant of the eighteenth century, or, rather, the peasant you see today, for he is still the same; his condition has changed, but not his character. Picture him, as the documents of the time depict him, so eager for land that he saves all his money to buy, and buys at any price. In order to purchase, he is bound, in the first place, to pay a tax, not to the government, but to some neighbours of his, who have no more authority, and no more to do with public business than he. Still he buys, and puts his heart into his land with his seed. The idea that this little corner of the vast universe belongs to him alone fills him with pride and independence. But the same neighbours pass along and compel him to work on their land without wages. If he tries to protect his harvest from the game, they prevent him. He cannot cross the river without paying them toll. He cannot take his produce to market and sell it till he has bought leave to do so from them; and when, on his return home, he wants to consume in his family the surplus of his produce – sown by his hands and grown under his eyes – he finds he must first send his grain to their mill to be ground, and to their oven to be cooked. The largest part of the income of his little estate goes to the same parties in the shape of rents, which cannot be redeemed or got rid of in any way.

Let him do what he like, he cannot but meet at every step of his life these same neighbours, who interfere with his enjoyments, impede his work, consume his produce; and when he has done with these, others, dressed in black, make their appearance, and sweep off the clearest part of his harvest. Picture, if you can, the condition, the wants, the character, the passions of such a man, and estimate the store of hatred and envy he is laying up in his heart![12]

The feudal system, though stripped of its political attributes, was still the greatest of our civil institutions;[13] but its very curtailment was the source of its unpopularity. It may be said, with perfect truth, that the destruction of a part of that system rendered the remainder a hundred-fold more odious than the whole had ever appeared.

Chapter 2

That we owe 'Administrative Centralization', not to the Revolution or the Empire, as some say, but to the old Regime.

I once heard an orator, in the days when we had political assemblies, call administrative centralization 'that noble conquest of the Revolution which Europe envies us'. I am willing to admit that centralization was a noble conquest, and that Europe envies us its possession; but I deny that it was a conquest of the Revolution. It was, on the contrary, a feature of the old regime, and, I may add, the only one which out-lived the Revolution, because it was the only one that was suited to the new condition of society created by the Revolution. A careful perusal of this chapter will perhaps convince the reader that I have more than proved this.

I must, at the outset, beg to be permitted to set aside those provinces known as *pays d'états*, which did actually, or, at least, had the appearance of partially controlling the administration of their own government.

The *pays d'états*, situated at the extremities of the kingdom, contained barely one fourth of the total population of France; and, with one or two exceptions, their provincial liberties were in a dying condition. I shall have occasion hereafter to return to them, and to show how far the central power had rendered them subject to the ordinary rules.*

I purpose to devote attention at present chiefly to those provinces which were styled, in administrative parlance, *pays d'élection*, though there were fewer elections there than anywhere else. They surrounded Paris on all sides, bordering each on the other, and constituting the fairest portion of France.

A first glance at the old government of the kingdom leaves an impression of a host of diversified rules, and authorities, and concurrent powers. France seems to be covered with administrative bodies and independent functionaries, who, having purchased their offices, cannot be displaced. Their functions are often so intertwined and similar that it seems they must clash and interfere with each other.

The courts are invested with some legislative authority. They establish rules, which are binding within the limits of their jurisdiction. They occasionally join issue with the government, blame its measures loudly, and decry its agents. Single judges make the police regulations in the cities and boroughs where they live.

City charters differ widely. Their magistrates bear different titles, or derive their authority from different sources. In one place we find a mayor, in another consuls, in a third syndics. Some of these are chosen by the king; others are appointed by the old seignior, or by the prince in whose domain the city lies; others are elected by the people for a year; others, again have purchased their office, and hold it for life.

*See Appendix.

These are all old ruined authorities. Among them, however, is found an institution either new of lately transformed, which remains to be described. In the heart of the kingdom, and close to the monarch, an administrative body of singular power has lately grown up and absorbed all minor powers. That is the Royal Council.

Though its origin is ancient, most of its functions are modern. It is everything at once: supreme court of justice, for it can reverse the decision of all ordinary tribunals and highest administrative authority, from which all subordinate authorities derive their power. As adviser of the king, it possesses, under him, legislative powers, discusses all and proposes most of the laws, levies and distributes the taxes. It makes rules for the direction of all government agents. It decides all important affairs in person, and superintends the working of all subordinate departments. All business originates with it, or reaches it at last; yet it has no fixed, well-defined jurisdiction. Its decisions are the king's, though they seem to be the Council's. Even while it is administering justice, it is nothing more than an assembly of 'givers of advice', as the Parliament said in one of its remonstrances.

This Council is not composed of nobles, but of persons of ordinary or low extraction, who have filled various offices and acquired an extensive knowledge of business. They all hold office during good behaviour.

It works noiselessly, discreetly, far less pretentious than powerful. It has no brilliancy of its own. Its proximity to the king makes it a partner in every important measure, but his greater effulgence eclipses it.

As the national administration was in the hands of a single body, nearly the whole executive direction of home affairs was in like manner intrusted to a single agent, the comptroller-general.

Old almanacs furnish lists of special ministers for each province, but an examination of the business records shows that these ministers had very little important business to transact. That fell to the lot of the comptroller-general, who gradually monopolized the management of all money affairs – in other words, the whole public administration. He was alternately minister of finance, of the interior, of public works, of commerce.

On the same principle, one agent in each province sufficed. As late as the eighteenth century, some great seigniors were entitled provincial governors. They were the representatives, often by hereditary descent, of feudal royalty. They enjoyed honours still, but they were unaccompanied by power. The substantial government was in the hands of the intendant.

That functionary was not of noble extraction. He was invariably a stranger to the province, a young man with his fortune to make. He obtained his office neither by purchase, election, nor inheritance; he was selected by the government from among the inferior members of the Council of State, and held his office during good behaviour. While in his province, he represented that body, and was hence styled in office dialect the absent commissioner (*commissaire départi*). His powers were scarcely less than those of the council itself, though his decisions were subject to appeal. Like the Council, he held administrative and judicial authority: he corresponded with ministers; he was, in his province, the sole instrument of the will of government.

Under him he appointed for each canton an officer called a sub-delegate (*subdélégué*), who also held office during good behavior. The intendant was usually the first noble of his family; the sub-delegate was always a commoner, yet the latter was the sole representative of the government in his little sphere, as the intendant was in his province. He was subject to the intendant, himself subject to the minister.

The Marquis d'Argenson tells us in his Memoirs that one day Law said to him, 'I never could have believed beforehand what I saw when I was comptroller of finances. Let me tell you that this kingdom of France is governed by thirty intendants. You have neither Parliament, nor estates, nor governors; nothing but thirty masters of requests, on whom, so far as the provinces are concerned, welfare or misery, plenty or want, entirely depend.'

These powerful officials were, however, outwardly eclipsed by the remains of the old feudal aristocracy, thrown into the shade by its lingering splendour; hence it was that even in their day one saw so little of them though their hand was everywhere felt. In society, the nobility took precedence of them in virtue of their rank, their wealth, and the respect always paid to what is ancient. In the government, the nobility surrounded the king and constituted the court; noblemen led the armies and commanded the fleet; they performed those duties, in a word, which are most noticed by contemporaries, and too often best remembered by posterity. A seignior of high rank would have felt himself insulted by the offer of a place of intendant; the poorest gentleman of his house would have disdained to accept it. In their eyes the intendant were the types of usurped authority, new men, employed to look after burghers and peasants; at best, very poor company. For all this, these men governed France, as Law said, and as we shall soon discover.

Let us begin with the right of levying taxes, which may be said to involve all other rights.

It is well known that a portion of the taxes were farmed out to financial companies, which levied them under the directions of the Royal Council. All other taxes, such as the *taille,* capitation-tax, and twentieths, were established and levied directly by the agents of the central administration, or under their all-power control.

Every year the Council fixed and distributed among the provinces the amount of the *taille* and its numerous accessories. The session and decision of the Council were secret; the *taille* increased year after year, and no one was aware of it.

The *taille* was a very old tax; in former times it had been apportioned and levied by local agents, who were independent of government, and held office in virtue of their birth, or by election, or by purchase. Such were the ' seignior', the 'parochial collector', the 'treasurers of France', the 'select-men' (*élus*). These titles were still in existence in the eighteenth century; but some of the persons who bore them had ceased wholly to have to do with the *taille*, while others were only concerned with it in a subordinate and secondary capacity. The whole real authority on the subject was in the hands of the intendant and his agents; it was he who apportioned the *taille* among the parishes, directed and overlooked the collectors, granted delays or remissions.

More modern imposts, such as the capitation-tax, were

regulated by government without interference from the surviving officers of the old system. The comptroller-general, the intendant, and the Council fixed the amount of each impost, and levied it without the intervention of the taxables. -

Let us pass from money to men.

Surprise has been expressed at the docility with which the French bore the burden of the conscription during and after the Revolution; but it must be borne in mind that they had long been used to it. The militia system which had preceded it was more onerous, though the contingents raised were smaller. From time to time, in the country parts, young men were drawn by lot to serve in militia regiments for a term of six years.

As the militia was a comparatively modern institution, none of the feudal authorities interfered with it; it was wholly under the control of the central government. The entire contingent, and the proportion to be borne by each province, were regulated by the Council. The intendant fixed the number of men to be furnished by each parish. His sub-delegate presided over the lottery, awarded exemptions, decided who were to remain at home and who were to march. It was his duty to hand over the latter to the military authorities. There was no appeal from him but to the intendant and the Council.

It may be added here that, except in the *pays d'états*, all public works, including those which were exclusively local, were decided upon and undertaken by the agents of the central power.

Other authorities, such as the seignior, the department of finance, the road trustees (*grands voyers*), were nominally entitled to co-operate in the direction of these works. But practically these old authorities did little or nothing, as the most cursory glance at the records shows. All highways and roads from city to city were built and kept in repair out of the general public fund. They were planned and the contracts given out by the Council. The intendant superintended the engineering work, the sub-delegate mustered the men who were bound to labour. To the old authorities was left the task of seeing to parish roads, which accordingly became impassable.

The chief agent of the central government for public works was the Department of Bridges and Roads (*ponts et chaussées*).

Here a striking resemblance to our modern system becomes manifest. The establishment of Bridges and Roads had a council and a school; inspectors, who travelled each year throughout France; engineers residing on the spot, and intrusted, under the orders of the intendant, with the direction of the works. Most of the old institutions which have been adopted in modern times – and they are more numerous than is generally supposed – have lost their names while retaining their substance. This one has preserved both – a very rare instance.

Upon the central government alone devolved the duty of preserving the peace in the provinces. Mounted police (*maréchaussée*) were scattered over the kingdom in small detachments, ready to act under the orders of the intendants. It was with these troops, and, in case of need, with the aid of the regular army, that the intendant met all sudden outbreaks, arrested vagabonds, repressed mendicity, crushed the riots which the price of food constantly excited. It never happened that the government was driven to call upon its subjects for assistance, as had been common enough at one time, except in cities, where there was usually a civic guard, composed of men selected and officers appointed by the intendant.

The courts had preserved and frequently exercised the right of making police regulations; but they were only applicable to the territory within the court's jurisdiction, and not unfrequently to a single place. They were liable to rejection by the Council, and were often so rejected, especially regulations made by inferior courts. On the other hand, the Council constantly made regulations that were applicable to the whole kingdom, as well on matters beyond the authority of the courts as on those which were within the scope of that authority. These regulations, or, as they were then called, Orders in Council (*arrêts du conseil*), were immensely numerous, especially toward the period of the Revolution. It is hardly possible to mention a branch of social economy or political organization which was not remodelled by Orders in Council during the last forty years of the old regime.

In the old feudal society, the seignior's extensive rights were counterpoised by extensive obligations. He was bound to succour the indigent on his domain. A trace of this principle is to be found in the Prussian code of 1795, where it is said, 'The seignior must see to it that poor peasants receive education. He should, as far as he can, procure means of subsistence for those of his vassals who own no land. If any of them fall into poverty, he is bound to aid them.'

No such law had existed in France for many years. When the seignior's rights were taken from him, he shook off his obligations. No local authority, or council, or provincial, or parochial association had taken his place. The law obliged no man to take care of the poor in the rural districts; the central government boldly assumed charge of them.

Out of the proceeds of the taxes a sum was annually set apart by the Council to be distributed by the intendant in parochial charities. The needy were instructed to apply to him. In times of distress it was he who distributed corn or rice. Annual Orders in Council directed that benevolent work-houses should be opened at places which the Orders took care to indicate; at these, indigent peasants could always obtain work at moderate wages. It need hardly be observed that charity dispensed from such a distance must often have been blind and capricious, and always inadequate.[14ab]

Not content with aiding the peasantry in times of distress, the central government undertook to teach them the art of growing rich, by giving them good advice, and occasionally by resorting to compulsory methods. With this view it distributed from time to time, by the hands of its intendants and sub-delegates, short pamphlets on agriculture, founded agricultural societies, promised prizes, kept up at great expense nurseries for the distribution of seeds and plants. Some reduction of the burdens which weighed on agriculture would probably have proved more efficacious; but this was never contemplated for a moment.

At times the Council endeavoured to force prosperity on the people, whether they would or no. Innumerable Orders compelled mechanics to make use of certain specified machinery, and to manufacture certain specified articles;[15] and as the intendants were not always able to see that their regulations were enforced, inspectors-general of industry were appointed to travel through the provinces and relieve them of the duty.

Orders were passed prohibiting the cultivation of this or that agricultural product in lands which the Council considered unsuited to it. Others required that vines planted in what the Council regarded as bad soil should be uprooted. To such an extent had the government exchanged the duties of sovereign for those of guardian.

Chapter 3

That what is now called 'the Guardianship of the State' (*Tutelle Administrative*) was an Institution of the old Regime.

Municipal liberty outlived the feudal system in France. Long after the seigniors had ceased to administer the government of the rural districts, the cities retained the right of self-government. As late as the close of the seventeenth century, several towns continued to figure as litle democratic republics, with magistrates freely elected by the people. Municipal life was here still active and public; the citizens were proud of their rights and jealous of their independence.[16]

Elections were not generally abolished till 1692; after that date municipal business was transferred to offices (*mis en offices*), that is to say, the king sold to certain citizens of each town the right of governing the others forever.

This was destroying, not the freedom of the cities alone, but their prosperity also; for, though the sale of offices has often been followed by happy results in the case of judges, whose independence is the first condition of their usefulness, it has never failed to be most disastrous in every administrative branch of government, because there responsibility, subordination, and zeal are the conditions of efficiency. The government of the old monarchy made no mistake in the matter; it took good care to steer clear of the system it imposed on the towns – it never sold posts of intendant or sub-delegate.

History may well note with scorn that this great revolution

was accomplished without the least political design.[17] Louis XI had curtailed municipal franchises because their democratic tendency frightened him; Louis XIV abolished, though he did not fear them, for he sold them back again to all the towns which could afford to purchase. His object, indeed, was less to destroy their liberties than to traffic in them. When he did abolish them, it was, so to speak, a mere financial experiment, and, singular to relate, the game was kept up for eighty years. Seven times during that period did the towns purchase the right of electing their magistrates, and seven times was it taken away as soon as they had learned to appreciate its value. The motive of the measure was never varied or concealed. In the preamble to the edict of 1722, the king avowed that 'the necessities of our finances compel us to resort to the most effective remedy'. The remedy was effective enough, but it was ruinous to those upon whom this new impost was laid. 'I am struck,' says an intendant to the comptroller-general in 1764, 'with the enormous aggregate of the sums that have been paid from time to time for the redemption of municipal offices. Had these sums been laid out in works of utility in each city, the citizens would have been great gainers; as it is, the offices have only been a burden.' I am at a loss to find another feature as shameful as this in the whole range of the old regime.

It seems difficult to tell precisely how towns were governed in the eighteenth century; for not only did the source of municipal power change continually, in the manner just described, but each city had preserved some shreds of its old constitution and its peculiar local customs. No two cities in France were, perhaps, alike in every respect, though the contrasts between them are deceptive, and conceal a general similarity.

In 1764, the Council undertook to make a general law for the government of cities. It obtained from its intendants reports on the municipal organization of each town within their province. I have discovered a portion of these reports, and a perusal has completely satisfied me that municipal matters were managed very similarly in all. There are superficial and apparent diversities; substantially the plan was the same everywhere.

In most cases, cities were governed by two assemblies. This is true of all the large cities, and of most of the small ones.

The first assembly was composed of municipal officers, whose number varied in different localities. This was the executive of the *commune*, the city corporation (*corps de ville*), as it used to be called. When the city had obtained or purchased from the king its municipal franchise, members of this assembly were elected for a fixed term. When the king succeeded in selling the municipal offices (which did not always happen, for this kind of merchandise was cheapened by each submission of the municipal to the central authority), they had a life-interest in the posts they bought. In neither case did the municipal officers receive a salary: in both they enjoyed privileges and exemptions of taxes. All were equal rank; they discharged their functions collectively. No magistrate was charged with any particular supervision, authority, or responsibility. The mayor presided over the corporation, but did not administer the government of the city.

The second assembly, known as the 'general assembly', elected the corporation (wherever elections were still held), and participated in the chief affairs of the city.

In the fifteenth century, the general assembly consisted of the whole population. One of the reports mentioned above observed that this usage was 'in accordance with the popular sympathies of our forefathers'. Municipal officers were chosen by the whole people. The people were consulted from time to time, and to them account was rendered by outgoing officials. This custom is still occasionally met with at the close of the seventeenth century.

In the eighteenth century the people no longer constituted the general assembly. That body was almost invariably representative. But it must be carefully borne in mind that it was, in no single city, elected by the people generally, or imbued with a popular spirit. It was invariably composed of *notables*, some of whom were entitled to seats in virtue of their individual station, while others were delegates from guilds and companies, and were instructed as to their course by their constituents.

With the advance of the century, the number of notables *ex officio* increases in these assemblies, while the deputies from industrial associations fall off, or disappear entirely. But deputies from guilds are still present; that is to say, mechanics are excluded to make room for burghers. But the people are not so easily duped by sham liberties as many imagine; they cease to take an interest in public affairs, and live at home as unconcernedly as if they were foreigners. In vain do the magistrates endeavour to revive the patriotism which did such wonders in the Middle Age; no one listens to them. No one takes the least thought for the most momentous interests of the city. The polls – deceitful relic of departed liberty – are there still, and the magistrates would be glad if people would vote; but they resolutely abstain. History teems with similar sights. Very few monarchs, from Augustus to our day, have failed to keep up the outward forms of freedom while they destroyed its substance, in the hope that they might combine the moral power of public approval with the peculiar conveniences of despotism. But the experiment has usually failed, and it has soon been found impossible to maintain a deceitful semblance of that which really has no existence.

In the eighteenth century, then, municipal government in cities had universally degenerated into oligarchy. A few families controlled the public affairs in favour of private interests, without the knowledge of or any responsibility to the public. The disease pervaded every municipal organization in France. It is perceived by all the intendants, but the only remedy they can suggest is the still farther subordination of local authorities to the central government.

They were already under pretty extensive subjection. Not only did the Council modify city governments generally, from time to time,[18] but not unfrequently the intendants proposed for particular cities special laws, which the Council passed without preliminary inquiry, and often without the knowledge of the people; and these laws went into effect without the formality of registration. 'This measure,' said the inhabitants of a city at which such an Order had been levelled, 'has astonished all classes; nothing of the kind was expected.'

Cities were prohibited from establishing town-dues, or levying taxes, or hypothecating, selling, leasing, or administering their property, or going to law, or employing their surplus funds without an order in Council first rendered on the report of the intendant.[19] All public works in cities were executed according to plans and specifications approved by an order in Council. Contracts were adjudged by the intendant or his sub-delegates; the state engineer usually exercised a general superintendance over all. Those who imagine that all we see in France is new will not read this without surprise.

But the Council had even a larger share of the direction of city affairs than might be inferred from these rules. Its power was, in fact, greater than the law allowed.

I find, in a circular addressed to intendants by the comptroller-general about the middle of last century, the following language: 'You will pay particular attention to the proceedings of municipal assemblies. You will require a full report of all their proceedings and debates, and transmit the same to me with your observations thereon.'

The correspondence between the intendants and their sub-delegates shows that the government had a hand in the management of all the cities in the kingdom, great and small. It was consulted on all subjects, and gave decided opinions on all; it even regulated festivals. It was the government which gave orders for public rejoicing, fireworks, and illuminations. I find it mentioned that an intendant once fined some members of the burgher guard twenty *livres* for absenting themselves from the *Te Deum*.

Municipal officers were impressed with a suitable consciousness of the nonentity. Some of them wrote their intendant, 'We pray you most humbly, monseigneur, to grant us your good will and protection. We shall try to prove ourselves worthy of it by our submission to the orders of your highness.' Others, who style themselves grandly 'city peers', write to say that they 'have never resisted your will, monseigneur'.

It was thus that the burghers were being prepared for government, and the people for liberty.

If this close subjection of the cities had but preserved their financial standing! But it did nothing of the kind. It is said that, were it not for centralization, our cities would ruin themselves.

How this may be, I know not; but it is quite certain that, in the eighteenth century, centralization did not save cities from ruin. The financial history of the period is full of city troubles.[20]

Let us pass from cities to villages. We shall find new authorities, new forms, but the same dependence.

I have discovered many indications that, in the Middle Ages, the people of villages formed communities apart from the seigniors. The seigniors used them, superintended, and governed them; but they owned property exclusively, elected their rulers, and administered their government on democratic principles.

This old parochial system may be traced through all the nations which were once organized on a feudal basis, even to the dependencies to which they transported their decaying laws. It is easily discernible in England. Sixty years ago it was in full vigour in Prussia, as the code of Frederick the Great is there to prove. Some vestiges of it still lingered in France in the eighteenth century.

I remember that the first time I examined the archives of an intendant's office, in order to discover what a parish really was under the old regime, I was quite struck with the discovery, in that poor enslaved community, of several features which I had noticed in the rural districts of America, and erroneously considered as peculiarities of New World institutions. Both communities were governed by functionaries acting independently of each other, and under the direction of the community at large; in neither was there a permanent representative body, or municipal assembly proper. In both, from time to time, the people at large met to elect magistrates, and transact important business. They resembled each other, in fact, as closely as a living body resembles a corpse. Nor is this a matter of surprise, for the two systems, different as their destinies were, had the same origin.

When the rural parish of the Middle Ages was removed beyond the reach of the feudal system and left uncontrolled, it became the New England township. When it was cut loose from the seignior, but crushed in the close grasp of the state in France, it became what remains to be described.

In the eighteenth century parochial officers differed in number and title in the several provinces. Old records show that when the parishes were in full vigour, the number of these officers was greater than when the stream of parochial life became sluggish. In the eighteenth century we find but two in most parishes: the collector, and another officer usually known as the syndic. Generally speaking, these officials were elected, really or nominally, but they served far more as instruments of the state than as agents of the community. Collectors levied the *taille* under the orders of the intendant. Syndics, receiving orders from day to day from the sub-delegates, acted as their deputies in all matters bearing on public order or government; such, for instance, as militia business, state works, and the execution of general laws.

It has already been observed that the seignior had no part in these details of government. He neither superintended nor assisted the officials. His real power gone, he despised contrivances used to keep up its semblance, and his pride alone forbade him to take any share in their establishment. Though he had ceased to govern, his residence in the parish and his privileges precluded the formation of a sound parochial system in the stead of that in which he had figured. Such a personage, so isolated in his independence and his privileges, could not but weaken or militate against the authority of law.

His presence drove to the cities all persons of means and information, as I shall have occasion to show hereafter. Around him lived a herd of rough, ignorant peasants, quite incapable of administering their collective business. It was Turgot who described a parish as 'a collection of huts not more passive than their tenants.'

The records of the eighteenth century abound with complaints of the inefficiency, the carelessness, and the ignorance of parochial collectors and syndics. Everybody deplores the fact – ministers, intendants, sub-delegates, even men of rank, but nobody thinks of looking for its true cause.

Until the Revolution the government of rural parishes in France preserved some traces of that democratic aspect which characterized it during the Middle Ages. When municipal officers were to be elected, or public affairs discussed, the village bell summoned the peasantry, poor and rich alike, to the church door. There was no regular debate followed by a vote, but all were free to express their views, and a notary, officiating in the open air, noted, in a formal report, the substance of what was said.

The contrast between these empty semblances of liberty and the real impotence which they concealed furnishes a slight indication of the ease with which the most absolute government may adopt some of the forms of radical democracy, and aggravate oppression by placing the oppressed under the ridiculous imputation of not being aware of their real state. The democratic parish meeting was free to express its wishes, but it was as powerless to enforce them as the municipal councils or cities; nor could it utter a word till its mouth had been opened by authority. No meeting could be convened until permission had been obtained in express terms from the intendant: this granted, the villagers, who called things by their right names, met 'by his good will and pleasure'. No meeting, however unanimous, could impose a tax, or sell or buy, or lease, or go to law, without permission from the Royal Council. The church which a storm had unroofed, or the presbytery wall which was falling to pieces, could not be repaired without a decree of Council. This rule applied with equal force to all parishes, however distant from the capital. I have seen a petition from a parish to the council praying to be allowed to spend twenty-five *livres*.

In general, the parishioners were still entitled to elect magistrates by universal suffrage; but the intendant frequently took pains to recommend a candidate, who never failed to obtain the votes of the small electoral body. Again, he would occasionally declare of his own authority than an election just held was null and void, would appoint a collector and syndic, and temporarily disfranchise the community. Of this course I have noticed a thousand examples.

No more wretched station than that of these parochial functionaries can be conceived. They were subject to the whim of the lowest agent of the central government, the sub-delegate. He would fine or imprison them, and they could lay no claim to the usual guarantees of the subject against arbitrary oppression. An intendant wrote in 1750, 'I have imprisoned a few of the principal grumblers, and made the community pay the expense of sending for the police. By these measures I have checkmated them without difficulty.' Naturally enough, under these circumstances, parochial office, instead of being an honour, became a burden from which all sought to escape.

Yet still, these last traces of the old parochial system were dear to the peasant's heart. To this very day that system is the only branch of government which he thoroughly understands and cares for. Men who cheerfully see the whole nation submit to a master, rebel at the bare idea of not being consulted in the government of their village. So pregnant with weight are hollow forms!

The remarks I have made upon cities and villages apply also to almost every corporate body which had a separate existence and corporate property.

Under the old regime, as in our own day, neither city, nor borough, nor village, nor hamlet, however small, nor hospital, nor church, nor convent,[21] nor college, could exercise a free will in its private affairs, or administer its property as it thought best. Then, as now, the administration was the guardian of the whole French people; insolence had not yet invented the name, but the thing was already in existence.

Chapter 4

That administrative Tribunals (*la justice administrative*) and official Irresponsibility (*Garantie des Functionnaires*) were Institutions of the old Regime.

In no country in Europe were the courts more independent of the government than in France; nor was there any in which more abnormal tribunals existed. The one involved a necessity for the other. Judges whose position was beyond the King's reach, whom he could neither dismiss, nor displace, nor promote, and over whom he had no hold either by ambition or by fear, soon proved inconvenient. That led to the denial of their jurisdiction over cases to which the administration was a party, and to the establishment of another class of courts, less independent, which presented to the subject's eye a semblance of justice, without involving, for the monarch, any risk of its reality.

In countries like Germany, where the judges were never as independent of the government as they were in France at this time, no such precaution was ever taken, and no administrative tribunals ever established. The monarch held the common courts in such subjection that he did not need extraordinary ones.

Very few of the royal edicts and declarations, or of the Orders in Council, issued during the last century of the old monarchy, were unprovided with a clause stating that all disputes that might arise, and lawsuits that might grow out of them, must be referred to the intendants and to the Council. The ordinary form of words was, 'His majesty ordains that all disputes which may arise concerning the execution of the present decree, its accessories and corollaries, shall be tried before the intendant, and decided by him, subject to appeal to the Council. We forbid our courts and tribunals to take cognizance of any such disputes.'

In cases arising out of laws or old customs which made no similar provision, the Council constantly intervened by process of evocation, and took the suit out of the hands of the common judges to bring it before itself. The Council registers are full of such decrees of evocation. Frequently they gave to the practice the force of theory. A maxim, not of law, took root in the public mind to the effect that suits, in which state interests were involved, or which turned on the interpretation of a law, were not within the jurisdiction of ordinary courts, and that these latter were restricted to the decision of cases between private individuals. We have embodied this idea in a set form, but its substance belongs to the old regime.

In those days, the intendant and Council were the only court that could try cases growing out of questions of taxation. They alone were competent to decide suits concerning common carriers and passenger vehicles, public highways, canals, river navigation, and generally all matters in which the public interest was concerned.

Nothing was left undone by the intendants to extend their jurisdiction. Representations to the comptroller-general, and sharp hints to the Council, were incessant. One of the reasons assigned by a magistrate of this rank for issuing a writ of evocation is worth preserving. 'Ordinary judges,' says he, 'are bound by rule to repress illegal acts; but the Council can always overstep rules for a salutary purpose.'

This principle often led intendants and Council to assume jurisdiction over cases whose connection with the administration was so slight as to be invisible, and even over cases which had obviously no connection with it at all. A gentleman went to law with his neighbour. Dissatisfied with the tone of the court, he begged the Council to evoke the case. The intendant, to whom it was referred reported that, 'though the interests involved were wholly of a private nature, his majesty could always, if he chose, take cognizance of all classes of suits, without rendering account of his motives to any one'.

Individuals arrested for riot were usually tried on evocation before the intendant or the Provost of Police (*prévôt de la maréchaussée*). In times of scarcity, evocations of this kind were common, and the intendants appointed several 'graduates' to assist them in their duties. They formed a sort of prefect's council, with criminal jurisdiction. I have seen sentences rendered by these bodies condemning culprits to the galleys and to the scaffold. At the close of the seventeenth century, criminal jurisdiction was still frequently exercised by intendants.

Modern legists assure us that we have made great progress in administrative law since the Revolution. They tell us that 'before that event the powers of the judiciary and those of the administration were intermingled and confused, but that since then they have been severed, and a line drawn between them'. A right appreciation of the progress here mentioned can only be formed when it is well borne in mind that if the judiciary under the old regime occasionally overstepped its natural sphere, it never filled the whole of that sphere. Both of these facts must be remembered, or a false and incomplete view will be taken of the subject. True, the courts were allowed to travel out of their sphere to make laws on certain subjects for the government of the public; but, on the other hand, they were denied cognizance of legitimate lawsuits, and thus excluded from a part of their proper domain. We have stripped the courts of the right of intruding into the administration of government, which they very improperly possessed under the old regime, but we have continued to suffer the government to intrude into the courts of law; yet it is even more dangerous for the government than for the judiciary to transcend its scope; for the interference of the latter in the administration of government only injures the public business, whereas the interference of government in the administration of justice tends to deprave the public mind, and to render men servile and revolutionary at one and the same time.

In one of the nine or ten constitutions which have been established in France within the last sixty years, and designed to last forever, an article was inserted declaring that no government official could be prosecuted before the common courts until permission had been obtained from the executive. The idea seemed so happy that, when the constitution was destroyed, the article in question was rescued from destruction, and has ever since been carefully sheltered from revolution. Officials commonly allude to the privilege secured to them by this article as one of the great triumphs of 1789, but here again they are in error. The old monarchy was quite as solicitous as more modern governments to protect its servants from responsibility to the courts, like mere citizens. Between the two eras the only substantial difference is this: before the Revolution government could not come to the rescue of its agents without having recourse to arbitrary and illegal measures; since then it has been legally authorized to let them violate the law.

When, under the old regime, an agent of the central government was prosecuted before any of the ordinary courts, an Order in Council usually forbade the judges to proceed with the case, and referred it to commissioners named in the order. The ground for the proceeding was, according to the opinion of a councillor of that day, because the ordinary judges were sure to be biased against a government official, and thus the king's government was likely to be brought into contempt. Cases of evocation were not rare occurrences. They took place daily, and the lowest officials were as often protected by them as the highest. The most slender connection with government secured immunity from all authorities, save the Council only. A farmer liable to *corvées* prosecuted an overseer of the Bridge and Road department for having maltreated him. The Council evoked the case. The chief engineer reported confidentially to the intendant that 'the overseer was no doubt much to blame, but that was no reason why the case should be allowed to take its course. It is of the highest importance to the department of Bridges and Roads that the ordinary courts should not take cognizance of complaints against the overseers made by workmen bound to service, for if they did, the works would soon be brought to a stand by the lawsuits which the public dislike of these officials would excite.'

On another occasion, a state contractor had taken from a neighbouring field materials which he required, and used them. The intendant himself wrote to the comptroller-general, 'I cannot lay sufficent stress on the injury the government would incur if contractors were left at the mercy of the ordinary courts, for their principles are wholly at variance with those by which the administration is guided.'

A century has elapsed since these lines were written, and yet these public officers would pass for contemporaries of our own.

Chapter 5

How Centralization crept in among the old Authorities, and supplanted without destroying them

Let us briefly recapitulate the points established in the three preceding chapters.

A single body, placed in the centre of the kingdom, administering government throughout the country; a single minister

managing nearly all the business of the interior; a single agent
directing the details in each province; no secondary administrative bodies, or authorities competent to act without permission: special tribunals to hear cases in which government is
concerned, and shield its agents. What is this but the same
centralization with which we are acquainted? As compared with
ours, its forms are less sharply marked, its mode of action less
regular, its existence less tranquil; but the system is the same.
Nothing has been added, nothing taken away from the old plan;
when the surrounding edifices were pulled down, it stood
precisely as we see it.

Frequent imitations of the institutions I have just described
have since made their appearance in various places,[22] but they
were then peculiar to France. We shall see presently how great
an influence they exercised over the French Revolution and its
sequel.

But how did these modern institutions find place among the
ruins of the old feudal society?

By patient, adroit, persevering labour, rather than by violent
arbitrary effort. At the outbreak of the Revolution, the old
administrative system of France was still standing, but a new
system had been built up inside it.

There is no reason for believing that this difficult exploit was
the fruit of a deep scheme laid by the old government. On the
contrary, it appears to have been accomplished almost unconsciously, instinct teaching the government and its various
agents to acquire as much control as possible. The old officials
were left in possession of their titles and their honours, but
stripped of their power. They were led, not driven out of their
domain. The idleness of one, the selfishness of another, the vices
of all, were skilfully turned to account. No attempt was made to
convert them, but one and all were quietly replaced by the
intendant, whose name had never even been heard at the time
they were born.

The only obstacle in the way of the change was in the judiciary
department; but there, as elsewhere, the government had
contrived to seize the substance, leaving its rivals the outward
show of power. It did not exclude the Parliaments from

administrative business, but it gradually absorbed their duties till there was nothing for them to do.[23] On some few rare occasions, as, for example, in times of scarcity, when popular excitements tempted the ambition of magistrates, it allowed the Parliaments to exercise administrative authority for a brief interval, and let them make a noise which has often found an echo in history; but it soon silently resumed its functions, and discreetly assumed sole control of men and things.

A close study of the struggles of the Parliaments against the power of the king will lead to the discovery that they were invariably on political issues, and never on points of administration. Quarrels usually began on the creation of new taxes — that is to say, the belligerents contended for legislative authority, to which neither had any claim, and not for administrative power.

This becomes more apparent as we approach the revolutionary era. As the people's feelings become inflamed, the Parliament mixes more in politics; and simultaneously, the central government and its agents, with skill enhanced by experience, usurp more administrative power. The Parliament grows daily less like an administration, and more like a tribune.

Day after day, the central government conquers new fields of action into which these bodies cannot follow it. Novelties arise, pregnant with cases for which no precedents can be found in parliamentary routine: society, in a fever of activity, creates new demands, which the government alone can satisfy, and each of which swells its authority; for the sphere of all administrative bodies is defined and fixed; that of the government alone is movable, and spreads with the extension of civilization.

Impending revolution unsettles the mind of the French, and suggests a host of new ideas which the central government alone can realize: it is developed before it perishes. Like everything else, it is brought to perfection, as is singularly proved by its archives. There is no resemblance between the comptroller-general and the intendant of 1780 and the like officials in 1740: the system has been transformed. The agents are the same but their spirit is different. Time, while it extends and exercises the power of the government, imparts to it new skill and regularity.

Its latest usurpations are marked by unusual forbearance; it rules more imperatively, but it is far less oppressive.

This great institution of the monarchy was thrown down by the first blow of the Revolution: it was raised anew in 1800. It is not true that the principles of government which were then adopted were those of 1789, as so many persons have asserted; they were those of the old monarchy, which were restored, and have remained in force every since.

If it be asked how this portion of the old regime could be bodily transplanted into and incorporated with the new social system, I reply that centralization was not abolished by the Revolution, because it was, in fact, its preliminary and precursor; and I may add, that when a nation abolishes aristocracy, centralization follows as a matter of course. It is much harder to prevent its establishment than to hasten it. Everything tends toward unity of power, and it requires no small contrivance to maintain diversions of authority.

It was natural, then, that the democratic Revolution, while it destroyed so many of the institutions of the old regime, should retain this one. Nor was centralization so out of place in the social order created by the Revolution that it could not easily be mistaken for one of its fruits.

Chapter 6

Of official Manners and Customs under the old Regime.

It is impossible to read the correspondence of intendants of the old regime with their superiors without being struck with the resemblance between the officials of that day and those of our own. Like institutions produced like men; across the Revolutionary gulf which divides them they appear hand in hand. As much may be said of the people governed. Never was the power of legislation to shape men's minds more powerfully illustrated.

Already in those days ministers were seized with a mania for seeing with their own eyes the details of everything, and managing everything at Paris. The mania increased with time and practice. Toward the close of the eighteenth century, a work-house could not be established in any corner of a distant province but the comptroller must insist on overseeing its expenditure, providing it with rules, choosing its site. If a poor-house were founded, the same minister required to know the names of all paupers relieved, their exits and their entrances. Before the middle of the century, in 1733, M. D'Argenson wrote, 'Ministers are overloaded with business details. Everything is done by them and through them and if their information be not coextensive with their power, they are forced to let their clerks act as they please and become the real masters of the country.'

Comptrollers-general were not content with business reports; they insisted on minute information about individuals. Intendants expected the same from their sub-delegates, and rarely failed to repeat, word for word, in their reports, what these subordinates stated in theirs, as though they were stating matters within their own knowledge.

A very extensive machinery was requisite before the government could know everything and manage everything at Paris. The amount of documents filed was enormous, and the slowness with which public business was transacted such that I have been unable to discover any case in which a village obtained permission to raise its church steeple or repair its presbytery in less than a year. Generally speaking, two or three years elapsed before such petitions were granted.

The Council itself confessed, in a decree of 29 March 1773, that 'administrative forms cause infinite delays, and frequently give rise to very just complaints; yet these forms are all necessary'.

I was under the impression that a taste for statistics was peculiar to the government officials of our own day: this I find to be an error. Toward the close of the old regime, printed forms were constantly sent to the intendant, who sent them on to his sub-delegates, who sent them on to the syndics, who filled the blanks. The subjects on which the comptroller thus sought information were the character of lands and of their cultivation, the kind and quantity of produce raised, the number of cattle, and the customs of the people. Information thus obtained was fully as minute and as reliable as that which sub-prefects and mayors furnish in our own day. Sub-delegates seem, from these tabular reports, to have formed in general an unfavourable judgment upon the character of the people. They reiterate the opinion that 'the peasent is naturally idle, and would not work if he could live without it'. That economical doctrine appears to be very generally received among these government officials.

Nor is the official style of the two periods less strikingly similar. Official writers then, as now, affected a colourless, smooth, vague, diffuse style; each writer merged his identity in the general mediocrity of the body to which he belonged. Read a prefect, you have read an intendant.

When, toward the close of the century, the peculiarities of Diderot and Rousseau spread into the language of the day, the affected sensibility of these writers was adopted by the officials and even by state financiers. Official style, usually dry enough, then became unctuous and even tender. A sub-delegate complained to the intendant of Paris that his 'feelings were so sensitive that he could not discharge the duties of his office without moments of poignant grief'.

The government distributed, as it still does, certain sums in charity in each parish, on condition that the parishioners raised something on their side for the same purpose. When the sum raised by them was sufficient, the comptroller made a memorandum on the margin of the scheme of distribution, 'Good – express satisfaction'; but when it was considerable, he wrote, 'Good – express satisfaction and sensibility.'

Government officials, none of whom were of noble descent, already formed a class apart, with feelings, traditions, virtues, and notions of honour and dignity all their own. They constituted the aristocracy of the new society. Ready to take their rank as soon as the Revolution had cleared the way.

A marked characteristic of the French government, even in those days, was the hatred it bore to everyone, whether noble or not, who presumed to meddle with public affairs without its knowledge. It took fright at the organization of the least public body which ventured to exist without permission. It was disturbed by the formation of any free society. It could brook no association but such as it had arbitrarily formed, and over which it presided. Even manufacturing companies displeased it. In a word, it objected to people looking after their own concerns, and preferred general inertia to rivalry. Still, as the French could not exist without some sort of liberty, they were permitted to discuss as freely as they chose all sorts of general and abstract theories of religion, philosophy, morals, and even politics. Provided its agents were not meddled with, the government had no objection to attacks on the fundamental principles of society, and even on the existence of a God. Officials fancied these were no concerns of their.

Though the newspapers of those days, or, as they were usually called, the gazettes, contained more poetry than politics, they were none the less viewed with a jealous eye by the government. Careless about books, it was very strict with regard to journals, and being unable to suppress them, it undertook to make them a government monopoly. A circular, dated 1761, which I have seen, announced to all the intendants in the kingdom that the *Gazette de France* would be thereafter composed under the eye of the king (Louis XV), his majesty desiring to render it interesting and superior to all others. You will, therefore,' continues the circular, 'have the goodness to let me have a report of all events of interest within your province, especially such as bear upon natural philosophy and natural history, together with other singular and striking occurrences.' To the circular was attached a prospectus of the *Gazette,* informing the public that, though it appeared oftener and contained more matter than its rival, its subscription price would be considerably less.

Armed with these documents, an intendant applied to his sub-delegates for information, but the latter replied that they had none to give. Then came a second letter from the minister, complaining bitterly of the dearth of news from the province in question, and winding up with, 'His majesty commands me to say to you that it is his will that you give your serious attention to this affair, and issue the strictest orders to your subordin-ates.' Under the pressure, the sub-delegates did their best. One reported that a salt-smuggler had been hanged, and had displayed great courage; another, that a woman in his neighbourhood had been delivered of three girls at one birth; a third, that a terrible storm had taken place, but happily, had done no mischief. A fourth declared that he had not been able, notwithstanding great exertions, to discover any news of interest, but that he took pleasure in subscribing personally to so useful a gazette, and would recommend all his neighbours to do the like. Still, these remarkable efforts seem to have produced inadequate results, for it appears from a fresh letter that 'the king, who has graciously deigned to give his attention to the best means of perfecting the *Gazette,* and wishes to secure for this journal the superiority and fame which it deserves, has expressed much dissatisfaction at the manner in which his desires have been seconded'.

History, it is easily perceived, is a picture-gallery containing a host of copies and very few originals.

It must be admitted, however, that the central government of France never followed the example of those southern governments which seem to have sought to be despotic only in order to blight their realms. The former was always active, and often intelligently so. Its activity was often fruitless and even mischievous, however, because it essayed to achieve feats beyond its reach, and even impossibilities.

It seldom undertook, or soon abandoned projects of useful reform which demanded perseverance and energy, but it was incessantly engaged in altering the laws. Repose was never known in its domain. New rules followed each other with such bewildering rapidity that its agents never knew which to obey of the multifarious commands they received. Municipal officers complained to the comptroller-general of the extreme instability of the minor laws. 'The financial regulations alone,' say they, 'vary so constantly that it would require the whole time of a municipal officer, holding office for life, to acquire a knowledge of the new regulations as they appear from time to time.'

When the substance of the laws was allowed to remain the same, their execution was varied. Those who have not studied the actual working of the old regime in the official records it left behind can form no idea of the contempt into which the laws fall, even in the minds of their administrators, when there are no political meetings or newspapers to check the capricious activity and set bounds to the arbitrary tendencies of government officials.

Very few Orders in Council omitted to repeal former and frequently quite recent enactments, which, though quite regular, have never been carried into effect. No edict, or royal declaration, or registered letters patent was strictly carried out in practice. The correspondence of the comptrollers-general and the intendants shows plainly that the government was constantly in the habit of tolerating exceptions to its rules. It rarely broke the law, but it daily bent it to either side, to suit particular cases or facilitate the transaction of business.

An intendant wrote to the minister, in reference to an application of a state contractor to be relieved from paying town dues, 'It is certain that, according to the strict letter of the laws I have cited, no one can claim exemption from these dues, but all who are acquainted with business are aware that these sweeping provisions, like the penalities they impose, though contained in most of the edicts, declarations, and decrees establishing taxes, were not intended to be literally construed, or to exclude exceptional cases.'

These words contain the whole principle of the old regime. Strict rules, loosely enforced – such was its characteristic.

To attempt to form an opinion of the age from its laws would lead to the most ridiculous errors. A royal declaration of 1757 condemned to death all writers or printers of works assailing religion or government. Booksellers in whose shops they were found, peddlers who hawked them, were liable to the same penalties. Was this the age of Saint Dominic? No, it was exactly the period of Voltaire's reign.

Complaints are heard that Frenchmen show contempt for law. Alas! when could they have learned to respect it? It may be broadly said that, among the men of the old regime, the place in the mind which should have been occupied by the idea of law was vacant. Petitioners begged that established rules might be departed from in their case as seriously and as earnestly as if they had been insisting on the honest execution of the law; nor were they ever referred to the law unless government intended to give them a rebuff. Custom, rather than volition, still inculcated submission to authority on the part of the people; but whenever they did break loose, the least excitement gave rise to violent acts, which were themselves met, not by the law, but by violence on the other side, and arbitrary stretches of power.

Though the central power had not acquired in the eighteenth century the strong and healthy constitution it has since possessed, it had, notwithstanding, so thoroughly destroyed all intermediate authorities, and left so wide a vacant space between itself and the public, that it already appeared to be the mainspring of the social machine, the sole source of national life.

Nothing proves this more thoroughly than the writings of its assailants. During the period of uneasiness which preceded the Revolution, a host of schemes for new forms of society and government were brought to light. These schemes sought various ends, but the means by which they were to be reached were invariably identical. All the schemers wanted to use the central power for the destruction of the existing system, and the substitution of their new plan in its stead: that power alone seemed to them capable of accomplishing so great a task. They all assumed that the rights and powers of the state ought to be unlimited, and that the only thing needed was to persuade it to use them aright. Mirabeau the father, whose aristocractic prejudices led him to denominate the intendants intruders, and to declare that if the government had the sole right of appointing magistrates, the courts of justice would soon be mere 'bands of commissioners', relied on the central power alone for the realization of his chimerical plans.

Nor were these notions confined to books; they pervaded men's minds, gave a colour to society and social habits, and were conspicuous in every transaction of everyday life.

Nobody expected to succeed in any enterprise unless the state helped him. Farmers, who, as a class, are generally stubborn and indocile, were led to believe that the backwardness of agriculture was due to the lack of advice and aid from the government. A letter from one of them, somewhat revolutionary in tone, inquired of the intendant 'why the government did not appoint inspectors to travel once a year through the provinces, and examine the state of agriculture throughout the kingdom? Such officers would teach farmers what to plant, what to do with their cattle, how to fatten, raise, and sell them, and where to send them to market. They would, of course, be paid officials. Some honorary distinction should be conferred on successful agriculturists.'

Inspectors and honorary distinctions! These are the last encouragements a Suffolk farmer would have thought of expecting.

The masses were quite satisfied that the government alone could preserve the public peace. The mounted police alone commanded the respect of the rich, and inspired terror among the people. Both viewed that force rather as the incarnation of public order than as one of its chief instruments. The provincial assembly of Guienne observed that 'everyone has noticed how quickly the sight of a mounted policeman will subdue the most riotous mob'. And everybody wanted, accordingly, to have a troop of them at his door.[24] Petitions to that effect overloaded the registers of the intendants: no one seemed to suspect that the protector might be a master in disguise.

Nothing astonished the exiles who fled to England so much as the absence of any such force there. Some express surprise, others contempt at the phenomenon. A man of some merit, but who had not been taught to expect such a contrast, exclaimed, 'It is positively true that an Englishman congratulates himself on being robbed, with the reflection that, at all events, there are no mounted police in his country. An Englishman is sorry to see riots, but when rioters escape scot free into the bosom of society, he consoles himself with the remark that the law must be observed to the letter, at whatever cost. These false notions, however, are not universally adopted. There are wise men who think differently, and their view must ultimately prevail.'

He never dreamed that these eccentricities of the English might possibly have some connection with their liberties. He accounted for them on scientific principles. 'In countries where a damp climate and a want of elasticity in the air gives a gloomy cast to the character of the people, serious subjects are sure to be popular. Hence it is that the English are naturally inclined to busy themselves about their government, while the French are not.'

Government having assumed the place of Providence, people naturally invoked its aid for their private wants. Heaps of petitions were received from persons who wanted their petty private ends served, always for the public good.[25] The chests which contained them were, perhaps, the only spot where all classes of society under the old regime freely intermingled. Sad reading, this: farmers begging to be reimbursed the value of lost cattle or horses; men in easy circumstances begging a loan to enable them to work their land to more advantage; manufacturers begging for monopolies to crush out competition; business men confiding their pecuniary embarrassments to the intendant, and begging for assistance or a loan. It would appear that the public funds were liable to be used in this way.

Men of rank were not unfrequent applicants for favours. They might be recognized by the lofty tone in which they begged. They came to solicit from the intendant delays in which to pay their share of the land-tax, which was their chief burden; or they asked that it be remitted altogether. I have read a great number of petitions of this kind from noblemen, some of very high degree; the ground alleged is usually the inadequacy of the petitioner's income, or his pecuniary straits. Men of rank always addressed intendants simply 'Sir': on these occasions they addressed him 'Monseigneur', as everybody else did.

Pride and poverty are often amusingly combined in these petitions. One reads as follows: 'Your warm heart can never surely insist on the payment of a strict twentieth by a man of my rank, as you might with men of the common sort.'

In times of scarcity, which recurred frequently during the eighteenth century, the people of each province flew to the intendant, and seemed to expect food from him as a matter of course.[26] The act was redeemed by wholesale denunciations of the government. All the sufferings of the people were laid to its charge; it was loudly blamed for the severity of the weather.

Let no one again express surprise at the wonderful ease with which centralization was re-established in France at the beginning of this century. It had been overthrown by the men of 1789;

but its foundations were deep in the minds of its very destroyers, and upon these it was rebuilt anew stronger than ever.

Chapter 7

How the Capital of France had acquired more Preponderance over the Provinces, and usurped more Control over the nation, than any other Capital in Europe.

It is not situation, or size, or wealth which makes some capital cities rule the countries in which they stand; that phenomenon is caused by the prevailing form of government.

London, which is as populous as many a kingdom, has, up to this time, exercised no sovereign control over Great Britain.

No citizen of the United States ever supposes that New York could decide the fate of the American Union, not does any citizen of the State of New York fancy that that city could even direct state affairs at will; yet New York contains as many inhabitants today as Paris did when the Revolution broke out.

Moreover, Paris bore to the rest of the kingdom the same proportion, so far as population was concerned, during the religious wars as it did in 1789; yet it was powerless at the former period. At the time of the Fronde, Paris was nothing more than the largest French city; in 1789 it was France.

In 1740 Montesquieu wrote to a friend, 'France is nothing but Paris and a few distant provinces which Paris has not yet had time to swallow up.' In 1750 the Marquis de Mirabeau, a man of chimerical views, but occasionally profound in his way, said of Paris without naming it, 'Capitals are necessities, but if the head grow too large, the body becomes apoplectic and wastes away. What will the consequence be, if by drawing all the talent of the kingdom to this metropolis, and leaving to the provincials no chance of reward or motive for ambition, the latter are placed in a sort of quasi dependence, and converted into an inferior class of citizens?' He adds that this process is effecting a silent revolution by depopulating the provinces of their notables, leading men, and men of ability.

The foregoing chapters have explained pretty fully the causes of this phenomenon; the reader's patience may be spared their repetition here.

The Revolution did not escape the notice of government, but it only viewed the fact in its bearing on the capital, whose rapid increase seemed to presage increased difficulties of administration. Numerous royal ordinances, especially in the seventeeth and eighteenth centuries, endeavoured to check its growth. The monarchy steadily concentrated in Paris all the national life of France, and yet desired to see Paris remain small. People were forbidden to build new houses, or were bound to build them in the most costly manner, in the worst localities. But each successive ordinance admitted that, notwithstanding its predecessors, Paris had increased steadily. Six times did Louis XIV exert his omnipotent will to check the expansion of the city, but each effort was a failure; the capital expanded in spite of decrees. Its power swelled even more rapidly than its volume, which was due less to its own exertions than to events beyond its walls.

For, simultaneously with its extension, the local franchises of the rural districts were fading away, all symptoms of independent vigour were vanishing, provincial characteristics were being effaced, the last flicker of the old national life was dying out. Not that the nation was growing sluggish; on the contrary, it never knew a more active time; but the only mainspring of movement was at Paris. One illustration, chosen out of a thousand, may make this plainer. I find reports to the minister on the book business, in which it is stated that, during the sixteenth and at the beginning of the seventeenth century, there were large printing-offices in many provincial cities, but that now there are no printers to be found, and no work to be done. Yet it is not to be questioned but there were far more books printed at the close of the eighteenth century than during the sixteenth. The secret is, simply, that mind had ceased to radiate from any point but the centre: Paris had swallowed up the provinces.

This preliminary revolution was fully accomplished before the French Revolution broke out.

The famous traveller, Arthur Young, left Paris a few days after the assembling of the States-General, and before the capture of the Bastille; he was struck with the contrast between city and country. In Paris, all was activity and noise; political pamphlets appeared in such quantities that ninety-two were counted in one week. 'I never saw such a fever of publishing,' said he, 'even at London.' Outside of Paris he could find nothing but inertia and silence; no pamphlets, and but few journals. The provinces were roused and ready to move, but not to take the initiative; when the people met, it was to hear the news from Paris. Young asked the people of each city what they purposed doing. 'Their answer was always the same, "We are but a provincial city; you must go and see what they are going to do at Paris." These people,' he adds, 'dare not hold an opinion till they know how it is received at Paris.'

Surprise has been expressed at the remarkable ease with which the *Constituante* assembly destroyed at a blow provinces in some cases older than the monarchy, and parcelled out the kingdom into eighty-three distinct sections, as if it had been virgin soil in the New World. Europe was not prepared for any such act, and viewed it with surprise and horror. 'This is the first time,' said Burke, 'that men have so barbarously torn their country to pieces.' It did look as though they had torn living bodies, but in reality they had only dismembered corpses.

At the very time that Paris was becoming all-powerful, another noteworthy change was taking place within its borders. It had long been a city of trade, business and pleasure; it now became an industrial and manufacturing city. This change gave it a new and formidable character.

It had long been inevitable. Even in the Middle Ages Paris had been the most industrious, as it was the largest city of the kingdom; latterly, the distance between it and its rivals had increased. Arts and industrial energy followed the government. As Paris became more and more the arbiter of taste, the only centre of power and of art, the focus of national activity, the manufacturing life of the country gradually concentrated itself there.

Though I place, in general, but little reliance on the statistical tables of the old regime, I believe it may be safely asserted that during the sixty years which preceded the French Revolution, the number of workmen at Paris was more than doubled, though the whole population of the city during the same period only increased one third.

Independently of these general causes, peculiar motives attracted mechanics from all parts of France to Paris; and when they came, they lived mostly together, and ultimately monopolized whole wards. The burdens laid on mechanics by the fiscal policy of the government were lighter at Paris than in the provinces; nor was it so easy anywhere as there to obtain the freedom of a trade-company. Residents of the suburbs of Saint Antoine and of the Temple enjoyed peculiar privileges in this respect. Louis XVI enlarged still further the prerogatives of the Saint Antoine suburb, in the design of collecting an immense number of operatives there, or, as that unfortunate monarch phrased it, 'being desirous of showing a new mark of our favour to the workmen of the Saint Antoine suburb, and relieving them from burdens which are alike injurious to their interests and to the freedom of trade'.

Toward the period of the Revolution the number of factories, manufacturers, and blast-furnaces had become so great at Paris as to alarm the government. Industrial progress had aroused strange fears in the mind of officials. A decree of council in 1782 declares that 'the king, fearing lest the rapid increase of factories should lead to so large a consumption of firewood as to deprive the city of its proper supply, prohibits the establishment of new works of this kind within fifteen leagues of the capital.' No one suspected the real danger to be apprehended from the agglomeration of workmen.

It was thus that Paris became the mistress of France, and thus that the army that was to master Paris was mustered.

It is generally admitted nowadays, I believe, that administrative centralization and the omnipotence of Paris have had much to do with the fall of the various governments we have had during the last forty years. I shall have but little difficulty in proving that the ruin of the old monarchy was in a great measure due to the same causes, and that they exercised no small influence in bringing about that revolution which was the parent of all the others.

Chapter 8

That Frenchmen had grown more like each other than any other People.

The careful student of the old regime in France soon meets with two apparently contradictory facts.

It appears that everybody in the upper and middle classes of society, the only classes which are heard of, is exactly like his neighbour.

At the same time, this homogeneous mass is split into an immense multitude of small bodies, and each body contains an exclusive set, which takes no concern for any interests but its own.

When I think of these infinite subdivisions, and the want of union and sympathy they must have produced, I begin to understand how a great revolution could overthrow such a society, from top to bottom, in a moment. The shock must have levelled, at a blow, all party walls, and left behind it the most compact and homogeneous social body every seen in the world.

I have already described how provincial peculiarities had gradually worn off. That change tended powerfully to assimilate the French people. National unity loomed through the surviving distinctions of rank. The laws were uniform. As the eighteenth century advanced, the number of edicts, declarations, and Orders in Council, which applied the same rules with equal force to all parts of the kingdom, became larger and larger. Subjects as well as rulers entertained ideas of a general uniform system of legislation that shoud bear equally on all: this was a prominent feature in all the schemes of reform which saw the light during the thirty years preceding the Revolution. Two centuries before, the basis for such schemes may be said to have been wanting.

Not only had all the provinces grown like each other, but the men also. A marked resemblance began to exist between men of all ranks and stations; or, at all events, among those who were not comprised in the class known as 'the people'.

This is clearly shown in the *cahiers* of the various classes presented in 1789. Their authors had evidently different interests to serve, but in all other respects they were alike.

At former meetings of the States-General, on the contrary, the interests of the middle classes were common to the nobility, their aims were the same, their intercourse free from antagonism; but they seemed to be two distinct races.

Time had maintained and occasionally aggravated the privileges which kept them apart, but in all other respects it had singularly laboured to produce a resemblance between them.

The impoverishment of the nobility had gone on steadily for several centuries. A man of rank observed sadly in 1755, 'Notwithstanding their privileges, the nobility are falling daily deeper into difficulties and destruction, while the Third Estate inherits their fortunes.' No change had been made in the laws which protected the property of the aristocracy, or in their economical condition. Yet they grew poorer everywhere as they lost their power.

One is almost inclined to fancy that human institutions, like the human body, contain, besides the particular organs appointed to perform specific functions, a central hidden force which is the vital principle. When this force is subdued, though the organs seem to act as usual, the whole machine languishes and dies. The French nobility still retained the use of entails (which, according to Burke, were more frequent and more binding in France than in England), laws of primogeniture, irredeemable ground-rents, and, generally, the beneficial rights they derived from feudal customs; they had been released from military service, but paid fewer taxes than ever, thus getting rid of the burden while they retained the privilege. They enjoyed, moreover, many other pecuniary advantages which their fathers had never had, and yet they grew poorer gradually as they mixed less in the theory and practice of government. It was their poverty which mainly led to the extensive subdivision of landed property that has already been noted.[27] Men of rank sold their land piecemeal to the peasantry, reserving nothing but seigniorial rents, which furnished a nominal, not a substantial competency. Several French provinces, such as Limousin, which Turgot describes, were full of petty impoverished noblemen, who had no land left, and who lived on the produce of seigniorial rights and ground-rents.

'In this province,' said an intendant, 'at the beginning of the century, there were several thousand noble families, but not fifteen out of the whole number had an income of twenty thousand livres.' I find a memorandum addressed by the intendant of Franche-Comté to his successor in 1750, in which it is said that 'the nobility of this section of country are of high rank, but very poor, and as proud as they are poor. The contrast between their former and their present condition is humiliating. It is a very good plan to keep them poor, in order that they shall need our aid and serve our purposes. They have formed,' he adds, 'a society into which no one can obtain admission unless he can prove four quarterings. It is not incorporated by letters patent; but it is tolerated, as it meets but once a year, and in the presence of the intendant. These noblemen hear mass and dine together, after which they return home, some on their Rosinantes, some of foot. You will enjoy this comical assembly.'

All over the Continent, in the countries where the feudal system was being displaced and no new aristocracy founded, as was the case in France, the nobility were relapsing into poverty. Their decline was peculiarly marked among the German nations bordering on the Rhine. England alone presented a contrast. There the old noble families had not only kept, but largely increased their fortunes, and were the chiefs of the nation in wealth as well as in power. The new families which had grown up by their side competed with them but could not surpass them in magnificence.

In France, the commoners (*roturiers*) inherited all the property lost by the nobility, they seemed to fatten on their substance. The laws did not hinder commoners from ruining themselves, or help them to acquire wealth, yet they did acquire it constantly, and became as rich or richer than men of rank. They often invested their means in the same kind of property as the nobles held; though usually residents of the city, they often owned country estates, and occasionally even seigniories.

Both classes were educated alike, and led similar lives, hence more points of resemblance. The commoner was as well informed as the nobleman, and had obtained his information from the same source. Both were equally and similarly enlightened; both had received the same theoretical and literary education. Paris had become the sole preceptor of France, and shaped all minds in the same form and mould.

There was, no doubt, at the close of the eighteenth century, a difference between the manners of the noble and the commoner, for nothing resists the levelling process so long as that superficial varnish called manners. But at bottom all the classes which ranked above the people were alike. Their ideas were the same; so were their habits, tastes, pleasures, books, and language. They differed in point of rights alone.

I doubt whether the same fact existed to the same extent in any other country. Common interests had closely knit together the various social classes in England, but they differed widely in habits and ideas; for political liberty, so long enjoyed by that admirable power, though it unites men by close relations and mutual dependence, does not always assimilate them one to another; it is despotism which, in the long run, inevitably renders them mere duplicates one of the other, and types of selfishness.

Chapter 9

That these Men, who were so alike, were more divided than they had
ever been into petty Groups, each independent of and indifferent to
the others.

Let us now glance at the reverse of the picture, and see how
these same Frenchmen, who had so many features in
common, were, notwithstanding, split into more isolated groups
than any other people or their own ancestry.

There is reason to believe that, at the time the feudal system
was established in Europe, the class since known as the nobility
did not form a *caste,* but was composed originally of the chief
men of the nation, thus forming a real aristocracy. That is a
question which I did not purpose to discuss in this place. I
merely observe that in the Middle Ages the nobility had become
a caste; that is to say, its distinguishing mark was birth.

It resembled an aristocracy inasmuch as it was the governing
body; but birth alone decided who should stand at the head of
that body. All who were not of noble birth were excluded from
its ranks, and filled a station in the state which might vary in
dignity, but was always subordinate.

Wherever the fuedal system took root in Europe, it led to the
establishment of castes; in England alone it gave birth to an
aristocracy.

I have always been surprised that a fact so strikingly peculiar
to England, and which is the only true key to the peculiarities of
her laws, her spirit, and her history, should have obtained so
little notice among philosophers and statesmen. Custom seems
to have blinded the English to its importance. It has often been
half noticed and half described, but never, I think, fully and
clearly realized. Montesquieu, who visited Great Britain in
1739, certainly did write, 'I am in a country which does not
resemble the west of Europe'; but he went no farther.

The contrast between England and the rest of Europe arose,
indeed, less from her Parliament, her liberty, her freedom of the
press, and her jury system, than from another and more
important peculiarity. England was the only country where
castes had been not altered, but thoroughly abolished: noblemen

and people engaged in the same avocations, entered the same professions, and, what is more significant, inter-married with each other. The daughter of the greatest nobleman in the land might marry, without dishonour, a man of no hereditary rank.

If you want to ascertain whether castes, and the ideas, habits, and barriers to which they give rise, are really abolished in any nation, look at the marriages which take place there. There you will find the decisive test. Sixty years of democracy have not wholly effaced privileges of caste in France; old families, mixed and confounded with new ones in everything else, still scorn connection with them by marriage.

It has often been said that the English nobility were more prudent, more skilful, more open than the nobility of any other country. The truth is, that there had not been, for a long period of time any nobility at all in England, in the old circumscribed meaning of the word.

The revolution which destroyed it is lost in the night of time, but the English tongue is a surviving witness of the change. Many centuries since, the meaning of the word 'gentleman' changed in England, and the word 'roturier' ceased to exist. When Molière wrote Tartuffe in 1664, it would have been impossible to give a literal English version of the line,

> Et tel que l'on le voit, il est bon gentilhomme.

Language can be made to throw farther light on the science of history. Follow, for instance, the meanings of the word gentleman throughout its career. Our word 'gentilhomme' was its father. As distinctions of classes became less marked in England, its signification widened. Century after century, it was applied to lower and lower classes in the social scale. The English at last bore it with them to America, where it was indiscriminately applied to all classes. Its history is, in fact, that of democracy.

In France, the word 'gentilhomme' never acquired more latitude than it possessed at first. Since the Revolution it has become disused, but not modified. The word which described members of the caste was preserved unaltered, because the caste itself was retained as widely distinct as ever from other classes of society.

I will go farther. I maintain that the caste had grown more distinct and exclusive than ever; that the movement of French society had been exactly opposite to that which took place in England.

While the citizen and the noble had grown more like each other, the distance between them had increased; their mutual resemblance had rather alienated than united them.

During the Middle Ages, when the feudal system was in full vigour, the holders of seigniorial lands (who were technically styled vassals), whether nobles or not, were constantly associated with the seignior in the government of the seigniory. That was, in fact, the principal condition of their tenure. They were bound by their titles not only to follow their seignior in arms, but to assist him, for a given time each year, in rendering justice in his court, and administering the government of the seigniory. Seigniorial courts were the mainspring of feudal government; they figure in all the old laws of Europe, and I have found marked traces of them in many parts of Germany even in our own time. A learned feudist, Edme de Fréminville, who thought proper, thirty years before the Revolution, to write a voluminous work on feudal rights and the renewal of court rolls, informs us that he has seen 'many seigniorial titles by which the vassals bound themselves to attend, every fortnight, at the seignior's court, there to sit, jointly with him or his judge in ordinary, in judgment upon disputes and lawsuits between the people of the seigniory'. He adds, that he has 'found as many as eighty, a hundred and fifty, and even two hundred vassals, a great proportion of whom were *roturiers*, pledged to this service in a seigniory'. This I quote, not as a proof of the custom – such evidence abounds – but as an instance of the early and long-continued association of the peasantry with men of rank. They were constantly engaged together in the transaction of the same business. What the seigniorial courts did for small rural landholders, the Provincial States, and, at a later period the States-General, effected for the middle class in cities.

It is impossible to read the extant records of the States-General and Provincial States of the fourteenth century without being amazed at the weight and power exercised by the Third Estate in these assemblies.

As individuals, the burghers of the fourteenth century were, no doubt, very inferior to those of the eighteenth; collectively, they occupied a higher and more solidly established rank. Their right to take part in the government was uncontroverted; their share in political assemblies was always large, often paramount. The other classes were daily reminded of the necessity of making terms with them.

It is quite striking to notice how easily the nobility and the Third Estate then combined for purposes of action or defence – no easy matter to contrive at a later day. Many of the States-General of the fourteenth century derived an irregular and revolutionary character from the disasters of the time; but the Provincial States of the same period, on which there is no reason to suppose any abnormal influence was operating, contain singular evidence of this harmony. In Auvergne the Three Estates combined to carry out most important measures, and appointed commissioners, chosen equally from each, to superintend their excecution. Champagne witnessed a similar spectacle at the same time. Nor is it necessary to do more than hint at the famous league between the nobles and citizens of several cities, by which the leaguers bound themselves, at the beginning of the same century, to defend their national franchises and provincial privileges against the encroachments of the royal power.[28ab] Our history, at that age, is full of similar episodes, which seen to have been borrowed from the history of England. They disappear entirely in later times.

With the disorganization of the seigniorial government, the increasing infrequency or total cessation of meetings of the States-General, and the ruin of national and local liberties together, the middle classes ceased to associate in public life with men of rank. There was no longer any necessity for their meeting and coming to a mutual understanding. They became daily more independent of each other, and more complete strangers. By the eighteenth century the change was accomplished; the two classes only met accidentally in private life. They were not only rivals, but enemies.

A feature which appears peculiar to France was the seeming aggrandizement of individual noblemen at the cost of the order. While the nobility, as an order, was losing its political power, men of rank were acquiring new privileges and augmenting their old ones. The former had lost its corporate authority, but still the new master chose his chief servants more exclusively than ever from among its members. It was easier for a commoner (*roturier*) to become an officer under Louis XIV than Louis XVI. Commoners often obtained office in Prussia at a time when the fact was unexampled in France. All the new privileges were hereditary and inseparable from blood. The more the nobility ceased to be an aristocracy the more it became a caste.

Let us take the most odious of these privileges, the exemption from taxes: it is easily seen that from the fifteenth century to the French Revolution it was constantly on the increase. It became more valuable as the taxes swelled. When the *taille* was but 1,200,000 livres under Charles VII, the privilege of not being bound to contribute was not worth much; but it was considerable when the tax yielded 80,000,000, under Louis XVI. When the taille was the only tax from which the nobility were exempt, their privileges might pass unnoticed; but when similar taxes had been created in a thousand different shapes and with a thousand different names, when four other imposts had been placed on the same footing as the taille, and new impositions, such as royal *corvées* on all public works, military duty, &c, had been laid on every class save the nobles only, their privileges appeared immense.[29] True, the inequality, great as it was, seemed still greater, for the nobleman's farmer had often to pay the very taxes which his master flattered himself he escaped; but, in these matters, the semblance of injustice is more mischievous than the reality.

Louis XIV, when labouring under the financial difficulties which at last overwhelmed him, toward the close of his reign, created two taxes, a capitation-tax and a land-tax of a twentieth, which were to be paid by all his subjects indiscriminately. But, as though the privilege of the nobility was so intrinsically respectable that it deserved consideration even in cases where it did not apply, care was taken to preserve a distinction in the manner of levying it.[30abc] It was exacted of the people harshly and with marks of degradation; the nobles were respectfully and gently requested to pay.[31]

The taxes had been unequal all over Europe, but the inequality was more plainly seen and severely felt in France than abroad. The bulk of the taxes in Germany were indirect, and the exemption from direct taxes, enjoyed by the nobility, was only partial – they paid less than other people. They were taxed specially, too, in lieu of the military service they had once been bound to render.

Now, of all the methods that have been devised for the division of nations into classes, unequal taxes are the most pernicious and effective. They tend to isolate each class irremediably; for when the tax is unequal, the line is drawn afresh every year between the taxables and the exempts; the distinction is never allowed to fade. Every member of the privileged class feels a pressing and immediate interest in keeping it up, and maintaining his isolation from the taxable community.

All, or nearly all public measures begin or end with a tax. Hence, when two classes of citizens do not feel the taxes alike, they cease to have common interests and feelings in common; they do not require to meet for consultation; they have no opportunity and no desire to act in concert.

Burke draws a flattering picture of the old constitution of France, and makes a point in favour of the institution of nobility, that commoners might obtain rank by procuring office; he evidently infers an analogy between this feature of our institutions and the open aristocracy of England. Nor can it be denied that Louis XI bestowed titles freely in order to reduce the power of the nobility, and that his successors did the same thing to get money. Necker states that in his time as many as four thousand offices carried with them noble rank. No similar feature existed elsewhere in Europe. Yet the analogy which Burke seeks to establish between France and England was none the less false.

The real secret of the staunch attachment of the middle classes of England to their aristocracy did not lie in the fact that it was an open body; it flowed rather from the undefined extent and unknown limits of that body. Englishmen bore with their aristocracy less because they could obtain admission within its pale, than because they never knew when they were within, and could always consider themselves part and parcel of it, could share its authority, and derive *éclat* or profit from its power.

In France, on the contrary, the barrier which separated the nobility from the other classes, though easily surmounted, was always conspicuous, and known by outward and odious marks. The parvenu who overstepped it was separated from his former associates by privileges which were onerous and humiliating for them.

The plan of raising commoners to the nobility, therefore, far from weakening their hatred of the superior class, increased it beyond measure. New nobles were viewed by their old equals with most bitter envy. Hence it was that the Third Estate evinced far more dislike of the new than of the old nobility, and demanded constantly that the entrance to the ranks of the nobility should be, not enlarged, but narrowed.

At no time in our history was it so easy to become a noble as in 1789, and at no time had the nobility and the commonalty been so distinct and separate. Not only did the nobles exclude from their electoral colleges everyone who was the least tainted with plebeian blood, but the commoners exhibited equal anxiety to keep out of their ranks all who looked like men of rank. In certain provinces, new nobles were rejected by one party because they were not deemed noble enough, by the others because they were too noble. This happened, it is said, to the celebrated Lavoisier.

The burghers presented a very similar spectacle. They were as widely distinct from the people as the nobles from them.

Nearly the whole middle class under the old regime lived in the cities. Two causes had produced this result: the privileges of men of rank and the *taille*. Seigniors residing on their estates could afford to be good-natured and patronizing to the peasantry, but they were insolent to a degree to their neighbours of a higher rank. And the more political power they lost, the more proud and overbearing they become. Nor could it be otherwise; for when they were stripped of their authority, they no longer needed to conciliate partners in the business of government, while, on the other hand, they tried to console themselves for the sacrifice of substantial authority by an immoderate abuse of its outward semblance. Their absence from their estates was rather an increased inconvenience than a relief to their neighbours; absenteeism had not even that advantage, and privileges exercised by attorney were only the more intolerable.

I question, however, whether the taille and the other taxes which had been placed on the same footing were not still more effective causes than these.

It would be easy to explain, and that in a few words, why the taille was a more oppressive tax in the country than in the cities; but the reader may not consider such an explanation requisite. It will suffice, therefore, to say that the middle classes domiciled in cities were enabled, in many various ways, to evade the tax, wholly or partially, which they could not have done had they been living on their property in the country. Above all, a city residence saved them from the risk of being chosen to levy the taille. This they dreaded more than the tax itself, and very justly, for there was not, in the whole range of society under the old regime, or even in any society, I believe, a position worse than that of parochial collector of the taille. I shall have occasion to demonstrate this hereafter. Yet, with the single exception of men of rank, no resident of a village could escape the office. Rather than submit to the burden, rich commoners leased their estates and went to live in the nearest city. Turgot is consistent with the secret documents which I have had occasion to consult when he declares that 'the collection of the taille converts the landholding commoners of the country into city burghers'. This, it may be observed by the way, was one of the reasons why France was more plentifully sprinkled with towns, and especially small towns, than any other country of Europe.

Enclosed within city walls, the rich commoner lost his rural tastes and feelings. He ceased to take an interest in the toils and concerns of the class he had deserted. His life had henceforth but one object: he aspired to become a public functionary in his adopted city.

It is a grave error to suppose that the rage for office-seeking, which stamps the French of our day, the middle classes especially, sprung up since the Revolution: it dates from a much more ancient period, though constant encouragement has steadily developed and intensified it.

The offices of the old regime were not always like ours, but I think they were more numerous; there was no end to the small ones. Between 1693 and 1709 alone, it had been calculated that forty thousand were created, all within reach of the most slender commoner. I have myself counted, in a provincial town of no great size, in the year 1750, the names of one hundred and nine persons engaged in administering justice, and a hundred and twenty-six more busied in executing their orders. The middle classes really coveted government places with unexampled ardour. The moment a man acquired a little capital, instead of investing it in trade, he bought an office directly. Not even the close companies or the taille have proved as injurious to the commercial and agricultural interests of France as this mania for places. When no offices were vacant, the place-hunters set their imagination to work and soon invented new ones. I find a published memorial of a Sieur Lemberville, in which he proves that inspectors of this or that branch of industry are absolutely needed, and winds up by offering himself for the future office. Who has not known a Lemberville? A man possessed of some education and means did not think it decorous to die without having been a public functionary. 'Each in his way,' said a contemporary, 'wants to be something by his majesty's favour.'

The only substantial difference between the custom of those days and our own resides in the price paid for office. Then they were sold by government, now they are bestowed; it is no longer necessary to pay money; the object can be attained by selling one's soul.

Interest, to a still greater extent then locality or habits of life, drew a line between the middle classes and the peasantry. Complaint is made about the privileges of the nobles, and very justly; but what must be said of those of the middle classes? Thousands of offices carried with them exemptions from this or that impost. One exempted its holder from serving in the militia, another from performing *corvées,* a third from paying the taille. 'Where is the parish,' said a writer of the time, 'that does not contain, besides nobles and clergy, a number of inhabitants who have procured some exemption from taxes by obtaining office under government?' The number was so great, in fact, as to produce at times a sensible falling off in the product of the *taille;* and, now and then, this inconvenience led to the abolition of several useless offices. I have no doubt that exemptions were as frequent among the middle classes as among the nobility, and even more so.

These wretched privileges excited the envy of those who did not enjoy them, and filled their possessors with selfish pride. Nothing more common, during the whole of the eighteenth century, than hostility and jealousy between cities and the surrounding country. Turgot declares that 'the towns are monopolized by selfishness, and are always ready to sacrifice the village and country parts in their district'. On another occasion, he reminds his sub-delegates how 'often' they have been 'obliged to repress the tendency of cities to usurp the rights and encroach upon the privileges of the villages and country parts in their district.'

The middle classes contrived to make strangers and enemies of the lower classes in the cities also. Most of the local taxes were devised so as to fall mainly upon the latter. Turgot remarks somewhere that the middle classes usually contrived to escape the payment of town dues; and this I have found to be correct.

But the most striking characteristic of the middle classes was their fear of being confounded with the people, and their violent desire to escape in some way from popular control.

'If it be the king's pleasure,' said the burghers of a city in a memorial to the comptroller-general, 'that the office of mayor become elective, it would be fitting that the choice of the electors should be restricted to the principal notables, and even to the presidial.'

We have had occasion to notice how steadily the kings pursued the policy of stripping the cities of their political rights. This is the leading feature of their tactics from Louis XI to Louis XV. The burghers often aided in the accomplishment of these schemes, and sometimes suggested them.

At the time of the municipal reform of 1764, an intendant consulted the municipal officers of a small town on the subject of retaining an elective magistracy, chosen partly by the lower classes. They replied that, to tell the truth, 'the people had never abused the franchise, and it would no doubt be agreeable to confirm them in the right of choosing their masters; still it was better, for the sake of order and the public tranquillity, that the matter should be left to the decision of the notables'. The sub-delegate of the same town reported that he had invited to a secret conference 'the six leading citizens of the place', who were unanimously of opinion that the best thing to do was to have the magistrates elected, not by the assembly of notables, as the municipal officers proposed, but by a small committee selected from the various bodies which composed the assembly. The sub-delegate, who was more favourable to popular freedom than these citizens, reported their opinion, but added that 'it was hard for mechanics to be deprived of control over moneys exacted from them in virtue of taxes imposed by those among their fellow-citizens who, by reason of the exemption from taxes they enjoyed, were often disinterested in the matter'.

To complete the picture, let us glance at the middle classes independently of their relations to the people, as we examined the nobility independently of its bearing on the middle classes.

The first striking feature in this small part of the nation is infinite subdivision. The French people really seem to resemble those pretended elementary substances which science is unceasingly resolving into new elements the closer it examines them. I have studied a small town in which I found the names of thirty-six different bodies of citizens. These various bodies, small as they were, were constantly hard at work reducing their size; they were ever throwing off some foreign particle or other, and trying to reduce their condition to that of simple elements. This operation had cut down some of them to not more than three of four members. They were none the less quarrelsome and consequential on that account. Peculiar privileges, among which the least decorous were still marks of honour, distinguished each class from the others, and endless was the struggle for precedence among them. Intendant and courts were stunned with the clamour of their quarrels. 'It has just been decided that the holy water must be given to the presidial before the city corporation. The Parliament hestitated, but the king evoked the case, and decided it in Council. It was high time; the whole city was in a ferment on the subject.' If one body is granted precedence over another at the assembly of notables, the injured corporation withdraws; it will abandon its public duties rather than see, as it says, its dignity insulted. The corporation of barbers in the city of La Flêche decided 'to express in this manner the natural grief which it felt at the precedence awarded to the bakers'. A portion of the notables of a city refused to perform their functions, 'because', said the intendant, 'some mechanics had obtained admission to the assembly, and with these the leading citizens could not humble themselves by associating'. Another intendant observed, 'If the rank of alderman be given to a notary, that will disgust the other notables, for the notaries are men of low birth, not sons of notables, and have been clerks in their youth.' The six leading citizens, who I have mentioned above, who were so ready to strip the people of their political rights, were greatly perplexed when called upon to designate who should be notables, and what should be the order of precedence among them. On this point they expressed their views rather by doubts and hints than straightforward suggestions: 'They were afraid,' they said 'of hurting the feelings of their fellow-citizens.'

The friction between these small bodies sharpened the peculiar vanity of the French, but extinguished the proper pride of the citizens. Most of these corporations existed in the sixteenth century, but then, after having transacted the business of their exclusive association, they mingled with the other citizens for the transaction of the general concerns of the city. In the eighteenth century no such intermixture took place, for symptoms of municipal life had become rare, and city business was managed by hired agents. Each of these small societies lived for itself alone, thought of nothing but its own affairs, had no interest in any concerns but those which were exclusively its own.

Our ancestors had no such word as 'individuality', which we

have coined for our use. They did not need it, because in their time there were no individuals wholly isolated and unconnected with some group or other; but each of the small groups of which French society was composed was intensely selfish, whence arose a sort of collective individuality, so to speak, which prepared men's minds for the true individuality of the present day.

The strangest feature of the old society was the similarity which existed among all these individuals thus grouped in different sets; they were so alike that when they changed their surroundings it was impossible to recognize them; moreover, in their hearts they regarded the petty barriers which split them into rival cliques as equally contrary to public interest and common sense. In theory they were all for unity. Each held to his set because others did the like; but they were all ready to fuse together into one mass, provided no one obtained peculiar advantages, or rose above the common level.

Chapter 10

How the Destruction of political Liberty and Class Divisions were the Causes of all the Diseases of which the old Regime died.

Of all the fatal diseases which assailed the constitution of the old regime, the most deadly was the one I have just described. Let us return to the source of this strange and terrible malady, and see how many other troubles had the same origin.

Had the English wholly lost their political liberties and all the local franchises dependent thereon during the crisis of the Middle Ages, it is reasonable to suppose that the classes which comprise their aristocracy would have held themselves quite aloof from the people, as the corresponding classes did in France. It was the spirit of liberty which compelled them to remain within reach of the people, in order to come to an understanding with them when required.

It is curious to note how ambition prompted the English nobility to mix familiarly with their inferiors, and to treat them as equals when necessity seemed to require it. Arthur Young, from whom I have quoted already, and whose work is one of the most instructive that can be consulted on Old France, relates how, while he was staying at the country-house of the Duke of Liancourt, he expressed a wish to converse with some of the most skilful and intelligent farmers of the neighbourhood. The duke sent his intendant for them, upon which the Englishman remarks: 'An English nobleman, in the like case, would have asked three or four farmers to dinner with his family, and would have had them sit by the side of the noblest ladies. I have seen that a hundred times over in our island, but you may travel from Calais to Bayonne without seeing anything of the kind here.'

Beyond a doubt, the British aristocracy was naturally more haughty and more averse to familiarity with its inferiors than the same class in France, but the necessities of its position imposed restraints. It was willing to sacrifice anything for power. For centuries the only alterations in the taxes were made in favour of the poorer classes. Notice, I beg, how widely neighbours may be made to differ by different political principles![32] In the eighteenth century, in England, the only exemptions from taxes were enjoyed by the poor, in France by the rich. There the aristocracy had assumed all the burdens in order to enjoy the power of governing; here they steadily refused to pay taxes, as their only consolation for the loss of political power.

During the fourteenth century, the maxim N'impose qui ne veut (no taxation without the consent of the taxables), appears to have been as solidly established in France as in England. It was frequently quoted; deviations from it were regarded as acts of tyranny, absolute conformity with it constitutional. At this period our institutions were analogous, in many respects, to those of the English. But thenceforth the destinies of the two nations began to deviate, and became more unlike from century to century. They might be compared to two lines, which, starting from adjacent points in slightly different directions, separate more widely the more they are prolonged.

I venture to assert that when the nation, wearied out by the long disorders which had accompanied the captivity of King John and the insanity of Charles VI, allowed the kings to impose a tax without its consent, the nobles basely concurring on condition that they should be exempt, they sowed the seed of all the abuses and mischiefs which troubled the old regime during its existence, and led to its violent death; and I admire the singular sagacity of Commines when he says, 'When Charles VII gained the right of imposing the taille at will without the consent of the States, he greatly changed his spirit (*son âme*) and that of his successors, and dealt his kingdom a wound that will bleed for a long time to come.'

See how the wound has been enlarged by time; trace the consequences of this one act.

Forbonnais remarks with truth, in his learned 'Researches on French Finances', that, during the Middle Ages, monarchs usually lived on the produce of their domains; 'and as extraordinary necessities,' he adds, 'were met by extraordinary taxes, they bore equally on the clergy, the nobility, and the people.'

Most of the general taxes, voted by the three orders during the fourteenth century, were of this character. Nearly all the taxes established at this time were indirect, that is to say, they bore on all consumers indiscriminately. When the tax was direct, it bore, not on property, but on incomes. For instance, nobles, clergy, and commoners were required to abandon to the king a tithe of their income. And the rule with regard to taxes laid by the States-General applied with equal force to those which were laid by the Provincial States within their territories.

It is true that even then the direct tax, called *taille,* did not bear on men of rank, who were exempt in consideration of serving gratuitously as soldiers in time of war. But the *taille,* as a general tax, was restricted in its operation; it applied to seigniories more than to the kingdom.

When the king first undertook to impose a tax of his own will and mere motion, he was well aware that policy indicated the selection of one which did not bear upon the nobility, and which they – who were the most powerful class in the kingdom, and the only rivals of the sovereign – would not be provoked to resist; and, accordingly, he chose the *taille*.

Inequalities enough existed already between the various

classes of Frenchmen; this new distinction was more sweeping than all, and aggravated while it confirmed the others. Thenceforth, in proportion to the increased necessities which were produced by the enlarged ambition of the central power, the *taille* increased and multiplied, till the original amount levied was decupled, and every new tax was a *taille*.[33] Year by year the tax gathering divided society anew, and re-erected the barrier between the taxables and the exempts. The first condition of the tax being its imposition, not on those who could afford to pay it, but on those who could not afford to resist it, government was driven into the monstrous anomaly of sparing the rich and burdening the poor. It is said that Mazarin once intended to supply a pressing exigency by a tax on the principal houses in Paris; but, meeting with more resistance than he had anticipated, he simply added the five millions he wanted to the *taille* levy. His design had been to tax the most wealthy citizens; in fact, he taxed the poorest; but the treasury got the money.

Taxes so unequal yielded a limited revenue; but there was no limit to the necessities of the throne. Still, king after king refused to convoke the States in order to obtain subsidies, and refrained from taxing the nobility lest the annoyance should provoke them to insist on a return to constitutional usage. Hence those prodigious and mischievous financial *tours de force*, which marked the history of the French treasury during the last three centuries of the monarchy.

A careful study of the financial and administrative history of the old regime shows to what straits and dishonest shifts the want of money will reduce a government, however mild it may be, so long as it is unchecked, and fears neither publicity on the one hand, nor revolution – that safeguard of popular liberty – on the other.

That history teems with instances of royal properties sold, then resumed as inalienable; of violated contracts; vested rights trampled; public creditors sacrificed at every crisis; the public faith constantly broken.[34]

Privileges, granted as perpetual, were constantly revoked. If it were possible to sympathize with the sufferings of martyrs to vanity, one would pity those unfortunate new-made noblemen who, during the seventeenth and eighteenth centuries, were so often called upon to pay for honours and unjust privileges, whose price they had fully paid at the time of the original purchase. Louis XIV, for instance, annulled all the titles of nobility that had been granted during the ninety-two years previous, though most of them had been granted by himself. Their possessors could only retain them on paying more money, 'all these titles having been granted by surprise', says the edict. An example which Louis XV took care to imitate eighty years afterward.

It was pronounced illegal for militia-men to serve by substitute, as the practice would tend to enhance the value of recruits.

Cities, corporations, hospitals, were forced to repudiate their engagements in order to lend their money to the king. Parishes were hindered from undertaking useful works for fear that the *taille* might be less regularly paid if their resources were divided.

It is related that M. Orry and M. Trudaine, who were respectively comptroller-general and director-general of the department of Bridges and Roads, formed a plan for the commutation of seigniorial *corvées* on highways into an annual payment in money, to be applied to repairing the roads of each canton. There is much instruction in the reason which deterred these able officals from executing their design; they were afraid, it is said, that it would be impossible to prevent the treasury from embezzling the money, and obliging the people both to labour on the roads and to pay for their repairs besides. I do not hesitate to say that no private individual could escape ruin if he conducted his affairs as the great monarch in all his glory managed the public business.

All the old medieval institutions, whose faults were aggravated as everything around them improved, may be traced to a financial origin; the same is true of the pernicious innovations of a later date. To pay the debts of a day, powers were created which lasted centuries.

A particular tax, called the freehold duty (*droit de franc fief*), had been laid at a very remote period on commoners who possessed estates noble. This duty created the same division among lands as existed among men; and each helped the other.

The freehold duty hindered the fusion of the nobility and the people on the neutral ground of real estate; and I dare say it was more effective then anything else in keeping them apart. It opened a gulf between the nobleman and his neighbour. In England, nothing so powerfully aided the fusion of the two classes as the abolition, in the seventeeth century, of all the distinguishing marks which served to separate feudal lands from freeholds.

During the fourteenth century the feudal freehold duty was light, and only exacted at long intervals. During the eighteenth, when the feudal system was nearly abolished, it was rigorously levied every twenty years, and amounted to a twelvemonth's income of the land. Sons paid it on succeeding to their father. The agricultural society of Tours stated, in 1761, that 'this duty was infintely injurious to the progress of agricultural science. No tax levied by the king's government is so vexatious or so onerous in the country parts as this one'. Another contemporary observed that 'this imposition, which was originally paid but once in a lifetime, has become a very cruel exaction'. The nobility wished to see it abolished, for it operated to hinder commoners from buying their estates;[35] but the necessities of government involved its maintenance, and even its extension.

The Middle Ages have been unjustly blamed for much of the mischief produced by the trade-corporations. There is every reason to believe that, in the origin, trade-companies and trade-unions were formed merely for the purpose of uniting the members of each craft together, and establishing a sort of free government for each branch of industry, in order to assist and control the operatives. It does not appear that Saint Louis contemplated anything beyond this.

It was not till the beginning of the sixteenth century, when the revival of civil and religious liberty was in full progress, that the idea of placing labour on the footing of a privilege to be purchased of government was first broached. It was not till then that each craft became a small, close aristocracy, and a start was given to those monopolies which were so injurious to the progress of the arts and so odious to our ancestors. From the time of Henry III, who generalized, if he did not actually create the evil, to that of Louis XVI, who extirpated it, it may be said that the system of trade-companies acquired fresh strength and extension every year; and this, while the progress of society as steadily aggravated their inconvenience, and common sense revealed their absurdity. Year after year the close corporation system was adopted by new trades, while the privileges of the old companies were constantly on the increase. The evil reached its climax at the period which is usually termed the glorious portion of the reign of Louis XIV; for that was the time when the government stood in most urgent need of money, and was most firmly resolved not to appeal to the country.

Letronne remarked very justly in 1775, 'Government established trade-corporations solely for the purpose of obtaining money from them, either by the sale of patents, or by the creation of offices which the corporations were bound to buy up. The edict of 1673 carried out thoroughly the principles of Henry III by obliging all corporations to purchase charters from government; the next step was compelling all trades not incorporated to form companies. This wretched business yielded three hundred thousand livres.'

We have already seen how the constitutions of cities were overthrown, not from political motives, but in order to supply the public coffers with resources.

The same pecuniary necessities, coupled with a fixed aversion to appeal to the States, led to the sale of offices – a feature in the old regime which gradually assumed such proportions that history may be searched in vain for a parallel. It owed its origin to fiscal ingenuity. But is was so well contrived that for three centuries it fed the vanity of the middle classes, and directed the whole of their energies toward the acquisition of place; it stamped on the national heart that rage for offices, which became the source alike of our revolutions and our servitude.

As the finances became more embarrassed, new offices were created, with exemptions from taxation or privileges by way of salary; and, as they were created to supply the wants of the treasury, and not the requirements of the public service, an immense number of them were useless or positively mischievous.[36] As ealy as 1664, when Colbert instituted an inquiry into the subject, it was discovered that the capital invested in this miserable business nearly amounted to five hundred millions of livres. It is said that Richelieu abolished a hundred thousand offices. They rose anew under fresh names. For a trifle of money, people trafficked away the right of directing and controlling their own servants. The net result of this system was a government machine, so vast, so complicated, so cumbrous, and so inefficient, that it was actually found necessary to let it stand idle, while a new instrument, constructed with more simplicity and better adapted for use, performed the work which these countless functionaries were supposed to do.[37]

It may be affirmed that none of these detestable institutions could have lasted twenty years if it had been lawful to discuss their merits. None would have been established or extended if the States had been consulted, or if their complaints had been noticed when they were convened. On the rare occasions when the States met during the later ages of the monarchy, they were uniformly presented as a grievance. These assemblies frequently traced all the abuses of which they complained to the king's usurpation of the right of levying taxes arbitrarily, or, to use the energetic expressions of the fifteenth century, 'of his enriching himself out of the substance of the people without the advice and consent of the three Estates'. They did not confine their remonstrances to their own wrongs; they strenuously demanded, and often succeeded in enforcing respect for the rights of the provinces and cities. Some members protested at every session against the inequality of the public burdens. They repeatedly demanded the abolition of trade-corporations. They assailed the sale of offices century after century with increasing warmth. 'To sell offices,' they said, 'is to sell justice, which is infamous.' When the system of venal offices was firmly established, they complained of its abuse as persistently as ever. They exclaimed against the creation of useless and dangerous privileges; but all was in vain. These institutions were barricades against the people. They were devised in order to obviate the necessity of convening the States, and to conceal from the public eye taxes which the government dared not exhibit in an honest light.

Nor were the good kings any better in this respect than the

bad ones. It was Louis XII who systematized the sale of offices, and Henry IV who first sold hereditary ones. So weak was personal virtue against the vice of the system!

It was the desire to avoid meeting the States which led to the original grant of political power to the Parliaments, whence the judiciary became mixed with government in a manner that could not but be prejudicial to business. Policy dictated the establishment of new guarantees in the room of those that were taken away; for the French, who are patient enough under moderate despotisms, do not like the sight of them; and it is always wise to surround absolute power in France with a fence which, though it may not impede its movements, may conceal them from the public eye.

In fine, it was through fear lest the nation, whose money the kings wanted, should insist upon the restoration of its liberties, that class divisions were kept up; for by this means organized resistance or a common understanding was rendered impossible, and the government was certain of having to deal with each small clique separately. In the long course of French history, there reigned many distinguished sovereigns, several who were men of wit, some who were men of talent, while nearly all were men of courage; but there was not a single one who tried to efface class distinctions, or to promote union otherwise than as a condition of dependence. I am wrong; there was one who did desire to see the people united, and tried with all his heart to unite them, and that one – wonderful mystery of God's judgments! – was Louis XVI!

The great crime of the old kings was the division of the people into classes. Their subsequent policy followed as a matter of course; for when the wealthy and enlightened portion of a people are debarred from combination for public purposes, self-government becomes impossible, and tyranny become a necessity.

Turgot, in a secret report to the king, observes sadly, 'The nation is composed of several disunited classes and a divided people; hence no one takes thought for anything but his own private interest. Public spirit is a thing unknown. Villages and cities have no mutual relations with each other, nor have the counties (*arrondissements*) in which they are situate. They are even unable to come to an understanding for the repair of the common roads. An incessant warfare is carried on between rival claims and pretensions; the decision is invariably referred to your majesty or your servants. An order from you is required before people will pay taxes, or respect the rights of their neighbours, or even exercise their own.'

It was no slight task to reunite people who had been strangers to each other, or foes for so many centuries. It was very difficult to teach them to come to an understanding for the transaction of their common business. Division was a comparatively easy achievement. We have furnished the world with a memorable illustration of the difficulty of the reverse process. When, sixty years ago, the various classes into which French society was divided were suddenly brought together, after a separation of several centuries, their only points of contact were their old sores; they only met to tear each other in pieces. Their rival jealousies and hatreds survive to this day.

Chapter 11

Of the kind of Liberty enjoyed under the old Regime, and of its
Influence upon the Revolution.

It is impossible to form an accurate conception of the government of the old regime, and of the society which produced the Revolution, without pursuing somewhat farther the perusal of this book.

The spectacle of a people so divided and narrowed into cliques, with a royal authority so extensive and powerful, might lead to the impression that the spirit of independence had disappeared with public liberty, and that all Frenchmen were equally bowed in subjection. Nothing of the kind was the case. The government was sole and absolute manager of the public business, but it was not master of individual citizens.

Liberty survived in the midst of the institutions already

prepared for despotism; but it was a curious kind of liberty, not easily understood today. A very close inspection can alone discern the precise proportions of good and evil which it contained.

While the central government was displacing all the local authorities, and absorbing the whole power of the kingdom, its action was often impeded by institutions which it had either created or refrained from destroying, by old usages and customs, by rooted abuses. These nurtured a spirit of resistance in the minds of individuals, and preserved the characters of a good many from losing all their temper and outline.

The central government had the same character, used the same means, sought the same ends that it does today, but its power was less. Bent on making money out of everything, it had sold most of the public offices, and made away with the privilege of disposing of its patronage at will.[38] One of its passions had been the detriment of the other; its avarice had counteracted its ambition. It could not carry out its measures without employing agents whom it had not trained to the work, and whom it could not discharge for inefficiency. Its positive commands were thus often neutralized by the loose manner in which they were carried out. This strange radical vice of the system operated as a sort of check against the omnipotence of government – a breakwater, irregular in form and badly built, but still serving to break the shock and weaken the force of authority.

Again, the government had not as many favours to dispose of, in the shape of charitable assistance, honours, and money, as it has today; its power of seduction, like its power of control, was less.

It was not itself aware of the exact limits of its powers. None of them were solidly established or regularly recognized. Its sphere was immense, but it traversed it with uncertain step, groping its way through obscure and unknown paths. And that obscurity, which veiled the limits of its powers, and shrouded all its rights, favourable as it was to the encroachments of royalty, was likewise favourable to the defence of popular freedom.

With the consciousness of its recent rise and slender origin, the administration was invariably timid in the face of obstacles. It is a striking sight to see, in the correspondence of the ministers and intendants of the eighteenth century, how quickly this government, which was so overbearing and despotic when all was submission, lost its presence of mind at the first show of resistance, was alarmed by the mildest criticism, and terrified at the least noise. On these occasions it stopped short, hesitated, tried to compromise matters, and often withdrew from the contest at the sacrifice of a portion of its legitimate authority. Such was the course best suited to the weak selfishness of Louis XV and the benevolence of his successor. These sovereigns, besides, never supposed for a moment that anyone thought of dethroning them. They were strangers to the harshness and distrust which fear has since often planted in the hearts of rulers. They never perceived that they were trampling people under foot.

Many of the prejudices, and privileges, and false notions which stood in the way of the foundation of wholesome liberty, encouraged in many minds a spirit of independence and even insubordination.

The nobility held the government proper in supreme contempt, though they had occasional relations with its agents. Even after their power was gone, the nobles preserved some relic of the pride of their ancestors, who rebelled alike against servitude and against law. They took no thought for the liberty of the masses, and willingly allowed the government to lay its hand heavily on them; but they had no notion of submitting to it themselves, whatever reistance might cost. At the outbreak of the Revolution, the language and tone of the nobility toward the king and his agents were infinitely more haughty than those of the Third Estate, though the latter was on the point of overturning the throne, by whose side the former were to fall. The nobility claim the invention of nearly all the guarantees of the rights of the subject that were enjoyed during our thirty-seven years of representative government. Their old *cahiers*, in spite of their errors and prejudices, breathe the spirit of a great aristocracy.[39] It will always be a subject of regret that the French nobility was destroyed and uprooted instead of being subjected to the control of the laws. The error deprived the nation of a portion of its substance, and dealt liberty a wound that will never heal. The nobility had been the first class in the kingdom, and had enjoyed undisputed greatness for so many centuries, that it had acquired a high-mindedness, a self-reliance, a sense of responsibility, which rendered it the most solid portion of the social frame. Virile itself, it imparted virility to the other classes of society. Its extirpation weakened its very assailants. It can never be wholly restored – can never revive of itself; it may regain the titles and estates of its ancestors, but their spirit, never.

The clergy, who have since been abjectly servile in civil matters to any and every temporal authority, and the most audacious flatterers of any monarch who condescended to appear to favour the Church, were then the most independent body in the nation, the only one whose peculiar liberties were safe from assault.

When the provinces had lost their franchises, and the city charters were a mere name, when ten nobles could not meet to discuss business without the express permission of the king, the French Church held its periodical assemblies just as usual. Nor were the several ecclesiastical authorites without fixed limts.[40] Substantial guarantees shielded the lower clergy from the oppression of their superiors. No arbitary power in the hands of the bishop schooled them to passive obedience to the king. I have no intention of discussing the old constitution of the Church; I only observe that it did not teach the priests political servility.

Many ecclesiastics, moreover, were men of rank, and carried with them into the Church the pride and intractability of their class. All held a high rank in the state, and enjoyed privileges. The very feudal rights which militated so gravely against the moral power of the Church, imparted to its individual members a feeling of independence toward the civil authority.

Above all, the possession of real estate endowed the clergy with the feelings, and necessities, and opinions, and even the passions of citizens. I have had the patience to read most of the reports and debates of the old provincial assemblies, especially those of Languedoc, where the clergy took an unusual share in the details of government, and the reports of the provincial assemblies which were held in 1779 and 1787; and, bringing to bear on these documents our modern ideas, I have been amazed to find bishops and *abbés*, many of whom were as eminent in holiness as in learning, report ably on the opening of a road or the construction of a canal, argue with knowledge and science on the best means of increasing the agricultural yield of lands, of improving the condition or developing the industry of the people, and prove themselves always the equals, and often the superiors of the laymen with whom they were associated.[41]

I venture to think, in opposition to the generally received opinion, that systems which debar the Catholic clergy from the possession of landed property, and provide for their remuneration in money, serve no interests but those of the Papacy and the temporal power, and deprive the people of a very important element of liberty.

For a man whose best qualities are under foreign control, and who can have no family in the land he inhabits, there can be but one substantial motive for patriotism – the ownership of real estate. Remove that motive, and he ceases to belong to any one place rather than another. A stranger to civil society, he lives where chance has planted him, without sharing any of the interests which surround him. His conscience is in the hands of the Pope, his livelihood in those of the sovereign. He has no country but the Church. In political troubles, he thinks of nothing but its dangers and its advancement. If it be free and prosperous, what matters the rest? His normal political state is indifference. An excellent member of the Christian city, he is but a poor citizen of any other. Feelings and ideas such as his, in a body intrusted with the education of youth and the censorship of morals, cannot but enervate the national spirit for all the concerns of public life.

To form a correct idea of the changes that can be wrought in men's minds by changes in their condition, one must read once more the *cahiers* presented by the clerical order in 1789.

Though frequently intolerant, and sometimes obstinately wedded to their ancient privileges, the clergy gave proof on that occasion that they were as resolute foes to despotism and as staunch friends of civil and political liberty as the nobility or the

Third Estate.[42] They demanded that individual liberty should be secured, not by promises, but by a proceeding analogous in character to the writ of *habeas corpus*. They called for the destruction of state prisons, the abolition of unconstitutional courts and evocations, public debates, an irremovable judiciary; the distribution of offices among all classes of citizens, and the adoption of merit as the sole test of eligibility; a less oppressive and less ignominious recruiting system, to admit of no exemptions; the commutation of all feudal rights, which, they said, being part of the feudal system, were inimical to liberty; free labour; the abolition of inland custom-houses; an increase in the number of private schools, until there was one, and that a free school, in each parish; lay charitable institutions, such as workhouses, in the rural districts; all sorts of encouragements to agriculture.

So far as politics proper were concerned, they proclaimed loudly that to the nation alone belonged the indefeasible and inalienable right of making laws and imposing taxes. No Frenchman, they said, can be compelled to pay a tax which he did not vote either in person or by representative. They demanded free elections and annual meetings of the States-General, declared that it was their office to discuss all great public measures in presence of the nation, to make general laws which no special customs or privileges could defeat, to vote supplies, and control even the king's household. They insisted on the inviolability of the persons of deputies and the responsibility of ministers. They also demanded the establishment of provincial assemblies in every province and municipalities in every city. Of divine right not one word said they.

I doubt whether, on the whole, even taking into account the startling vices of some of its members, the world ever saw a more remarkable body than the Catholic clergy at the time the Revolution broke out. They were enlightened; they were national; their private virtues were not more striking than their public qualities; and yet they were largely endowed with faith, sufficient to bear them up against persecution. I began to study the old regime full of prejudice against the clergy; I have ended my task, and feel nothing but respect for them. They had no faults, in truth, but those which are inseparable from all corporations, whether political or religious, when they are solidly built and closely knit together, namely, a tendency to extension, an intolerant spirit, and an instinctive, and occasionally a blind devotion to the special interests of the corporate body.

Nor were the middle classes of the old regime less superior to their modern successors in point of independence and spirit. Many of the very vices of their organization led to this result. It has already been mentioned that they were even more given to place-hunting, and that there were more places within their reach than there are now; but mark the difference between the two. Government could neither give nor take away these places. They increased the dignity of their incumbents, without in any way rendering them slaves to the ruling power. Thus the very cause of the servility of so many men today was formerly the most powerful motive for independence and self-respect.

The immunities which, unhappily, divided the middle and lower classes, converted the former into a species of sham aristocracy, and armed it occasionally with pride and a spirit of resistance worthy of the genuine. The public good was often forgotten in the little private cliques which they formed; but the clique interests never.[43] There were common privileges, there was a corporate dignity to be defended, and there was no chance of concealment for the complaisant coward. People were, so to speak, actors on a very small but uncommonly conspicuous stage, with the same audience always before them, and always ready to applaud or hiss.

The art of stifling the sound of resistance was not brought to such perfection as it has been since. France was not so well deafened as it is in our day. It was, on the contrary, well adapted for the transmission of sound, and, though no political liberty could be seen, one had only to speak loud to be heard at a great distance.

The oppressed were secured a hearing in the courts of justice. The political and administrative institutions of the country were those of a despotism, but we were still a free people in our courts of law. The administration of justice under the old regime was cumbrous, complicated, slow, and costly – grave faults, no doubt; but it was never servile to the supreme power; and this is the very worst form of venality. That capital vice, which not only corrupts the judge, but soon infects the whole body of the people, was unknown in the old courts. Judges were not only irremovable, but looked for no promotion; both conditions are essential to independence for the power of punishing may be dispensed with if that of rewarding be retained.

True, the royal authority had stripped the common courts of their jurisdiction over cases in which the govenment was interested, but it had not stripped them of their terrors. They might be prevented from judging cases, but they could not be hindered from receiving complaints and expressing their opinions. And as the judicial idiom had preserved the plain simplicity of the old French tongue, which called things by their right names, it was not uncommon for judges to qualify the measures of the government with such epithets as arbitrary and despotic.[44] The irregular interference of the courts in the administration of government, which often proved a hindrance to the transaction of business, occasionally served as a safeguard of liberty; the greater evil was limited by the lesser.

In the heart of the magistracy and around it, the new ideas of the day had not wholly crushed out the vigorous habits of thought of olden time. No doubt the Parliaments thought more of themselves than of the public good; but still, when it was necessary to defend their independence and their honour, they were always intrepid, and gave heart to all who surrounded them.

When the Parliament of Paris was dissolved in 1770, every one of the magistrates who composed it submitted to the loss of rank and power rather than yield to the king. More than this: courts of another kind, such as the Court of Aids (*cour des aides*), which were neither assailed nor menaced, voluntarily exposed themselves to the same fate when that fate had become a matter of certainty. Nor was even this all. The leading advocates who had practised before the Parliament spontaneously shared its fate. They resigned glory and profit, and preferred silence to pleading before a dishonoured magistracy. I know of nothing grander than this in the history of any free people; and yet this took place in the eighteenth century, close to Louis the Fifteenth's court.

The nation had borrowed many habits from the courts. It was from the courts that we learned the only portion of the education of a free people which we owe to the old regime, that is to say, the principle that all decisions should be preceded by discussion, and subject to appeal; the use of publicity, and the love of forms. The government itself had borrowed largely from the language and usages of the courts. The king felt bound to assign reasons for his edicts; the Council's Orders were preceded by long preambles, intendants notified the public of their ordinances by the ministry of bailiffs. All the old administrative bodies, such as the Treasury Board, and the select-men, transacted business publicly, and heard rival petitioners or applicants by counsel. All their habits and forms were so many barriers against the arbitrary power of the sovereign. But the people proper, especially in the rural districts, had no means of resisting oppression except by violence.

Most of the means of defence I have just pointed out were beyond their reach; no one could avail himself of them unless his position in society was such that he could make himself seen and heard. But outside the ranks of the people, anyone in France who had the courage might, if he chose, yield a conditioned obedience, and resist even while he yielded.

The king addressed the nation in the language of a chief, not a master. At the commencement of the reign of Louis XVI, the monarch declared in the preamble of an edict, 'We glory in commanding a free and generous nation.' One of his ancestors had expressed the same idea in older style, when, on thanking the States-General for the boldness of their remonstrances, he exclaimed, 'We had rather speak to freemen than to slaves.'

The men of the eighteenth century were strangers to that passionate love for ease which is the mother of servitude; which, equally tame and tenacious, combines with several of the private virtues, such as family affection, regular habits, respect for religion, lukewarm but assiduous devotional habits; which tolerates honesty, and justifies heroism, and is remarkably successful in producing respectable men and cowardly citizens. They were better and worse.

The French of those days loved merriment and adored pleasure; their habits were perhaps more irregular, their passions and ideas more disorderly than those of their descendants, but they were strangers to the modern and decent sensuality of our day. Persons in the higher classes sought ornament rather than comfort, honour rather than money. Comfort did not even absorb the attention of the middle classes; more delicate and higher enjoyments were constantly sought in preference. Money was never the great end of life. 'I know my countrymen,' proudly wrote a contemporary; 'skilled in melting and scattering the metals, they are not calculated to worship them, and are quite prepared to return to their old idols, valour, glory, and, I will add, magnanimity.'

Care must be taken not to measure the baseness of men by their degree of submission to the sovereign power: that gauge would be a false one. Submissive as the men of the old regime were to the will of the king, they were strangers to submission of another kind; they had not learned to bow the knee to illegitimate or disputed authority, which inspires not honour, but contempt, and secures submission through the fear of injury or the hope of reward. That degrading form of servitude was unknown in olden time. The king inspired feelings such as no absolute monarch of later times has ever been able to awaken, and which the Revolution so thoroughly uprooted that we can can hardly understand them. They loved him like a father, and respected him as they respected their God. When they submitted to his arbitrary commands, it was less from compulsion than from love, and their soul often remained their own, even in a state of complete subjection. For them, the greatest evil of obedience was constraint; it is the least in our time. The greatest evil now is the servility which prompts obedience. Let us beware how we despise our ancestors; we have no right to do so. Would to God that we could recover, even with their faults and their prejudices, a little of their greatness.

It would then be an error to consider the old regime as a period of servility and dependence. There was much more liberty then than there is now,[45ab] but it was an irregular and intermittent kind of liberty, bound up with the class system and notions of privileges and exemptions – a sort of liberty which encouraged rebellion against law as well as against oppression, and always left a portion of the people destitute of the most natural and obvious safeguards. Yet, stunted and deformed as it was, it was fertile. It was to that liberty that so many individuals owed the preservation of their natural character, with its colour and outline, when centralization was labouring to reduce the character of the whole nation to a dead level and one uniform line. It was that which kept self-respect alive, and often raised the love of glory above all other passions. it was that which formed those vigorous souls, those proud and bold geniuses, whose appearance on the scene we are soon to witness, and who made the French Revolution alike the admiration and the terror of subsequent generations. It would be strange indeed if such masculine virtues as theirs had been brought to light in a land where liberty was unknown.

But if this disorderly and unwholesome sort of liberty prepared the French to overthrow despotism, it unfitted them, to an unexampled degree, perhaps, for replacing it by the peaceful and free government of law.

Chapter 12

How the Condition of the French Peasantry was worse in some respects in the Eighteenth Century than it had been in the Thirteenth, notwithstanding the Progress of Civilization.

In the eighteenth century, the French peasantry were no longer a prey to small feudal despots. They rarely suffered violence at the hands of government. They enjoyed civil liberty and possessed land; but they were shunned by all the other classes of society and led a life of unexampled isolation. The consequences of this new and singular form of oppression deserve to be examined separately and with some attention.

At the very beginning of the seventeenth century, Henry IV

complained, says Peréfix, that the nobility were deserting the rural districts. The desertion had become general by the middle of the eighteenth: all the documents of the time – treatises on political economy, intendants' correspondence, reports of agricultural societies – concur in deploring the fact. It is, moreover, indisputably proved by the capitation registers. The capitation-tax was levied at the actual place of residence of the taxable: all the great and a portion of the lesser nobility paid it at Paris.

No men of rank remained in the country districts but those whose means did not allow them to move. A man of this class was strangely situate among the peasantry. He was no longer their ruler, and had no reasons for conciliating, or aiding, or guiding them, while, on the other hand, he did not share their burdens, and consequently felt no sympathy for sufferings which did not afflict him, or for wrongs to which he was a stranger. Though they had ceased to be his subjects, he had not become their fellow-citizen. The position is without parallel in history.

There resulted from it a sort of absenteeism of heart, if I may use the expression, which was even more effective than absenteeism of body. The man of rank who resided on his estate often thought and acted as his steward would have done in his absence. He viewed his tenants merely in the light of debtors, and rigorously exacted from them his full due according to law, thus rendering the remains of the feudal system harder to bear than its entirety had formerly been.[46ab]

He was often in involved and needy circumstances, and lived meanly in his chateau, his main thought being how he could save money for the winter at Paris. With their peculiar directness of mind, the people gave him the name of the least of all birds of prey; they called him the hobby.

There were individual exceptions, of course; but history regards classes only. No one denies that there were at this time many rich landowners who concerned themselves for the welfare of the peasantry, without being compelled to do so by duty or interest; but these were rebels against the law of their condition, which, in spite of themselves, enjoined indifference on the one side and hatred on the other.

It has been common to ascribe the general desertion of the country parts by the nobility to the policy of particular kings or ministers: some have traced it to Richelieu, others to Louis XIV. During the last three centuries of the monarchy it certainly was the aim of the monarchs to keep the nobility apart from the people, and to attract the former to the court. That aim was pursued with especial vigour in the seventeenth century, when the nobility were still feared by the kings. One of the questions addressed to intendants was, 'Do the noblemen of your province prefer remaining there, or leaving their homes?' The answer of one intendant regretted that in his province men of rank preferred the company of mere peasants to the society of the court and their duty to the king. The province of which this was said was Anjou, which afterward became La Vendée. These noblemen, who were said to be slow to perform their duty to the king, were the only ones who defended the French monarchy in the field, and died for it; they owed this glorious distinction solely to their influence over the peasantry, among whom they were censured for preferring to reside.

Care must be taken, however, not to ascribe the migration of the nobility into the capital to the direct influence of this or that king. The true and principal cause of the phenomenon lay not in the policy of individuals, but in the slow, unceasing operation of institutions; this is proved by the utter incapacity of the government to arrest the mischief, when in the eighteenth century it was so minded. When the nobility lost, irretrievably, their political rights, and the local franchises were taken away, the migration became universal. No stimulus was required to wean the nobles from the country; they had no wish to stay there: rural life had no charms for them.

What I have said of the nobility applies equally to rich landowners in general. Centralization stripped the rural districts of their rich and enlightened inhabitants. I might explain how, moreover, it prevented agriculture from arriving at perfection; for, as Montesquieu profoundly observes, 'The yield of land depends less on its fertility than on the freedom of its occupants.' But I do not wish to digress.

We have seen already how the middle classes deserted the

country parts and took refuge in cities. Nothing is better established by the documents of the old regime. One rarely sees, say they, more than one generation of rich peasants. The moment a farmer acquires a little property, he takes his son from the plow, sends him into the city, and buys him some small office. Hence arose the strange dislike which farmers even still seem to feel for the calling which has enriched them. The effect has outlived the cause.

In fact, the only well-bred man, or, as the English would say, the only gentleman who lived permanently among the peasantry, and associated with them, was the parish curate; and the curate would have become the master of the rural classes, in spite of Voltaire, had he not been so notoriously connected with the political hierarchy, whose odium he shared together with its privileges.[47]

The peasant, then, was widely separated from the upper classes of society. He was kept aloof from all who could help or guide him. The higher his fellows rose in influence and station, the more they avoided him. He seemed to have been picked out of the whole nation, and set aside.

No such state of things existed in any other great nation of civilized Europe, nor had it been of long duration in France. The peasant of the fourteenth century was liable to more oppression, but he had better claims to assistance. If the aristocracy tyrannized over him occasionally, they never abandoned him.

Villages in the eighteenth century were assemblages of poor, ignorant, and coarse persons; with unskilled magistrates, universally despised; with a syndic who could not read; with a collector who could not add up the accounts on which his neighbours' and his own fortune depended. Their old seigniors, despoiled of their authority, had come to consider it degrading to be concerned in their government. They viewed the distribution of the taille, the militia levy, the regulation of *corvées*, as servile duties only fit for a syndic. No one but the central power paid any attention to village affairs; and, as it was distant, and had nothing to fear from the villagers, it noticed them no further than was necessary to get money from them.

See, now, what became of this forsaken class, over which no

one tried to tyrannize, but which no one tried to aid or enlighten.

The weightiest of the feudal burdens had certainly been lightened or removed, but they had been succeeded by others perhaps even more oppressive. Peasants were relieved from many grievances which had afflicted their ancestors, but they endured sufferings which the latter had never known.

It is notorious that the increase of the taille – tenfold in two centuries – fell wholly on the agricultural classes. A word must be said here of the manner in which it was levied in the country, in order to show what barbarous laws may be established or maintained in a civilized age, when the leading minds of the nation have no personal interest in changing them.

I find a sketch of the taille, in a confidential circular of the comptroller-general to the intendants, dated 1772. It is a masterpiece of accuracy and brevity. 'In the greater part of the kingdom,' says the minister, 'the taille is arbitrarily distributed and levied, under a joint and several responsibility, on the persons of taxables and not on property; it varies constantly in consequence of the fluctuations in the means of those who pay it.' That is the whole story; impossible to sketch with more art the lucrative evil.

The sum to be paid by each parish was fixed yearly. As the minister observed, it varied incessantly, so that the farmer could never tell how much he would have to pay from year to year. In each parish a peasant was chosen at haphazard every year, and appointed collector; it was his business to distribute the tax among his fellow-parishioners.

I promised to describe the office of collector. Listen to the Provincial Assembly of Guienne: it is an impartial witness, being wholly composed of persons who are exempt in virtue of royal appointments. It declared in 1779: 'As no one is willing to take the office of collector, it must be held alternately by everyone. Hence the tax is levied every year by a new collector, about whose capacity and honesty no inquiry is made. The tax levy is what might be expected: it bears the mark of the collector's fears, his weaknesses, or his vices. How could it be otherwise? He is wholly in the dark. Who can tell the exact income of his neighbour, or the proportion it bears to that of others? Yet the collector is bound to decide the exact amount of each; and for the proceeds of the tax his property and his person are liable. He usually loses half his time, for two years, in running after the tax-payers. Those who cannot read are obliged to find a neighbour to take their place.'

A short while before, Turgot had said of another province, 'The post of collector often drives its incumbent to despair, and nearly always ruins him. In each village, all the families in easy circumstances are thus successively reduced to poverty.'

The unfortunate individual was, however, armed with pro-digious power – a tyrant as well as a martyr. While he was ruining himself, he held the fortune of everyone else in his hands. In the language of the provincial assembly, 'Family affection, personal friendships and spites, a desire for vengeance, a wish to conciliate, fears of displeasing a rich man who has work to give – all these render it almost impossible that he can discharge his duties justly.' Fear often made the collector pitiless. In some parishes he did not show his face without a band of bailiffs and followers at his back. 'Unless he is backed by bailiffs,' writes an intendant in 1764, 'the taxables will not pay.' 'At Villefranche alone,' says the provincial assembly quoted above, 'six hundred bailiffs and followers are always kept on foot.'[48]

To escape this violent and arbitrary taxation, the French peasant of the eighteenth century imitated the Jew of the Middle Ages. He assumed the garb of poverty if he was accidentally in easy circumstances; the idea of a competency terrified him. I find this proved by a document which does not date from Guienne, but from a hundred leagues from thence. The Agricultural Society of Maine announced in its report of 1761 that it had intended to distribute cattle as prizes, but had 'abandoned the design from apprehensions that the distribution of such prizes might awaken jealousies which the arbitrary mode of distributing the taxes might enable defeated competitors to gratify in future years.'

This system of taxation trained everyone, in fact, to spy out his neighbours, and denounce to the collector their progress towards affluence: all were educated to be informers and natural enemies. What more would one expect to hear of the dominions of a rajah of Hindostan?

There were parts of France, however, where the taxes were uniform and mild; these were some of the *pays d'états*.[49] It is true that these provinces had reserved the right of taxing themselves. In Languedoc, for instance, the taille bore wholly on landed property, and did not vary with the owner's means. Every thirty years the whole province was divided into three classes of lands, according to fertility, and the proportion to be borne by each estate was carefully fixed and recorded in a register. Everyone knew beforehand precisely how much he had to pay. If he failed to pay, he, or rather his land, was alone responsible. If he felt aggrieved by the levy, he had the right of demanding a comparison of his quota with that of any other resident of the parish he chose to select, by the process we now call an 'appeal for proportionate equality'.

It will be seen that this system is precisely the one which we pursue today; it has been extended to the whole country without alteration. It is worthy of remark, that while we have borrowed from the old regime the form of our public administration, we have abstained from imitating it in other respects. Our administrative methods are copied from those of the old provinces. We have taken the machine, but rejected its product.

The habitual poverty of the country people had given rise to maxims well calculated to keep them poor. Richelieu, in his Political Testament, says, 'If the people were well off, it would be difficult to restrain them within legal bounds.' Rulers in the eighteenth century did not go quite so far, but they believed the peasant would not work without the spur of need; misery appeared to them the only safeguard against idleness. I have heard the very same theory advanced in reference to the negroes in our colonies. So general has this belief been, that most political economists have felt it necessary to refute it at length.

It is well known that the primitive object of the taille was to enable the king to hire soldiers in lieu of the nobles and vassals who were bound to service; yet in the seventeenth century the military service was again exacted, as has been mentioned, under the name of militia, and this time the burden fell wholly upon the people, and almost exclusively on the peasantry.

That militia duty was often strenuously refused or evaded is well established by the immense number of police reports referring to the apprehension of refractory militia-men or deserters that are to be found in every intendant's office. It was, it seems the most odious of all the burdens that were laid on the peasantry. They fled into the woods to avoid serving, or resisted the levies with force of arms. This appears surprising in view of the ease with which a system of compulsory conscription is enforced today.

The intense aversion which the old regime peasantry felt for the militia system was due less to the principle of the law than to the manner in which it was executed; to the length of time during which the risk hung over men's heads (a man was liable till he was forty, unless he married); to the arbitrary revision of the lots, which often made a good number as fatal as a bad one; which often made a good number as fatal as a bad one; to the legal impossibility of procuring a substitute; to the disgust inspired by a hard, dangerous vocation, in which it was wholly impossible to rise; but, above all, to the reflection that this great burden bore on them alone, and on the most wretched individuals among them. The ignominious distinction established between them and other classes imbittered their actual wrongs.

I have examined the reports of several drawings for militia-men, in various parishes, in the year 1769. The exempts are enumerated: one is the servant of a gentleman; another, watchman at an abbey; a third is only valet of a burgher, it is true, but his master 'lives nobly'. No one, as a rule, was exempt but persons in easy circumstances. When a farmer, for instance, paid heavy taxes for several years, his sons were exempt: this was called encouraging agriculture. Political economists, much as they admired equality in other matters, made no objection to this privilege; they only desired to extend it to other cases, or, in other words, to increase the burden of the poorest and most unprotected peasantry. One of them observes that 'soldiers are so badly paid, so poorly lodged, dressed, and fed, and kept in such strict dependence, that it would be too cruel to choose them out of any class but the very lowest.'

Up to the close of the reign of Louis XIV the high-roads were not repaired at all, or were kept in repair at the cost of the state and of the road-side landowners: it was at that period that the plan of keeping them in repair at the expense of the peasantry, by *corvées*, was first commenced. It seemed so excellent a mode of securing good roads without paying for them, that in 1737 a circular of Comptroller-general Orry applied it to the whole of France. Intendants were authorized to imprison refractory peasants, or to send bailiffs for them.[50]

Thenceforth, measurably with the extension of trade and the desire for good roads, *corvées* were extended and increased.[51] A report made in 1779 to the Provincial Assembly of Berry states that the annual value of labour performed by the peasantry in *corvées* in that poor province was 700,000 *livres*. A similar estimate was made for lower Normandy in 1787. No better indication of the sad condition of the country-people could be found. Social progress enriched all other classes of society, but impoverished the peasantry. Civilization was a blessing to all but them.

It is stated in the correspondence of the intendants about the same period, that the peasantry must not be allowed to perform their regular *corvées* on private roads, for they are all required on the highways, or, as the phrase was, on the king's highway.[52] The strange notion that the cost of keeping the roads in repair ought to be borne by the poorest persons in the community, and those who travel the least – new as it was – took such root in the minds of those who were gainers by it, that they soon came to believe that no other system was feasible. An attempt was made in 1776 to commute *corvées* for a tax payable in money: the new tax was as unequally distributed as the old imposition.

Corvées, on ceasing to be seigniorial and becoming royal, were gradually applied to all public works. In 1719 they were exacted for the construction of barracks. '*The parishes must send their best workmen,*' said the ordinance, '*and give up all other work for this.*' *Corvées* were exacted for the conveyance of convicts to the galleys,[53] and of beggars to charitable institutions; for the removal of military baggage from place to place, when troops were moved.[54] This was no slight task at a time when every regiment was encumbered with heavy baggage: it was requisite to gather from the neighbourhood for many miles around an immense number of carts and oxen. This kind of compulsory labour, which was hardly felt at first, became a very heavy burden when the standing armies became large. I have seen pressing demands from contractors, insisting on the employment of *corvées* for the conveyance of timber from the forests to ship-yards.[55] Labour of this description was usually remunerated, but the price was low and unalterable. This ill-advised imposition sometimes became so burdensome as to frighten the receivers of the taille. In 1751 a receiver was apprehensive lest 'the expense to which the peasantry were put for the repairs of the roads would incapacitate them from paying the taille'.

Could these oppressive measures have been carried into effect if beside the peasantry there had stood rich and enlightened men, with the will and the power, if not to protect them, at least to intercede on their behalf with the master, who held the fortune of rich and poor alike in his hand?

I have read a letter, written in 1774 by a wealthy landholder to the provincial intendant on the subject of opening a road. The road, says he, would insure the prosperity of the village, and he explains why; then he recommends the establishment of a fair, which could not fail to double the price of produce; and, lastly, this excellent citizen advises the foundation of a school, with some small help from government, as the best method of procuring industrious subjects for the king. None of these ideas had occurred to him until he had been confined a couple of years by a *lettre de cachet* in his chateau. 'It is my exile on my estate,' he adds ingenuously, 'which has convinced me of the extreme utility of all these projects.'

It was especially in time of scarcity that observers noticed the rupture of the old bonds of patronage and dependence which had formerly linked the great landowners and the peasantry together. At these critical periods the central government was terrified by a consciousness of its weakness. It tried to recall to life the individual influences or the political associations it had destroyed, but they gave no sign, and it saw with surprise that the people it had killed were really dead.

When the suffering was very great, especially in the poorer provinces, some intendants, like Turgot, issued illegal ordinances, compelling the rich landowners to feed their peasantry till the harvest came round. I have seen letters from several curates, dated 1770, advocating the taxation of the richest landowners of their parishes, laymen and ecclesiastics alike – 'men who own large estates, on which they never reside, and which only serve to give them an income which they spend elsewhere'.

Villages were always infested with beggars, for, as Letronne remarks, the poor are relieved in the cities, but in the country, especially in winter, there is no one to help them, and they have no choice but to beg.

These unfortunate people were sometimes furiously persecuted. The Duke of Choiseul undertook in 1767 to put down mendicity throughout France. The intendant's correspondence bears witness to the rigor with which he proceeded. Orders were given to the police to arrest simultaneously all the beggars in the kingdom: it is said they seized fifty thousand. All able-bodied vagabonds were sent to the galleys; for the others, some forty poor-houses were opened in various parts of the kingdom. It would have answered better to have opened the hearts of the rich.

The government of the old regime, which was so mild and so timid, so fond of formalities and delays in dealing with the upper classes, was often rough and always prompt in dealing with the lower, especially with the peasantry. I have never been able to discover, in all the documents I have examined, a single instance where a burgher was arrested by order of an intendant, but peasants were arrested daily for *corvées*, militia duty, mendicity, and a thousand other matters. One class was entitled to be judged by an independent tribunal, after a long and public hearing; the other was dragged before the police magistrate (*prévôt*), who decided summarily and without appeal.[56]

'The immense distance which separates the people from other classes of society,' says Necker in 1785, 'tends to divert attention from the manner in which power may be used against individuals. Were it not for the gentleness and humanity of the

French character, and the spirit of the age, the subject would be an endless source of sorrow to those who can sympathize with sufferings which they do not share.'

But the oppressive character of the system was more conspicuous in the improvement it prevented than in the injury it caused. Free, and landholders as they were, the peasantry were almost as ignorant as, and often more wretched than the serfs their ancestors. In the midst of a prodigious development of art and science, they made no industrial progress; they remained dark and uncivilized in a world that glittered with intelligence. They had never learned to use the quickness and keenness of their race; they could not even succeed in their own calling – agriculture. A celebrated English agricultural writer described what he saw as being 'farms dating from the tenth century'. They excelled in nothing but warfare; for, as soldiers, they could not help mingling with other social classes.

Such was the depth of wretchedness and solitude in which the French peasantry were hermetically sealed. I was surprised and almost alarmed by discovering that, less than twenty years before the Catholic faith was abolished without resistance and the churches profaned, the government often adopted the following method of ascertaining the population of a canton: the curates reported the number of communicants at Easter; to this an approximate figure was added for children under age and sick persons; and the total was assumed to be the exact population. Yet the ideas of the time, strangely altered and disguised, were making their way into the peasant's mind by devious and crooked channels, though nothing of them appeared on the surface. Manners, customs, belief – all were unchanged: the peasant was not only resigned, he was in good spirits.

Care must be taken not to misunderstand the gaiety which the French have often exhibited in the greatest affliction. It is a mere attempt to divert the mind from the contemplation of misfortune which seems inevitable; it by no means indicates insensibility. Throw open a door by which these men may escape from the misery which they appear to bear so lightly, and they will rush through it with such force as to pass over any obstacle that stands in the way, without even noticing it.

We see these things very plainly from our point of view, but they were hidden from contemporaneous observers. The upper classes never easily read the mind of their inferiors, and least of all of the peasantry. Their education and their social habits endow the latter with habits of judging which are peculiar to themselves, and which other classes do not acquire; and when rich and poor have no interests, or grievances, or business in common, the obscurity which wraps their respective minds becomes impenetrable; they may live side by side for centuries without understanding each other. It is curious to note the astonishing feeling of security which pervaded the upper and middle classes of society at the time the Revolution began, to hear their ingenious lucubrations on the virtues of the people, on their gentleness, their affectionate disposition, their innocent pleasures, when '93 is close at hand. A ridiculous, but a terrible spectacle!

Let us stop here, before proceeding further, and observe, through all the small facts I have noticed, one of the greatest of God's laws for the government of society.

The French nobility will not mix with the other classes. Men of rank succeed in throwing off all their public burdens. They fancy that by doing so they may preserve their rank without its troublesome appendages, and at first sight it really seems they can; but before long an internal disease assails them, and reduces them gradually. They grow poorer as their privileges multiply. The middle classes, from which they had taken such care to keep aloof, grow rich and enlightened beside them, without them, in spite of them. The very men they had refused to accept as associates or fellow-citizens are about to become their rivals, their enemies, and, ere long, their masters. Though they have been relieved from the responsibility of guiding, protecting, assisting their vassals, they estimate that they have lost nothing, because their titles and their pecuniary privileges still remain intact. As they are still the first men in the country in rank, they persuade themselves that they still hold rule; and, in fact, they are still surrounded by those whom in notarial acts they style 'their subjects', while others are their vassals, their tenants, their farmers. But, in reality, they govern no one. They stand quite alone, and from the blow that threatens to overwhelm them, their only resource will be in flight.

Though the career of the nobility and that of the middle classes had differed widely, there was one point of resemblance between them: both had kept themselves aloof from the people. Instead of uniting with the peasantry, the middle classes had shrunk from the contact of their miseries; instead of joining them to combat the principle of inequality of ranks, they had only sought to aggravate the injustice of their position: they had been as eager for exceptional rights as the nobility for privileges. Themselves sprung from the ranks of the peasantry, they had so lost all recollection and knowledge of their former character, that it was not till they had armed the peasants that they perceived they had roused passions which they could neither gauge, guide, nor restrain, and of which they were destined to be the victims as well as the authors.

The ruin of the great house of France, which once promised to spread over the whole Continent, will always be a subject of wonder, but no careful student of its history can fail to comprehend its fall. With few exceptions, all the vices, all the errors, all the fatal prejudices which I have sketched, owed either their origin, or their continuance, or their development to the exertions made by most of our kings to create distinctions of classes in order to govern more absolutely.

But when the work was complete – when the nobility were isolated from the middle classes, and both from the peasantry – when each class contained a variety of small private associations, each as distinct from the others as the classes themselves, the whole nation, though homogeneous, was composed of parts that did not hold together. There was no organization that could resist the government, but there was none that could assist it. So it was that, the moment the groundwork moved, the whole edifice of the French monarchy gave way and fell with a crash.

Nor did the people, in taking advantage of the faults of their masters, and throwing off their yoke, wholly succeed in eradicating the false notions, the vicious habits, the bad propensities these masters had either imparted or allowed them to acquire. They have at times used liberty like slaves and shown themselves to be as incapable of self-government as they were void of pity for their old teachers.

I shall now pursue my subject, and, losing sight of the ancient and general predisposing causes of the great revolution, pass to some specific facts of more recent date, which determined finally its locality, its origin, and its character.

Chapter 13

How, toward the middle of the Eighteenth Century, literary Men became the leading Politicians of the Country, and of the Effects thereof.

France had long been the most literary nation of Europe, but her men of letters had never exhibited the mental peculiarities, or occupied the rank which distinguished them in the eithteenth century. Nothing of the kind had ever been witnessed either here or abroad.

They took no part in public business, as English authors did; on the contrary, they had never lived so much out of the world. They held no public office, and, though society teemed with functionaries, they had no public functions to discharge.

But they were not strangers to politics, or wholly absorbed in abstract philosophy and belles-letters, as most of the German literary men were. They paid sedulous, and, indeed, special attention to the subject of government. They were to be heard day after day discoursing of the origin and primitive form of society, of the primordial rights of the governed and governing power, of the natural and artificial relations of men one to the other, of the soundness or the errors of the prevailing customs, of the principles of the laws. They made thorough inquiries into the Constitution, and criticised its structure and general plan. They did not invariably devote particular or profound studies to these great problems. Many merely glanced at them in passing, often playfully, but none omitted them altogether. Abstract and literary views on political subjects are scattered throughout the works of that day; from the ponderous treatise to the popular song, none are wholly devoid of this feature.

The political systems of these writers were so varied that it would be wholly impossible to reconcile them together, and mould them all into a theory of government.

Still, setting details aside, and looking only to main principles, it is readily discerned that all these authors concurred in one central point, from whence their particular notions diverged. They all started with the principle that it was necessary to substitute simple and elementary rules, based on reason and natural law, for the complicated and traditional customs which regulated society in their time.

It will be ascertained, on close inquiry, that the whole of the political philosophy of the eighteenth century is really comprised in that single notion.

It was not new. For three thousand years it had been floating backward and forward through the minds of men without finding a resting-place. How was it that it contrived to engross the attention of all the authors of the day just at this time? How did it happen that, instead of lying buried in the brain of philosophers, as it had done so often, it became so absorbing a passion among the masses, that idlers were daily heard discussing abstract theories on the nature of human society, and the imaginations of women and peasants were fired by notions of new systems? How came it that literary men, without rank, or honours, or riches, or responsibility, or power, monopolized political authority, and found themselves, though strangers to the government, the only leading politicians of the day? I desire to answer these queries briefly, and to show how facts which seem to belong to the history of our literature alone exercised an influence over our revolution that was both extraordinary and terrible, and is still felt in our time.

It was not chance which led the philosophers of the eighteenth century to advocate principles so opposed to those on which society rested in their day. They were naturally suggested by the spectacle they had before them. They had constantly in view a host of absurd and ridiculous privileges, whose burden increased daily, while their origin was growing more and more indistinct; hence they were driven toward notions of natural equality. They beheld as many irregular and strange old institutions, all hopelessly jarring together and unsuited to the time, but clinging to life long after their virtue had departed; and they naturally felt disgusted with all that was ancient and traditional, and – each taking his own reason for his guide – they sought to rebuild society on some wholly new plan.[57]

These writers were naturally tempted to indulge unreservedly in abstract and general theories of government. They had no practical acquaintance with the subject; their ardours were undamped by actual experience; they knew of no existing facts which stood in the way of desirable reforms; they were ignorant of the dangers inseparable from the most necessary revolutions, and dreamed of none. There being no approach toward political liberty, the business of government was not only ill understood, it was not understood at all. Having no share in it themselves, and seeing nothing that was done by those who had, these writers lacked the superficial education which the habit of political freedom imparts even to those who take no part in politics. They were hence bolder in their projects of innovation, fonder of theory and system, more prone to despise the teaching of antiquity and to rely on individual reason than is usually the case with speculative writers on politics.

Ignorance of the same kind insured their success among the masses. If the French people had still participated in the government by means of States-General, if they had still taken part in the administration of the public business in Provincial Assemblies, it is certain that they would have received the lucubrations of these authors with more coolness; their business habits would have set them on their guard against pure theory.

Had they seen a possibility of changing the spirit without wholly destroying the form of their old institutions, as the English did, they might have been reluctant to adventure upon absolute novelties; but there was not a man whose fortune, or whose comfort, or whose person, or whose pride was not daily interfered with by some old law, or old institution, or old decayed authority, and each particular grievance seemed altogether incurable short of the total destruction of the constitution of the country.

We had, however, saved one right from the general wreck — that was the right of philosophizing freely on the origin of society, on the natural principles of government, and the primitive rights of man.

A rage for this political literature seized all who were inconvenienced by the legislation of the day, including many who were naturally but little prone to indulge in abstract speculations. Tax-payers, wronged by the unjust distribution of the taille, warmed over the principle of the natural equality of men. Farmers, whose harvests were spoiled by rabbits kept by their noble neighbours, rejoiced to hear that reason repudiated all privileges without exception. Popular passions thus disguised themselves in a philosophic garb; political aspirations were forcibly driven into a literary channel, and men of letters, taking the direction of public opinion, temporarily occupied the position which in free countries belongs to party leaders.

Nor could their claim to that place be disputed. A vigorous aristocracy will not only conduct public business, but will make public opinion, and give the keynote to authors, and authority to principles; but these prerogatives had passed away from the French nobility long before the eighteenth century; they had lost credit and power together. The place they had occupied in the public mind was vacant, and no one could gainsay the authors for seizing upon it.

The aristocracy rather favoured than impeded their usurpation. Forgetting that established theories, sooner or later, inevitably become political passions, and find expression in acts, they made no objection to the discussion of doctrines that were wholly subversive of their private rights, and even of their existence. They considered them ingenious exercises for the mind, amused themselves by taking part in them, and peacefully enjoyed their immunities and privileges, while they serenely discoursed on the absurdity of all existing customs.

Astonishment is expressed at the blindness with which the upper classes of the old regime helped to ruin themselves; but where could they have learned better? Ruling classes can no more acquire a knowledge of the dangers they have to avoid without free institutions, than their inferiors can discern the rights they ought to preserve in the same circumstances. More than a century had elapsed since the last trace of public life had disappeared in France. During the interval, no noise or shock warned conservatives of the impending fall of the ancient edifice. Appearances remaining unchanged, they suspected no internal revolution. Their minds had stood still at the point where their ancestors had left off. The nobility were as jealous of the royal prerogative in 1789 as they had been in the fifteenth century, as the reports of the States-General prove. On the other hand, on the very eve of his wreck in the democratic storm, the unhappy Louis XVI, as Burke very truly observes, could see no rival to the throne outside the ranks of the aristocracy; he was as suspicious of the nobles as if he had been living in the time of the Fronde. He felt as certain as any of his ancestors that the middle and lower classes were the surest supports of the throne.

But of all the strange phenomena of these times, the strangest to us, who have seen so many revolutions, is the absence of any thought of revolution from the mind of our ancestors. No such thing was discussed, because no such thing had been conceived. In free communities, constant vibrations keep men's minds alive to the possibility of a general earthquake, and hold governments in check; but in the old French society that was so soon to topple over, there was not the least symptom of unsteadiness.

I have read attentively the cahiers of the Three Estates presented to the States-General in 1789; I say the Three Estates – nobility and clergy as well as Third Estate. I observe that here a law and there a custom is sought to be changed, and I note it. Pursuing the immense task to the end, and adding together all the separate demands, I discover with terror that nothing less is demanded than the simultaneous and systematic repeal of all the laws, and abolition of all the customs prevailing in the country; and I perceive at once that one of the great revolutions the world ever saw is impending. Those who are to be its victims tomorrow suspect nothing; they delude themselves with the notion that this elaborate old society can be transformed without a shock, and with the help of reason alone. Unhappy creatures! how had they forgotten the quaint old maxim of their fathers four hundred years ago, 'He that is too desiring of liberty and franchess must needs fall into serfage.'

That the nobles and middle classes, shut out as they had been for so long from public life, should exhibit this singular inexperience, was not surprising; but it was singular that the members of the government, ministers, magistrates, and intendants, should be equally blind. Of these, many were able men at their trade; they were thoroughly versed in the administrative science of the period; but of the great science of government in the abstract, of the art of watching social movements and foreseeing their results, they were as ignorant as the people themselves; for this branch of the business of public men can only be taught by the practical working of free institutions.

This is finely illustrated in the memorial which Turgot presented to the kind in 1775, in which he advised the creation of a representative assembly. It was to be freely elected by the people, to meet for six weeks every year, but to exercise no effective authority. It might devote attention to administrative details, but without meddling with the government; express opinions rather than wishes; discuss laws without making them. 'Such an assembly,' said he, 'would enlighten the king without fettering him, and afford a safe outlet for public opinion. It would not be authorized to impede necessary measures of government, and could be easily restrained within these limits by his majesty in case it tried to overstep them.' It would have been difficult to misapprehend more grossly the tendency of a measure or the spirit of the age. Toward the close of revolutions, it has certainly often happened that Turgot's idea has been successfully realized, and the forms of liberty established without its substance. Augustus performed the experiment with success. When a nation has been wearied by long strife, it will submit to be duped for peace sake; and in these cases history apprises us that it will suffice to collect from various parts of the country obscure dependents of government, and make them play the part of a political assembly at a fixed rate of wages. This performance has been repeatedly witnessed. But at the outset of revolutions such enterprises have always failed, for they excite, without satisfying, men's minds. Every citizen of a free state is aware of this truth; Turgot, with all his administrative science, knew nothing of it.

Now when it is borne in mind that this French nation, which had so little experience of business, and so little to do with its own government, was, at the same time, the most literary of all the nations of the world, it may be easily understood how writers became a power in the state, and ended by ruling it.

In England, political writers and political actors were mixed, one set working to adapt new ideas to practice, the other circumscribing theory by existing facts; whereas in France, the political world was divided into two separate provinces without intercourse with each other. One administered the government, the other enunciated the principles on which government ought to rest. The former adopted measures according to precedent and routine, the latter evolved general laws, without ever thinking how they could be applied. The one conducted business, the other directed minds.

There were thus two social bodies; society proper, resting on a framework of tradition, confused and irregular in its organization, with a host of contradictory laws, well-defined distinctions of rank and station, and unequal rights; and above this, an imaginary society, in which everything was simply, harmonious, equitable, uniform, and reasonable.

The minds of the people gradually withdrew from the former to take refuge in the latter. Men became indifferent to the real by dint of dwelling on the ideal, and established a mental domicile in the imaginary city which the authors had built.

Our revolution has often been traced to American example. The American Revolution, no doubt, exercised considerable influence over ours, but that influence was less a consequence of the deeds done in America than an inference from the prevailing ideas in France. In other European countries the American Revolution was nothing more than a strange and new fact; in France it seemed a striking confirmation of principles known before. It surprised them, it convinced us. The Americans seemed merely to have carried out what our writers had conceived; they had realized what we were musing. It was as if Fénelon had been suddenly transported into the midst of the Sallentines.

It was something entirely new for men of letters to direct the political education of a great nation: this, more perhaps than anything else, contributed to form the peculiar character and results of our revolution.

The people imbibed the temper and disposition of the authors with their principles. They were so long sole tutors of the nation, and their lessons were so wholly unchecked and untried by practical experience, that the whole nation acquired, by dint of reading them, their instincts, their mental complexion, their tastes, and even their natural defects. When the time for action came, men dealt with political questions on literary principles.

The student of our revolution soon discovers that it was led and managed by the same spirit which gave birth to so many abstract treatises on government. In both he finds the same love for general theories, sweeping legislative systems, and symmetrical laws; the same confidence in theory; the same desire for new and original institutions; the same wish to reconstruct the whole Constitution according to the rules of logic, and in conformity with a set plan, instead of attempting partial amendments. A terrible sight! For what is a merit in an author is often a defect in a statesman, and characteristics which improve a book may be fatal to a revolution.

The political style of the day was somewhat indebted to the prevailing literature; it bristled with vague expressions, abstract terms, ambitious words, and literary phrases. The political passions of the day gave it currency among all classes, even the lowest. Long before the Revolution, the edicts of Louis XVI often spoke of natural laws and the rights of man. Peasants, in petitions, styled their neighbours 'fellow-citizens'; the intendant, 'a respectable magistrate'; the parish curate, the 'minister of the altar'; and God, the 'Supreme Being'. They might have become sorry authors had they but known orthography.

These peculiarities have taken such root in the French mind that they have been mistaken for its natural characteristics, whereas they are, in fact, only the result of a strange system of education. I have heard it stated that the taste, or, rather, the rage we have shown during the last sixty years for general principles, systems, and grand verbiage in political matters,

proceeded from an idiosyncracy of our race – a peculiarity of the
French mind; as though a feature of this kind would be likely to
remain hidden for ages, and only to see the light at the close of
last century.

It is singular that we should have retained the habits which
literature created, though we have almost entirely lost our old
love for letters. I was often surprised, during the course of my
public life, to see men who hardly ever read the works of the
eighteenth century, or, indeed, any others, and who despised
literary men, exhibit a singular fidelity to leading defects to
which the old literary spirit gave birth.

Chapter 14

How Irreligion became a general ruling Passion among Frenchmen in
the Eighteenth Century, and of the Influence it exercised over the
Character of the Revolution.

Ever since the great revolution of the sixteenth century, when
the spirit of free inquiry was evoked to decide which of the
various Christian traditions were true and which false, there had
constantly appeared, from time to time, inquisitive or daring
minds which disputed or denied them all. The train of thought
which in the time of Luther had expelled from the Catholic fold
several millions of Catholics drove a few Christians every year
out of the pale of Christianity. Heresy had been followed by
unbelief.

It may be said generally that in the eighteenth century
Christianity had lost a large portion of its power all over Europe;
but in most countries it had been reluctantly abandoned rather
than violently rejected. Irreligion had spread among sovereigns
and wits, but it had made no progress among the middle classes
and the people; it was a fashionable caprice, not a popular
opinion. 'A vulgar error prevails in Germany,' says Mirabeau in
1787, 'to the effect that the Prussian provinces are full of atheists.

The truth is, that, if there are a few freethinkers here and there, the people are as religious as any nation in the world, and among them fanatics are quite common.' He adds that it is a pity Frederick II does not authorize the marriage of Catholic priests, and allow married ecclesiastics to retain their rank and functions: 'This measure, I venture to say, would be worthy of so great a man.' In France irreligion had become a passion, general, ardent, intolerant, oppressive; but nowhere else.

The scenes that took place in France were without precedent. Established religions had often been violently attacked, but the fury which assailed them was always inspired by zeal for some new religion. Even the false and detestable religions of antiquity met with no violent or general opposition until Christianity arose to supplant them. Previous to that event they had died of old age, quietly, in the midst of doubt and indifference. In France the Christian faith was furiously assailed, but no attempt was made to raise up another religion on its ruins. Ardent efforts were made to eradicate from men's souls the faith that was in them, and leave them empty. A multitude of men engaged warmly in this ungrateful work. Absolute infidelity, than which nothing is more repugnant to man's natural instincts, or produces more discomfort of soul, appeared attractive to the masses. It had formerly given rise to a sickly languor: it now engendered fanaticism and propagandism.

The accidental coincidence of several leading writers, impressed with a sense of unbelief in Christianity, is not sufficient to account for this extraordinary event; for why should all these writers, without exception, turn their attention to this quarter in preference to others? How did it happen that not one out of all of them took the opposite side? Why was it that, unlike their predecessors, they found a ready ear and a predisposition in their favour among the people? The answer to these queries must be sought in peculiarities of time and place; in the same direction, too, we must look for the secret of the success of these writers. Voltaire's spirit had long existed in the world, but Voltaire's reign never could have been realized except in France during the eighteenth century.

Let us first acknowledge that the church in France was not

more open to attack than elsewhere. Fewer vices and abuses had in fact crept into the French Church than were seen in many foreign churches; the French clergy were more tolerant than their predecessors or their neighbours. The real causes of the phenomenon are to be found rather in the state of society than in that of the Church.

In searching for them, we must carefully keep in view the proposition established in the last chapter, namely, that the opposition aroused by the faults of government, being excluded from the political world, took refuge in literature, whereby men of letters became the real chiefs of the party that was to overthrow all the social and political institutions of the country.

That point established, the question presents itself in another form. It is not, What were the faults of the Church of that day as a religious institution? but, Wherein was it an obstacle to the progress of the Revolution, and an inconvenience to the writers who were its chief leaders?

The fundamental principles of the Church were at war with those which they desired to see prevail in the civil government of the country. The Church was founded on traditions: they professed the greatest contempt for all institutions claiming respect in virtue of their antiquity. It recognized a higher authority than individual reason; they allowed of no appeal from reason. It clung to the notion of a hierarchy; they insisted on levelling all ranks. The two could never come to an understanding, unless both admitted that political and religious societies, being essentially different, cannot be governed by like principles; and as they were far from any admission of this kind, it seemed to the reformers absolutely necessary to destroy the religious institutions of the time in order to reach the civil institutions, which were constructed on their basis and model.

The Church was, moreover, the first of all political bodies, and the most odious, though not the most oppressive. It had become a political body in defiance of its vocation and its nature; it shielded vice in high places, while it censured it among the people; it threw its sacred mantle over existing institutions, and seemed to demand for them the immortality it expected for itself. Attacks upon such a body were sure of public sympathy.

Besides these general reasons, the writers of the day had particular, and, so to speak, personal motives for directing their first attack against the Church. The clergy represented that portion of the government which was nearest and most diametrically opposed to them. Other authorities made themselves felt from time to time; but the Church, specially intrusted with the superintendence of ideas and the censorship of letters, was a daily thorn in their side. It opposed them when they stood forth on behalf of the general liberties of mankind, and consequently they were driven, in self-defence, to attack it as the outwork of the place they were assaulting.

The Church, moreover, appeared the weakest and most defenceless of all the outworks which lay before them. Its power had declined as that of the sovereign had gained strength. Once his superior, then his equal, it was now merely his subordinate. The pair had exchanged gifts; the Church had been glad to give its moral influence in return for the use of the physical power of the sovereign. He enforced submission to the Church, it taught respect for the crown. It was a dangerous bargain, so near revolutionary times, and sure to be disadvantageous to the power which relied on faith, not force.

Though the kings still styled themselves eldest sons of the Church, they were not particularly dutiful. They took far better case of their own authority than of that of the Church. They did not allow it to be openly molested, but neither did they prevent insidious and covert attacks upon it.

The species of constraint laid upon the enemies of the Church increased instead of diminishing their power. Oppression sometimes checks intellectual movement, but as often it accelerates it; it invariably happens that such a censorship of the press as then existed multiplies its power a hundred fold.

Authors were persecuted sufficiently to warrant complaint, but not to justify terror. They laboured under inconveniences, which goaded them on to the struggle without overwhelming them. Prosecutions against them were almost always noisy, slow, and fruitless; they were better calculated to encourage than to repress free speech. A thoroughly free press would have been safer for the Church.

'You think our intolerance,' Diderot wrote to Hume in 1768, 'more favourable to intellectual progress than your unrestricted liberty: D'Holback, Helvetius, Morelet, and Suard, are not of your opinion.' The Scotchman was, however, in the right; he had the experience of a freeman. Diderot judged like a man of letters, Hume like statesman.

If I ask the first American I meet, either at home or abroad, whether he considers religion to be of service to law and social order, he will answer unhesitatingly that civilized society, especially if it be free, can not exist without religion. Respect for religion is in his eyes the best safeguard for political stability and private security. Those who know least about government know this much. There is no country in the world where the boldest political doctrines of the eighteenth century philosophers have received so general a practical application as in America. But, notwithstanding the unlimited freedom of the press, their infidel doctrines have never made any progress there.

As much may be said of the English. Our irreligious philosophy was preached to them before our philosophers were born; it was Bolingbroke who completed Voltaire's education. Throughout the eighteenth century infidelity had famous champions in England.[58] Able writers, profound thinkers, embraced its cause. But they won no victories with it, because all who had anything to lose by revolutions hastened to the support of the established faith. Even men who mixed in France society, and did not reject the doctrines of our philosophers, considered them dangerous. Great political parties, such as exist in every free country, found it to be their interest to espouse the cause of the Church; Bolingbroke was seen to join hands with the bishops. Animated by this example, and encouraged by a consciousness of support, the clergy fought with energy in their own defence. Notwithstanding the vice of its constitution, and the abuses of all sorts which teemed within its organization, the Church of England stood the shock unmoved; writers and speakers sprang forth from its ranks, and defended Christianity with ardor. Infidel theories were discussed, refuted, and rejected by society, without the least interference on the part of government.

But why need we seek illustrations abroad? Where is the Frenchman who would write such books as these of Diderot of Helvetius at the present day? Who would read them? I might almost say, Who knows their titles? We have had experience enough of public life, incomplete as it has been, during the last sixty years, to lose all taste for this dangerous style of literature. See how each class in turn has learned, at the rough school of revolutions, the necessity of respecting religion. The old nobility were the most irreligious class of society before 1789, and the most pious after 1793; the first attacked, they were the first to recover. When the middle classes were struck down in the midst of their victory, they in their turn drew toward religion. Respect for religion gradually made its way into the breast of everyone who had anything to lose by popular disorders, and infidelity disappeared or lay hidden in the general dread of revolution.

Very different was the state of society toward the close of the old regime. Politicians were out of practice, and were so ignorant of the part which religion plays in the government of empires, that infidelity found proselytes among those who were the most vitally interested in the maintenance of order and the subordination of the people. Nor yet proselytes alone, but propagandists, who made an idle pastime of diseminating impiety.

The Church of France, which had up to that time been prolific in great orators, sank under the desertion of those whom a common interest should have rallied to its side, and made no sign. At one moment it seemed as though it would have compromised for the retention of its wealth and rank by the sacrifice of its faith.

The assailants of Christianity being as noisy as its adherents were mute, the latter began to fear that they were singular in their opinions, and, dreading singularity more than error, they joined the crowd without sharing its creed. Thus the whole nation was credited with the sentiments of a faction, and the new opinions seemed irresistible even to those whose conduct was the main secret of their imposing appearance. The phenomenon has been often witnessed since in France, in connection not only with religion, but with very different matters.

No doubt an extensive influence was exercised over our Revolution by the general discredit into which religious creeds had fallen at the close of the eighteenth century. Its character was moulded, and a terrible aspect imparted to its physiognomy by this peculiar circumstance.

I have endeavoured to trace the effects produced by irreligion in France, and I am satisfied that it was by unsettling men's minds, rather than by degrading their hearts or corrupting their morals, that it led them into such strange excesses.

When religion fled from men's souls, they were not left void and debilitated, as is usually the case; its place was temporarily occupied by ideas and feelings which engrossed the mind and did not allow it to collapse.

If the men of the Revolution were more irreligious than we are, they were imbued with one admirable faith which we lack: they believed in themselves. They had a robust faith in man's perfectibility and power; they were eager for his glory, trustful in his virtue. They had a proud reliance in their own strength; and though this often leads to errors, a people without it is not fit for freedom. They had no doubt but that they were appointed to transform society and regenerate the human race. These sentiments and passions had become a sort of new religion, which, like many religions which we have seen, stifled selfishness, stimulated heroism and disinterestedness, and rendered men insensible to many petty considerations which have weight with us.

I have studied history extensively, and I venture to affirm that I know of no other revolution at whose outset so many men were imbued with a patriotism as sincere, as disinterested, as truly great. The nation exhibited the characteristic fault, but likewise the characteristic virtue of youth, or, rather, the viture which used to be characteristic of youth; it was inexperienced, but it was generous.

For all this, infidelity produced immense evil.

Throughout most of the political revolutions that the world had experienced, the assailants of civil laws had respected religious creeds. In like manner, the leaders of religious revolutions had rarely undertaken to alter the form and character of civil institutions, and to abolish the whole framework of government. In the greatest social convulsions there had thus always remained one solid spot.

When the French Revolution overthrew civil and religious laws together, the human mind lost its balance. Men knew not where to stop or what measure to observe. There arose a new order of revolutionists, whose boldness was madness, who shrank from no novelty, knew no scruples, listened to no argument or objection. And it must not be imagined that this new species of beings was the spontaneous and ephemeral offspring of circumstances, destined to perish when they passed away; it has given birth to a race which has spread and propagated throughout the civilized world. preserving a uniform physiognomy, uniform passions, a uniform character. We found it in existence at our birth; it is still before us.

Chapter 15

How the French sought Reforms before Liberties.

It is noteworthy that of all the ideas and feelings which prepared the Revolution, the idea of political liberty, properly so called, was the last to make its appearance, as the desire for it was the first to vanish.

The old edifice of government had long been insecure; it shook, though no man struck it. Voltaire was hardly thinking of it. Three years' residence in England had enabled him to understand that country without falling in love with it. He was delighted with the skeptical philosophy that was freely taught among the English, but he was not struck with their political laws, which he rather criticized than praised. His letters on England, which are one of his master-pieces, hardly contain any allusion to Parliament: he envies the English their literary liberty, but cares little for their political liberty, as though the one could exist for any length of time without the other.

About the middle of the century, a class of writers devoted their attention to administrative questions; they had many points in common, and were hence distinguished by the general name of economists or physiocrats. They are less conspicuous in history than the philosophers; they exercised a less direct influence in causing the Revolution, but still I think its true nature can best be studied in their writing. The philosophers confined themselves, for the most part, to abstract and general theories on the subject of government; the economists dealt in theories, but also deigned to notice facts. The former furnished ideal, the latter practical schemes of reform. They assailed alternately all the institutions which the Revolution abolished; not one of them found favour in their eyes. All those, on the other hand, which are credited especially to the Revolution, were announced beforehand and warmly lauded by them: it is not easy to mention one whose substantial features are not to be found in some of their writings.

Their books, moreover, breathe that democratic and revolutionary spirit with which we are so familiar. They hate, not certain specific privileges, but all distinctions of classes; they would insist upon equality of rights in the midst of slavery. Obstacles they regard as only fit to be trampled on. They respect neither contracts nor private rights; indeed, they hardly recognize individual rights at all in their absorbing devotion to the public good. Yet they were quiet, peaceable men, of respectable character, honest magistrates, able administrators; they were carried away by the peculiar spirit of their task.

Their contempt for the past was unbounded. 'The nation,' said Letronne, 'is governed on wrong principles; everything seems to have been left to chance.' Starting from this idea, they set to work to demand the demolition of every institution, however old and time-honoured, which seemed to mar the symmetry of their plans. Forty years before the Constituent Assembly divided France into departments, one of the economists suggested the alteration of all existing territorial divisions and of the names of all the provinces.

They conceived all the social and administrative reforms effected by the Revolution before the idea of free institutions had once flashed upon their mind. They were in favour of the removal of all restrictions upon the sale and conveyance of produce and merchandise. But of political liberty they took no thought; and when it first occurred to them they rejected the idea. Most of them were strongly opposed to deliberative assemblies, to local and subordinate authorities, and to the various checks which have been established from time to time in free countries to counterbalance the supreme government. 'The system of counterpoises,' said Quesnay, 'is a fatal feature in governments.' A friend of his was satisfied that 'the system of counterpoises was the fruit of chimerical speculations'.

The only safeguard against despotism which they proposed was public education; for, as Quesnay said, Depotism is impossible in an enlightened nation.' 'Mankind,' says one of his disciples, 'have invented a host of fruitless contrivances to obviate the evils arising from abuses of power by governments, but they have generally neglected the only one that could really be of service, namely, a general permanent system of public education in the essence of justice and natural order.' Such was the literary nonsense they wanted to substitute in the place of political guarantees.

Letronne bitterly deplores the government's neglect of the rural districts, and describes them as having no roads, no industry, no intellectual progress; but he never seems to have imagined that they would have been better regulated if their affairs had been intrusted to the people themselves.

Even Turgot, with all his peculiar breadth of view and rare genius, was but little fonder than they of political liberty. He had no taste for it till late in life, when public opinion pointed in that direction. Like the economists, he conceived that the best of all political guarantees was public education afforded by the state; but he desired it to be conducted in a particular spirit, and according to a particular plan. His confidence in this intellectual course of medicine – or, as a contemporary styled it, this 'educational mechanism on fixed principles' – was unbounded. 'I will venture to answer,' said he to the king, in a memorial on the subject, 'that in ten years the nation will be so thoroughly altered that you shall not recognize it; and that, in point of enlightenment, morality, loyalty, and patriotism, it will surpass every other nation in the world. Children now ten years old will then be men, trained in ideas of love for their country, submissive to authority from conviction, not from fear, charitable to their fellow-countrymen, habituated to obey and to respect the voice of justice.'

It was so long since political liberty had flourished in France that its conditions and effects had been well-nigh forgotten. More than this, its shapeless relics, and the institutions which seemed to have been framed to take its place, rather aroused prejudice against it. Most of the surviving state assemblies exhibited the spirit as well as the forms of the Middle Ages, and hindered instead of assisting social progress. The Parliaments, which were the only substitutes for political bodies, could not arrest the mischief done by government, and often impeded it when it desired to do good.

The economists did not think it possible to use these old institutions as instruments for the accomplishment of the Revolution, nor did they approve the idea of intrusting the business to the nation as sovereign; they doubted the feasibility of effecting so elaborate and intricate a reform by the aid of a popular movement. Their designs, they thought, could be best and most easily accomplished by the crown itself.

The royal power had not taken its rise in the Middle Ages, and bore no medieval stamp. They discovered it in good as well as bad points. It shared their proclivity for levelling all ranks, and making all laws uniform. It detested as heartily as they did the old institutions which had grown out of the feudal system, or which favoured oligarchy. It was the best organized, the greatest and strongest government machine in Europe. Its existence seemed to them a very fortunate accident; they would have called it providential had it been the fashion then as now to allude to Providence on all possible occasions. Letronne observes that 'France is much more happily situated than England; for here reforms that will change the whole state of the country can be accomplished in a moment, whereas in England similar measures are always exposed to be defeated by party strife'.

Their idea, then, was not to destroy, but to convert the

absolute monarchy. 'The state must govern according to the laws of natural order (*règles de l'ordre essentiel*),' says Mercier de la Rivière; 'on these conditions it should be absolute.' 'Let the state,' said another, 'understand its duty thoroughly; this secured, it should be untrammelled.' All of them, from Quesnay to Abbé Bodeau, were of the same mind.

They were not satisfied with using the royal power to effect social reforms; they partly borrowed from it the idea of the future government they proposed to establish. The one was to be, in some measure, a copy of the other.

The state, said the economists, must not only govern, it must shape the nation. It must form the mind of citizens conformably to a preconceived model. It is its duty to fill their minds with such opinions and their hearts with such feelings as it may judge necessary. In fact, there are no limits either to its rights or its powers. It must transform as well as reform its subjects; perhaps even create new subjects, if it thinks fit. 'The state,' says Bodeau, 'moulds men into whatever shape it pleases.' That sentence expresses the gist of the whole system.

The immense social power conceived by the economists differed from the power they had before them in point of origin and character as well as magnitude. It was not of divine origin; it owed nothing to tradition; it was impersonal: it was called the state, not the king; it was not the heirloom of a family, it was the collective product and representative of the whole nation. Individual rights gave way to it as the sum of the rights of all.

They were quite familiar with the form of tyranny which we call democratic despotism, and which had not been conceived in the Middle Ages. No more social hierarchies, no distinctions of class or rank; a people consisting of individuals entirely equal, and as nearly alike as possible; this body acknowledged as the only legitimate sovereign, but carefully deprived of the means of directing or even superintending the government; over it a single agent, commissioned to perform all acts without consulting his principals: to control him, a public sense of right and wrong, destitute of organs for its expression; to check him, revolutions, not laws; the agent being *de jure* a subordinate agent, in fact a master: such was the plan.

Finding nothing in their neighbourhood conformable to this ideal of theirs, they went to the heart of Asia in search of a model. I do not exaggerate when I affirm that everyone of them wrote in some place or other an emphatic eulogium on China. One is sure to find at least that in their books; and as China is very imperfectly known even in our day, their statements on its subject are generally pure nonsense. They wanted all the nations of the world to set up exact copies of that barbarous and imbecile government, which a handful of Europeans master whenever they please. China was for them what England, and afterward America, became for all Frenchmen. They were filled with emotion and delight at the contemplation of a government wielded by an absolute but unprejudiced sovereign, who honoured the useful arts by plowing once a year with his own hands; of a nation whose only religion was philosophy, whose only aristocracy were men of letters, whose public offices were awarded to the victors at literary tournaments.

It is generally believed that the destructive theories known by the name of socialism are of modern origin. This is an error. These theories are coeval with the earliest economists. While some of them wanted to use the absolute power they desired to establish to change the forms of society, others proposed to employ it in ruining its fundamental basis.

Read the *Code de la Nature* by Morelly; you will find there, together with the economist doctrines regarding the omnipotence and the boundless rights of the state, several of those political theories which have terrified France of late years, and whose origin we fancy we have seen – community of property, rights of labour, absolute equality, universal uniformity, mechanical regularity of individual movements, tyrannical regulations on all subjects, and the total absorption of the individual in the body politic.

'Nothing,' says the first article of this code, 'belongs wholly to anyone. Property is detestable, and anyone who attempts to re-establish it shall be imprisoned for life, as a dangerous madman and an enemy of humanity.' The second article declares that 'every citizen shall be kept, and maintained, and supplied with work at the public expense. All produce shall be gathered into public garners, to be distributed to citizens for their subsistence. All cities shall be built on the same plan; all private residences shall be alike. All children shall be taken from their families at five years of age, and educated together on a uniform plan.' This book reads as if it had been written yesterday. It is a hundred years old: it appeared in 1755, simultaneously with the foundation of Quesnay's school. So true it is that centralization and socialism are native of the same soil: one is the wild herb, the other the garden-plant.

Of all the men of their age, the economists would seem the least out of place at the present day; their passion for equality is so violent, their love of liberty so variable, that they wear a false air of contemporaries of our own. When I read the speeches and writings of the men who made the Revolution, I feel that I am in the company of strangers; but when I glance at the writings of the economists, I begin to fancy that I have lived with them, and just heard them talk.

About 1750 the nation at large cared no more for political liberty than the economists themselves; when it fell into disuse, the taste for it, and even the idea of it, were soon lost. People sought reforms, not rights. Had the throne then been occupied by a monarch of the calibre and character of Frederick the Great, I have no doubt he would have accomplished many of the reforms which were brought about by the Revolution; and that not only without endangering his throne, but with a large gain of power. It is said that M. de Machault, one of the ablest ministers of Louis XV, conceived this idea, and communicated it to his master; but such enterprises are not executed at second-hand; a man capable of accomplishing them could not fail to conceive them himself.

Twenty years changed the face of things. France had a glimpse of political liberty, and liked it. Many indications prove this. The provinces began to desire once more to administer their own government. Men's minds became imbued with the notion that the people at large were entitled to a share in their own government. Recollections of the old States-General were revived. National history contained but this single item which the people loved to recall. The economists were carried away by the current, and compelled to clog their absolute scheme with some free institutions.

When the Parliaments were destroyed in 1771, the public, which had suffered severely from their evils, was profoundly affected by their fall. It seemed as if the last barrier against the royal prerogative had been destroyed.

Voltaire was indignant at the symptom. He wrote to his friends, 'Nearly all the kingdom is in a state of effervescence and consternation; the provinces ferment as violently as the capital. Yet the edict seems to me to be pregnant with useful reforms. To abolish all venal offices; to establish courts that will administer justice gratuitously; to prevent litigants from coming to Paris from all parts of the kingdom to ruin themselves; to burden the crown with the expense of the seigniorial courts – are not these great services rendered to the nation? Have not these Parliaments been barbarous and intolerant? Really I admire the "Welches" for taking the side of these insolent and indocile burghers. For my part, I think the king is right; if one must serve, I hold it better to serve a well-bred lion, who is naturally stronger than I am, than two hundred rats of my own breed.' And he adds, by way of excuse, 'Think how infinitely I ought to appreciate the kindness of the king in relieving seigniors of the cost of their courts.'

Voltaire had been absent from Paris for many years, and fancied that the public mind was just as he had known it. This was not the case. The French were not satisfied now with desiring to see their affairs well managed; they wanted to manage them themselves. It was already visible that the great revolution which was in preparation would be effected, not only with the consent of the people, but by their hands.

I think that from this moment the radical revolution, which was to ruin simultaneously the worst features of the old regime and its redeeming traits, became inevitable. A people so badly trained for action could not undertake reforms without destroying everything. An absolute sovereign would have been a less dangerous reformer. And, for my part, when I remember that this revolution, which destroyed so many institutions, and ideas, and habits that were inimical to liberty, also destroyed others without which liberty can hardly exist, I am inclined to think that, had it been accomplished by a despot, it would have left us perhaps fitter to become a free nation than it did, though it was done in the name of and by the sovereign people.

The preceding remarks must be carefully borne in mind by all who desire to understand the history of our Revolution.

At the time the French conceived a desire for political liberty, they were imbued with a number of notions on the subject of government which were not only difficult to reconcile with liberty, but were almost hostile to it.

In their ideal society there was no aristocracy but that of public functionaries, no authority but the government, sole and all-powerful, director of the state, tutor of individuals. They did not wish to depart from this system in the search for liberty; they tried to conciliate the two.

They attempted to combine an unlimited executive with a preponderating legislative body – a bureaucracy to administer, a democracy to govern. Collectively, the nation was sovereign – individually, citizens were confined in the closest dependence; yet from the former were expected the virtues and the experience of a free people, from the latter the qualities of a submissive servant.

It is to this desire of adjusting political liberty to institutions or ideas which are either foreign or hostile to it, but to which we were wedded by habit or attracted by taste, that we owe the many vain experiments of government that have been made during the last sixty years. Hence the fatal revolutions we have undergone. Hence it is that so many Frenchmen, worn out by fruitless efforts and sterile toil, have abandoned their second object and fallen back on their first, declaring that there is, after all, a certain pleasure in enjoying equality under a master. Hence we resemble the economists of 1750 more closely than our fathers of 1789.

I have often asked myself what was the source of that passion for political liberty which has inspired the greatest deeds of which mankind can boast. In what feelings does it take root? From whence does it derive nourishment?

I see clearly enough that when a people is badly governed it desires self-government; but this kind of love for independence grows out of certain particular temporary mischiefs wrought by despotism, and is never durable; it passes away with the accident which gave it birth. What seemed to be love for liberty turns out to be mere hatred of a despot. Nations born to freedom hate the intrinsic evil of dependence.

Nor do I believe that a true love for liberty can ever be inspired by the sight of the material advantages it procures, for they are not always clearly visible. It is very true that, in the long run, liberty always yields to those who know how to preserve its comfort, independence, and often wealth; but there are times when it disturbs these blessings for a while, and there are times when their immediate enjoyment can only be secured by a despotism. Those who only value liberty for their sake have never preserved it long.

It is the intrinsic attractions of freedom, its own peculiar charm – quite independently of its incidental benefits – which have seized so strong a hold on the great champions of liberty throughout history; they loved it because they loved the pleasure of being able to speak, to act, to breathe unrestrained, under the sole government of God and the laws. He who seeks freedom for anything but freedom's self is made to be a slave.

Some nations pursue liberty obstinately through all kinds of dangers and sufferings, not for its material benefits; they deem it so precious and essential a boon that nothing could console them for its loss, while its enjoyment would compensate them for all possible afflictions. Others, on the contrary, grow tired of it in the midst of prosperity; they allow it to be torn from them without resistance rather than compromise the comfort it has bestowed on them by making an effort. What do they need in order to remain free? A taste for freedom. Do not ask me to analyse that sublime taste; it can only be felt. It has a place in every great heart which God has prepared to receive it; it fills and inflames it. To try to explain it to those inferior minds who have never felt it is to waste time.

Chapter 16

That the reign of Louis XVI was the most prosperous Era of the old Monarchy, and how that Prosperity really hastened the Revolution.

It cannot be questioned but the exhaustion of France under Louis XIV commenced long before the reverses of that monarch. Symptoms of weakness may be detected in the most glorious years of his reign. France was ruined before she had ceased to conquer. Who has not read the terrible essay on Statistics of Administration which Vauban has left us? In memorials addressed to the Duke of Burgundy at the close of the seventeenth century, before the outbreak of the disastrous war of Succession, all the intendants allude to the growing decay of the nation, and do not speak as though it were of recent origin. One observes that population has greatly fallen off within his province of late years; another says that such a town, formerly rich and flourishing, now affords no demand for labour. One reports that there used to be manufactures in the province, but they have been abandoned; another, that the soil was more productive, and agriculture more flourishing twenty years ago than it is now. An intendant of Orleans was positive that population and production had fallen off twenty per cent within thirty years. Partisans of despotism and warlike sovereigns should be recommended to read these documents.

As these evils grew out of the faults of the Constitution, neither the death of Louis XIV nor even the advent of peace restored public prosperity. Writers on government and social economy, in the first half of the eighteenth century, invariably held to the opinion that the provinces were not recovering – that their decline was steadily progressive. They asserted that Paris alone was increasing in size and wealth. Intendants, ministers, men of business, agreed with men of letters on this point.

I confess that, for my part, I disbelieve this steady decline of France during the first half of the eighteenth century; but the universality of the belief in it, even among those who were best fitted to judge, shows that no sensible progress was being made. All the public documents of the time which I have seen, in fact, indicate a sort of social lethargy. The government revolved in the old routine circle, creating nothing new; cities made hardly any effort to render the condition of their inhabitants more comfortable and more wholesome; no private enterprise of any magnitude was undertaken.

About thirty or forty years before the Revolution broke out, the scene changed, Every portion of the social body seemed to quiver with internal motion. The phenomenon was unprecedented, and casual observers did not notice it; but it gradually became more characteristic and more distinct. Year after year it became more general and more violent, till the whole nation was aroused. Beware of supposing that its old life is going to be restored! 'Tis the awakening of a new spirit, which gives life only in order to destroy.

Everyone is dissatisfied with his condition, and seeks to change it. Reform is the cry on every side. But it is sought impatiently and angrily; men curse the past, and dream of a state of things opposite in every particular to that which they see before them. The spirit soon penetrates the government itself; transforms it inwardly without changing its outward form; leaves the laws as they were, but alters their administration.

I have said elsewhere that the comptroller-general and the intendants of 1740 were very different personages from the comptroller-general and the intendants of 1780. This is shown in detail in the official correspondence of the time. At both periods intendants were invested with the same authority, employed the same agents, used the same arbitrary means; but their objects were different. In 1740 intendants were engrossed with the business of keeping their province in order, levying militia, and collecting the taille; in 1780 their heads were full of schemes for enriching the public. Roads, canals, manufactures, commerce, and agriculture above all, absorbed their attention. Sully was then the fashionable model of an administrator.

It was at this period that the agricultural societies I have mentioned began to be established; that fairs began to be common, and prizes to be distributed. I have seen circulars from the comptroller-general which read more like agricultural treatises than public state papers.

The change that had come over the spirit of the governing

class was best seen in the collection of the taxes. Though the laws were as unequal, as arbitrary, as harsh as ever, their faults were materially alleviated in practice.

M. Mollien, in his Memoirs, observes that, when he 'began to study the fiscal laws, he was terrified by what he discovered; exceptional courts allowed to sentence men to fine, imprisonment, corporal punishment for mere omissions; tax-farmers exercising plenary authority over persons and property on the sole responsibility of their own oath, &c. Fortunately, he did not confine his studies to the letter of the law, and he soon discovered that there was as much difference between the text of the law and its application, as there was between the style of living of the old and modern school of financiers. The courts were always inclined to extenuate offences and mitigate penalties.'

The Provincial Assembly of Lower Normandy said, in like manner, in 1787, 'The tax levy may lead to abuses and vexations innumerable; we are, however, bound to admit that in practice the law has been carried out with moderation and discretion of late years.'

Official documents abundantly justify this assertion. They prove conclusively that life and liberty were respected; they indicate, moreover, a general concern for the ills of the poor: a new sentiment. The state rarely employed violence with the poor, but often remitted their taxes or granted them alms. The king subscribed to all the country work-houses or poor-houses, and occasionally founded new ones. I find that more than 80,000 *livres* were distributed by the state in charity, in Haute-Guienne alone, in the year 1779; 40,000 in Touraine in 1784; 48,000 in Normandy in 1787. Louis XVI would not always leave this branch of public business to his ministers; he often took charge of it himself. When a decree was drawn to fix the indemnity due to the peasantry for the damage done to their fields by the royal game in the neighbourhood of the captainries, the king drafted the preamble himself, and indicated the method which the peasants were to pursue in order to obtain speedy justice. Turgot describes this good and unfortunate sovereign bringing him the draft in his own handwriting, and saying, 'You perceive that I work, too, on my side.' If the old regime were described as it really was during the last years of its existence, the portrait would be flattering and very unfaithful.

Simultaneously with these changes in the mind of governed and governors, public prosperity began to develop with unexampled strides. This is shown by all sorts of evidence. Population increased rapidly; wealth more rapidly still. The American war did not check the movement: it completed the embarrassment of the state, but did not impede private enterprise; individuals grew more industrious, more inventive, richer than ever.

An official of the time states that in 1774 'industrial progress had been so rapid that the amount of taxable articles had largely increased'. On comparing the various contracts made between the state and the companies to which the taxes were farmed out, at different periods during the reign of Louis XVI, one perceives that the yield was increasing with astonishing rapidity. The lease of 1786 yielded fourteen millions more than that of 1780. Necker, in his report of 1781, estimated that 'the produce of taxes on articles of consumption increased at the rate of two millions a year'.

Arthur Young states that in 1788 the commerce of Bordeaux was greater than that of Liverpool, and adds that 'of late years maritime trade has made more progress in France than in England; the whole trade of France has doubled in the last twenty years'.

Due allowance made for the difference of the times, it may be asserted that at no period since the Revolution has public prosperity made such progress as it did during the twenty years prior to the Revolution.[59] In this respect, the thirty-seven years of constitutional monarchy, which were periods of peace and rapid progress for us, can alone compare with the reign of Louis XVI.

Considering the vices of the government and the burdens which weighed upon industry, the spectacle of this great and increasing prosperity is astonishing; so astonishing, indeed, that some political writers, finding themselves incapable of explaining the fact, have denied it altogether, on the same principle that

Molière's doctor refused to believe that a patient could be cured contrary to rule. How was it possible that France could prosper and grow rich with unequal taxes, diversified customs, town dues, feudal rights, trade guilds, venal offices, etc.? For all these, France did begin to grow rich and develop its resources on all sides; and for the simple reason that, independently of these misshapen and inharmonious machines, which seemed better calculated to retard than to accelerate social progress, society was held together and driven toward public prosperity by two very simple but very powerful agents: the one a government, strong without being despotic, which maintained order everywhere; the other a nation whose upper classes were the most enlightened and the freest people on the Continent, and in which individuals were at liberty to make money if they could, and to keep it when made.

Though the king used the language of a master, he was, in reality, the slave of public opinion. From public opinion he derived all his inspirations; he consulted it, feared it, flattered it. Absolute in theory, he was limited in practice. As early as 1784, Necker said in a public document, 'Foreigners rarely realize the authority wielded by public opinion in France; they cannot readily understand the nature of that invisible power which rules even over the royal palace. It does so, however.' He mentions the fact as a matter beyond dispute.

It is a superficial error to ascribe the greatness and power of a nation to the mechanism of its legislation; for in this matter the product is due less to the perfection of the instrument than to the strength of the power used. Look at England; how much more complicated, and varied, and irregular do her laws seem than ours![60] Yet where is the European nation whose public credit stands higher, or in which private property is more extensive, more varied, and safer, or society sounder or more opulent? The fact does not spring from the excellence of this or that law, but from the spirit which pervades the whole body of English legislation. The imperfection of special organs is immaterial, the vital spirit is so strong.

Measurably with the increase of prosperity in France, men's minds grow more restless and uneasy; public discontent is imbittered; the hatred of the old institutions increases. The nation visibly tends toward revolution.

More than this, those districts where progress makes the greatest strides are precisely those which are to be the chief theatre of the Revolution. The extant archives of the old district of Ile de France prove that the old regime was soonest and most thoroughly reformed in the neighbourhood of Paris. In no other *pays d'élection* were the liberty and property of the peasant so well secured. *Corvées* had disappeared long before 1789. The taille was more moderate, more regular, more evenly distributed there than in any other part of France. A perusal of the law which reformed it in 1772 is absolutely essential to those who would understand how powerful an intendant could be, whether for good or for evil. In this law the tax appears in a new light. Government commissioners visit each parish once a year and convene the whole community; the relative value of estates is settled publicly; the means of each citizen ascertained by fair discussion; the taille is distributed with the concurrence of all who are to pay it. The arbitrary power of the syndic, the old useless recourse to violence, are done away with. The taille retains its inherent vices, no doubt, under the best system of collection; it is levied on one class of taxables only, and weighs upon their industry as well as upon their property, but in all other respects it is a very different affair from the tax of the same name in the neighbouring districts.[61]

On the other hand, the old regime was nowhere in so high a state of preservation as on the borders of the Loire, especially near its mouth, in the swamps of Poitou and the moors of Brittany. That is the very place where the civil war broke out, and the Revolution was resisted with most obstinacy and violence. So that it would appear that the French found their condition the more insupportable in proportion to its improvement.

One is surprised at such an anomaly, but similar phenomena abound in history.

Revolutions are not always brought about by a gradual decline from bad to worse. Nations that have endured patiently and almost unconsciously the most overwhelming oppression, often burst into rebellion against the yoke the moment it begins to grow lighter. The regime which is destroyed by a revolution is almost always an improvement on its immediate predecessor, and experience teaches that the most critical moment for bad governments is the one which witnesses their first steps toward reform. A sovereign who seeks to relieve his subjects after a long period of oppression is lost, unless he be a man of great genius. Evils which are patiently endured when they seem inevitable, become intolerable when once the idea of escape from them is suggested. The very redress of grievances throws new light on those which are left untouched, and adds fresh poignancy to their smart: if the pain be less, the patient's sensibility is greater.[62] Never had the feudal system seemed so hateful to the French as at the moment of its proximate destruction. The arbitrary measures of Louis XVI – insignificant as they were – seemed harder to bear than all the despotism of Louis XIV. The short imprisonment of Beaumarchais aroused more emotion in Paris than the Dragonnades.

No one in 1780 had any idea that France was on the decline; on the contrary, there seemed to be no bounds to its progress. It was then that the theory of the continual and indefinite perfectibility of man took its rise. Twenty years before, nothing was hoped from the future; in 1780 nothing was feared. Imagination anticipated a coming era of unheard-of felicity, diverted attention from present blessings, and concentrated it upon novelties.

Besides these general reasons for the phenomenon, there were others of a particular nature and equally potent. Though the administration of the finances had been improved with the other departments, it was still marked by the faults which are inseparable from absolute governments. It was secret and irresponsible, and hence many of the mischievous practices of Louis XIV and XV were still in use. The very efforts which the government made to develop public prosperity, the assistance it occasionally lavished upon the needy, the public works it undertook, increased its expenses without proportionally increasing its revenue; hence the king's embarrassments were even greater than those of his predecessors. Like them, he often made his creditors suffer; like them, he borrowed on all sides privately, and without calling for tenders. His creditors were never sure of their interest; indeed, their only guarantee for their capital was the personal faith of the sovereign.

An observer who is reliable, for he was an eye-witness, and better placed for observation than most people, says on this subject, 'The French ran great risks in dealing with their own government. If they invested money in its securities, they were never sure of the time when the interest would be paid. If they built ships, mended roads, clothed soldiers for the government, they had no security for repayment of their advances, no certainty when the debt would be considered due; in fact, they were forced to calculate the chances of losing on a contract with ministers just as they would do on a bottomry bond.' He adds, very sensibly, 'At this time, especially when the development of industry created an unusual thirst for the acquisition of property, and a new liking for ease and comfort, those who had lent money to the state felt more keenly than they would have done at another time the bad faith of the creditor who, of all others, ought to have been the last to forget the sanctity of a contract.'

The abuses with which the French government was charged were not new, but the light in which they were viewed was. More crying faults had existed in the financial department at an earlier period, but since then changes had taken place, both in government and in society, which made them more keenly felt than before.

Within the last twenty years the government had acquired an unwonted activity, and had taken part in all kinds of new enterprises. It had thus become the largest consumer of industrial products, and the greatest contractor in the kingdom. A prodigious increase had taken place in the number of those who had money relations with it, who were interested in its loans, speculated in its bargains, or were its salaried servants. At no former period were private fortunes so deeply involved with the state finances. Bad financial management had formerly been a public evil, now it became disastrous to a thousand private families. In 1789 the state owed nearly 600 millions to creditors who were themselves in debt, and whose grievances were aggravated by the personal injury inflicted on them by the remissness of the state. And be it remarked that the irritation of this class of malcontents increased in proportion to their number; for a speculative mania, a thirst for riches, a taste for comfort spreading as business became extended, troubles of this kind appeared intolerable to those who, thirty years before, might have borne them without complaint.

Hence it happened that capitalists, merchants, maufacturers, and other business men or financiers – who are usually the most conservative class of the community, and the staunchest supporters of government, and who will submit patiently to laws which they despise or detest – were now more impatient and more resolutely bent on reform than any other section of the people. They were especially determined on a revolution in the financial department, never dreaming that a radical change in that branch of the government must involve the ruin of the whole.

How could a catastrophe have been avoided? On one side, a nation in which the desire for wealth increased daily; on the other, a government unceasingly engaged in exciting and disturbing men's minds, now inflaming their avarice, now driving them to despair – rushing to its ruin by both roads.

Chapter 17

How Attempts to relieve the People provoked Rebellion.

As the people had not appeared for a single instant on the public stage for a hundred and forty years, the possibility of their ever appearing there was forgotten, and their insensibility was regarded as a proof of deafness. Hence, when some interest began to be taken in their lot, they were discussed publicly as though they had not been present. It appeared as though it was supposed that the discussion would only be heard by the upper classes, and that the only danger was lest these might not be made to understand the case.

The very classes which had most to fear from popular fury declaimed loudly and publicly against the cruel injustice which the people had so long suffered. They took pleasure in pointing out to each other the monstrous vices of the institutions which weighed upon the people. They employed rhetoric to paint their sufferings and the inadequate rewards for their labour. Thus, in their endeavour to relieve the lower classes, they roused them to fury. I am not speaking of writers – I allude to the government, to its chief agents, themselves members of the privileged classes.

When the king endeavoured to abolish *corvées* thirteen years before the Revolution, he stated in the preamble of the ordinance, 'With the exception of a few provinces (*pays d'états*), nearly all the roads of the kingdom have been made gratuitously by the poorest portion of our subjects. The whole burden has fallen upon those who have no property but their labour, and whose interest in the roads is very slender; the landowners, who are really interested in the matter – for their property increases in value in proportion to the improvement in the roads – are privileged exempts. By compelling the poor to keep the roads in repair, to give their time and their labour for nothing, we have deprived them of their only safeguard against poverty and hunger, in order to make them toil for the benefit of the rich.'

When an effort was made, at the same time, to remove the restraints which the system of industrial corporations imposed on workmen, it was proclaimed in the king's name 'that the right to labour is the most sacred of all properties; that any law which infringes that right is essentially null and void, as being inconsistent with natural right; that the existing corporations are, moreover, abnormal and tyrannical institutions, the product of selfishness, cupidity and violence'. Such expressions were perilous indeed; but it was more dangerous still to utter them in vain. A few months later, corporations and *corvées* were re-established.

It was Turgot, it is said, who put these words in the king's mouth. Most of his successors followed the example. When the king announced, in 1780 that from that time forth the augmentations of the taille would be made public by registry, he took pains to add as a commentary, 'The persons liable to pay the taille have been not only tormented by the vexatious manner in which it is collected, but have been exposed besides to unexpected augmentations in the amount levied, and that to such an extent that the taxes paid by the poorest portion of our subjects have increased much more rapidly than those levied on the richer classes.' Again, when the king, not daring to equalize all the taxes, endeavoured to establish the principle of equality in the collection of those which were already paid by all classes in common, he said, 'His majesty hopes that the rich will not complain of being placed on the same level as the poor in the performance of a duty which they ought long ago to have shared more equally.'

In times of scarcity, especially, greater efforts seem to have been made to inflame the passions of the people than to supply their necessities. An intendant, desirous of stimulating the charity of the rich, would speak of 'the injustice and the harshness of those landowners who owe all they have to the labour of the poor, and who leave the unfortunate labourers, broken down in their service, to perish of hunger.' On a similar occasion, the king declared that it was 'his majesty's intention to protect the poor against schemes which compelled them to work for the rich at a rate of wages fixed by the latter, and thus exposed them to lack the very necessaries of life. The king will not permit one portion of mankind to be surrendered to the cupidity of another.'

To the close of the monarchical era, the struggle between the various administrative branches of government gave rise to all sorts of manifestations of this kind; each disputant accused his rival of being the cause of the people's misery. This is seen distinctly in the quarrel which took place between the king and the Parliament of Toulouse on the subject of the movement of breadstuffs. The Parliament declared that 'the false policy of the government endangered the subsistence of the poor', and the king replied that it was 'the ambition of the Parliament and the greed of the rich which caused the public distress'. Thus on both sides efforts were made to convince the people that their sufferings were the work of their superiors.

These matters were not stated in private letters; they are to be found in public documents, which the government and the Parliament took care to print by thousands. In the course of his explanations, the king told some harsh truths both of his predecessors and of himself. 'The state treasury,' said he once, 'has been embarrassed by the profusion of several reigns. Several of our inalienable domains have been sold far below their value'. 'Industrial corporations,' he is made to say on another occasion, with more truth than prudence, 'are the especial product of the fiscal greed of kings.' Farther on he says, 'If money has often been thrown away in useless expenses, and the taille has increased beyond measure, the fact must be charged upon the administrators of the finances, who, finding an increase of the taille the easiest, because the most secret method of meeting their difficulties, have had recourse to that plan, though almost any other would have been less burdensome to our subjects'.[63]

All this was addressed to the educated classes, in order to prove the merit of measures which certain private interests opposed. As for the people, it was taken for granted that they heard all, but understood nothing.

It must be admitted that the very benevolence which prompted the relief of these poor people concealed a large share of contempt for them. One is reminded of Madame de Duchatelet, who, according to Voltaire's secretary, had no objection to undress before her sevants, as she was not convinced that valets were men.

Nor was the dangerous language quoted above confined to Louis XVI or his ministers. The very privileged classes who were the most immediate objects of popular hatred never spoke otherwise. It must be acknowledged that the upper classes in France concerned themselves about the condition of the poor long before they learned to fear them: their interest in popular sufferings was prior to the first suspicion that those sufferings might eventuate in their ruin. This is especially visible in the ten years which preceded 1789. The peasantry were the theme of constant conversations, of abiding sympathy. Remedies for their evils were suggested incessantly. Light was thrown on their chief grievances, and the fiscal laws which pressed heavily on them were loudly censured. But their new friends were as thoughtless in their sympathy as they had formerly been in their insensibility.

Read the reports of the Provincial Assemblies which were convened in some parts of France in 1779, and, at a later period, throughout the kingdom; study the public documents which they have left us, and you will be touched with the humanity and amazed at the singular imprudence of their language.

The Provincial Assembly of Normandy declared, in 1787, that 'the money appropriated by the king to the roads has often been so used as to be convenient to the rich, but useless to the poor. It has often been employed to render the approach to a chateau more agreeable, while the entry of a bourg or village has been neglected.' At the same assembly, the two orders of the nobility and the clergy, after having described the vices of the system of *corvées*, offered spontaneously to devote 50,000 *livres* to the improvement of the roads, 'so that', as they say, 'the internal communications of the province may be made practicable without costing the people anything'. It would have been less onerous to the privileged classes to have substituted a general tax for the *corvées*, and to have paid their share; but even in abandoning the benefit of unequal taxation, they liked to preserve the name of being exempt. They sacrificed the useful portion of their rights, but they preserved what was odious.

Other assemblies, wholly composed of persons who were, and intended to remain, exempt from the taille, painted, in equally sombre colours, the evils which that tax inflicted on the poor. They drew a frightful sketch of its abuses, and scattered copies broadcast. And, singular to state, with these striking marks of interest in the people's welfare, they intermingled, from time to time, public expressions of contempt. The people had inspired sympathy without ceasing to inspire disdain.

The Provincial Assembly of Upper Guienne, pleading with warmth the cause of the peasantry, alluded to them as '*ignorant and gross beings, turbulent spirits, and rude and indocile characters*'. Turgot, who did so much for the people, used language very similar.[64]

Expressions as harsh were commonly used in documents

destined to a wide publicity, and intended to be seen by the peasantry. It was as if the writers had been living in one of those European countries like Gallicia, where the upper classes speak a different tongue from the lower, and cannot be understood by them. Feudal lawyers of the eighteenth century, who often evince an unusual spirit of justice, moderation, and tenderness for copyholders and other feudal debtors, still occasionally speak of *low peasants*. These insults appear to have been technical (*de style*), as the notaries say.

Toward 1789, the sympathy for the people grew warmer and more imprudent. I have had in my hands circulars, addressed by several Provincial Assemblies, in the early part of 1788, to the people of several parishes, inquiring for the details of their grievances. One of these was signed by an *abbé*, a nobleman of high degree, three men of rank, and a burgher, all members of the assembly and acting in its name. This commission directed the syndic of each parish to convene the peasantry, and inquire of them what complaints they had to make of the manner in which the taxes were levied upon them. 'We are aware,' it said, 'that most of the taxes, and especially the gavel and the taille, are disastrous in their effects upon farmers; but we desire to ascertain the particulars of each abuse.' Nor does the curiosity of the Assembly rest there. They want to know the number of persons who are exempt from taxation in the parish; whether they are noblemen, ecclesiastics, or commoners; what is the nature of their privileges; what is the value of their property; whether they reside on their estates; whether the parish contains much Church property, or, as the phrase then was, much land in mortmain, not merchantable; and what its value may be. Even these inquiries fall short of their requirements. They desire to know what sum of money would represent the share which each privileged person would have to bear in taxes, taille and its accessories, capitation-tax, *corvées*, if taxation weighed equally on all.

This was simply inflaming the passions of each individual by the recital of his wrongs, pointing out their authors to him, encouraging him by indicating the smallness of their number, stealing into his inmost heart to light up his cupidity, his envy, his hatred. It seemed as though the Jacquerie, the Maillotins, the Sixteen, had been wholly forgotten; and as if no one knew that the French, who are naturally the gentlest and even the kindest people in the world so long as they are in repose, become the most barbarous race alive when violent passions pervert their natural disposition.

I have, unhappily, been unable to procure all the answers which the peasants made to these murderous inquiries, but I have found a few of them, and they suffice to indicate the spirit of the whole.

They give with care the name of every privileged person, whether belonging to the nobility or the middle classes. Occasionally they describe, and invariably criticise his mode of life. They enter into curious calculations with regard to the value of his property; they enlarge upon the number and nature of his privileges, and especially upon the injury which they inflict upon the neighbourhood. They enumerate the bushels of wheat which he receives by way of dues; they estimate enviously his revenue, which they say is advantageous to no one. The curate's fees – his salary, as they have already begun to say – are excessive; they remark bitterly that the Church exacts money for everything, and that a poor man cannot even be buried gratuitously. As for the taxes, they are all ill-distributed and oppressive; not one obtains favour at their hands, and all are spoken of in violent language breathing absolute fury.

'The indirect taxes are odious,' they say; 'not a household but the tax-gatherer invades; nothing is sacred either from his eyes or his hands. The registry duties are crushing. The receiver of the taille is a tyrant whose cupidity shrinks from no measure of annoyance for honest people. The bailiffs are no better; no honest farmer is safe from their ferocity. The collectors are obliged to ruin their neighbours in order to save themselves from the voracity of these despots.'

The inquiry is no mere preliminary of the Revolution; it is part of it, speaks its language, wears its features.

One among the many points of difference between the religious revolution of the sixteenth century and the French Revolution is especially striking. In the sixteenth century, most of the nobility took the side of the new religion from ambitious or interested motives; while the people, on the contrary, embraced it from conviction, and without expecting any profit from the change. In the eighteenth century this was not the case. It was disinterested principle and generous sympathy which roused the upper classes to revolution, while the people were agitated by the bitter feeling of their grievances, and a rage to change their condition. The enthusiasm of the former fanned the flame of popular wrath and covetousness, and ended by arming the people.

Chapter 18

Of certain Practices by means of which the Government completed the revolutionary Education of the People.

The government had long laboured to plant and fasten in the popular mind several of those ideas which are now called revolutionary – principles of hostility to individual and private rights, and arguments in favour of appeals to violence.

The king set the example of treating the oldest and most solidly established institutions with contempt. Louis XV shook the monarchy, and hastened the Revolution as much by his innovations as by his vices, by his energy as by his dissipation. When the people saw the Parliament – an institution coeval with, and apparently as strong as the monarchy – fall and disappear, they inferred, in a vague manner, that a period of violence was at hand, when age would prove no guarantee of respectability, and novelty no indication of risk.

During the whole course of his reign, Louis XVI talked of nothing but reform. The Revolution overthrew very few institutions whose overthrow he did not foreshadow. He issued ordinances abolishing some of the worst, but he restored them soon afterward, as though he intended only to uproot them, leaving to others the task of pulling them down.

Some of the reforms which he effected changed violently and

unexpectedly old and respected customs; others did violence to acquired rights. They paved the way for the Revolution less by striking down obstacles which stood in its way than by showing the people how it might be brought about. The mischief was aggravated by the pure and disinterested motives of the king and his advisers; for no example is so dangerous as that of violence employed by well-meaning people for beneficial objects.

Long before, Louis XIV had publicly promulgated in his edicts the theory that all the lands in the kingdom had been in the origin conditionally granted by the state, which was therefore the only real landowner – the actual holders having mere possessory rights, and an imperfect and questionable title. This doctrine sprang out of the feudal system, but it was never openly professed in France till that system was on the point of death; courts of justice never admitted it. It was the mother of modern socialism, which thus, strange to say, seems to have been the offspring of royal despotism.[65]

During the subsequent reigns, the government took pains to teach the people, in practical lessons which they could easily understand, that private property was to be regarded with contempt. During the second half of the eighteenth century the government was seized with a mania for public works, it took possession without scruple of all the lands it required for its enterprises, and threw down the houses which stood in its way. The Department of Bridges and Roads was, then as now, smitten with admiration for the geometrical charm of the straight line. It would have nothing to do with roads in which there was the slightest curve; to avoid a bend, it would cut through a thousand estates. Properties thus injured or destroyed were always arbitrarily and tardily paid for; sometimes they were not paid for at all.[66]

When the Provincial Assembly of Lower Normandy took the administration of the province out of the hands of the intendant, it was ascertained that the price of all the lands taken by public authority during the twenty years previous was yet unpaid. The debt which the state thus owed to this little corner of France amounted to 250,000 *livres*. But few large landholders were injured; the burden fell chiefly on the smaller proprietors, for lands were very generally parcelled out into small lots. Here were a large number of persons whose own experience taught them that private rights were not for a moment to be balanced against the public interest: a doctrine they were not likely to forget when the time came for its application to their own benefit.

In many parishes persons had bequeathed sums of money to be employed in supporting charitable institutions for the benefit of the parishioners in certain specific cases. Most of these institutions were either destroyed or transformed during the later period of the monarchy, by mere Orders in Council, that is to say, by the arbitrary will of government. The fund was usually taken away from the village, and bestowed on neighbouring hospitals. Carrying out the principle still farther, the government simultaneously diverted the property of the hospitals from its original destination, and applied it to purposes of which the founder of the charity would doubtless have disapproved. Much of this property had been left to the hospitals, to be held by them inalienably: the government authorised them to sell it, and to pay over the price to the public treasury, which was to pay interest thereon. This, the administrators said, was making a better use of the bequest than the testator himself had done. They forgot that the very best way to teach men to violate the individual rights of the living is to disregard the wishes of the dead. No subsequent government has displayed such marked contempt for testamentary injunctions as the old monarchy. Never, on any occasion, did it evince any of those fastidious scruples which in England rally the whole weight of the social body to the support of the citizen's last will, and secure for his memory a respect that is never paid to his person.

Requisitions, compulsory sales of produce, the *maximum*, were all in use under the government of the old regime. I find that in times of scarcity the public officials would fix the price at which farm produce must be sold, and punish farmers who refused to send their grain to market by the imposition of a fine.

But the most pernicious of all lessons was that inculcated by judicial proceedings in criminal cases in which the people were concerned. Poor men were far better protected against the rich and the powerful than is generally supposed. But when they had to deal with the state, they were judged, as I said before, by abnormal tribunals composed of partial judges: the proceedings were speedy and delusive; the decision, which was final, might be anticipated by preliminary execution. 'His Majesty appoints the provost of police (*prévôt de la maréchaussée*) and his lieutenant to take cognizance of all movements and assemblages to which the scarcity of provisions may give rise; ordains that cases shall be heard and decided by them summarily and without appeal; and forbids all courts of justice to take cognizance of any such.' This Order in Council was the law throughout the eighteenth century. Police reports of the time show that, in cases of this character, suspected villages were surrounded at night; houses were entered before daybreak; peasants designated for arrest were seized without other warrant or authority. They were often detained for a length of time in prison before they could speak to a judge, though edicts declared that every person accused should be examined within twenty-four hours after his arrest. That provision of the law was neither less formal nor more respected than it is in our own day.

It was thus that a benign and solidly established government taught the people, day by day, the system of criminal procedure best adapted to the requirements of revolution and the desires of tyranny. It kept open school, and to the last gave to the lower classes this perilous education. Even Turgot faithfully copied his predecessors in this respect. When his legislation of 1775 on the subject of breadstuffs gave rise to resistance in the Parliament and riots in the country parts, he obtained from the king an ordinance which removed the cases of the rioters from the jurisdiction of the ordinary courts, and gave them exclusively to the cognizance of the provost. 'The police jurisdiction,' the ordinance said, 'is principally designed to repress popular disturbances when it is desirable that speedy examples be made.' Under this ordinance, peasants travelling out of their parish without a certificate signed by the curate and the syndic were liable to prosecution before the provost, arrest, and punishment as vagabonds.

It is true that, under terrible forms, the monarchy of the eighteenth century concealed moderate penalties. Its principle was rather to terrify than to injure; or, rather, it was arbitrary and violent from habit and indifference, but, at the same time, instinctively gentle. But summary judicial proceedings were none the less popular with government. The lighter the penalty, the easier the vice of its infliction was forgotten. The mildness of the sentence cloaked the harshness of the trial.

I venture to state – for I hold the proofs in my hand – that precedents and examples for very many of the proceedings of the revolutionary government were found in the records of the measures employed against the lower classes during the two last centuries of the monarchy. The old regime furnished the Revolution with many of its forms; the latter merely added the atrocity of its genius.

Chapter 19

How great administrative Changes had preceded the political
Revolution, and of the Consequences thereof.

Before the form of the government was altered, most of the laws regulating the condition of persons and the administration of public business had been repealed or modified.[67]

The destruction of trade-companies and their partial and incomplete restoration afterward had wholly changed the relation formerly existing between master and workman. That relation was now uncertain – constrained. Neither was the old dominical authority in a state of preservation, nor the guardianship of the state fully developed; so that, between the two, the mechanic, cramped and embarrassed, knew not to which side he ought to look for protection or control. This state of uncertainty and anomaly, in which all the lower classes of the large cities had been suddenly placed, led to very grave consequences when the people appeared on the political stage.

A year before the Revolution a royal edict overturned the whole judicial system. New jurisdictions were created, old ones abolished, all the old rules governing the competency of judges changed. Now I have already had occasion to remark that the number of persons who were employed in France, either in hearing cases or executing judgments, was immense. In fact, nearly all the middle class had something to do with the courts. Hence the effect of the law was to disturb the condition and means of several thousand families, whose situation was rendered uncertain and precarious. Nor was it less prejudicial to litigants, who, in the judicial confusion, had some trouble in finding out the law which was applicable to their case, and the court that was to hear it.

But it was especially the radical reform effected in the government proper, in 1787, which threw public business into disorder, and brought trouble into the home of every private family.

I stated that in the *pays d'élection*, that is to say, in three fourths of France, the whole government of each district (*généralité*) was placed in the hands of a single man, the intendant, who was not only uncontrolled, but without advisers.

In 1787 provincial assemblies were created, which became the real governors of the country. In every village an elective municipal body took the place of the old parochial assemblies, and, generally speaking, of the syndic also.

Thus a system diametrically opposed to the past, and completely subversive, not only of the old methods of transacting business, but of the relative positions of men, had to be applied to every part of the country by one uniform plan, quite independently of old usages and of the particular situation of the several provinces. So profoundly was the old government imbued with the unitarian spirit of the Revolution by whose hands it was to perish.

It was then plainly seen how large an influence habit exercises over the working of political institutions, and how much more easily men manage their affairs with obscure and complicated laws to which they are used than with a far simpler system which is new to them.

There were in France, under the old regime, all kinds of authorities, infinitely diversified according to locality, with powers of unknown and unlimited scope, so that the field of action of each was always common to several others; yet business was transacted in an orderly and tolerably easy manner. The new authorities, on the contrary, which were few in number, carefully limited in their sphere, and harmoniously adjusted, were no sooner put in force, than they encroached upon one another, and clashed, throwing everything into confusion and paralysing each other.

The new system, moreover, had a great fault, which alone would have rendered its execution difficult, at the outset especially; all the authorities it created were corporate.

Under the old monarchy, but two methods of governing were known. Where the government was in the hands of a single individual, he acted without the concurrence of any assembly. Where, on the other hand, assemblies were used, as was the case in *pays d'états* and in cities, the executive power was confided to no one in particular: the assembly not only governed and controlled the administration, it executed the laws, either directly or through the medium of temporary committees which it appointed.

These being the only two plans known, when one was abandoned the other was adopted. It is not a little singular that, in so enlightened a society, and one in which government had so long played a leading part, no one should have thought of combining the two systems, and drawing a distinction between the executive branch and that which was supervisory or directory, without disuniting them. This idea, simple as it is, never struck any one; it is a discovery which dates from this century, and almost the only discovery in administrative science that we can fairly claim. We shall perceive the effects of the contrary system when we see the old administrative methods applied to politics, the traditions of the detested old regime followed, and the plan of the Provincial States and small municipalities adopted by the National Convention. Causes which had formerly led to nothing but embarrassment in the transaction of public businesses then gave rise to the Reign of Terror.

The Provincial Assemblies of 1787 were authorized to administer their own government, and to supersede the intendant in almost all matters. They were intrusted with the distribution and levy of the taille, under the authority of the central government, and with the selection and general direction of all public works. All the agents of the Bridges and Roads, from the inspector to the overseer of works, were under their immediate orders. The assemblies decided according to their own discretion what was to be done, reported to the ministers, suggested the names of persons deserving reward. They were the guardians of the *communes*, heard most of the lawsuits which had formerly been brought before the intendant, &c., and discharged a variety of functions that were ill suited to a corporate and irresponsible body, especially when composed of persons who were entirely new to such duties.

The confusion was completed by an error; the intendant was stripped of his power, but the office was retained. After being deprived of their absolute authority, the intendants were expected to aid the assembly and supervise its acts – as though a fallen functionary could ever help to execute and enter into the spirit of laws which dispossess him.

A similar course was adopted with regard to the office of sub-delegate. District assemblies were appointed to discharge its functions under the direction of the Provincial Assembly, and on similar principles.

From all that we can learn of the proceedings of the Provincial Assemblies of 1787, including their own reports, it would appear that from the first they found themselves at war, sometimes open, sometimes secret, with the intendants, who employed all their superior business experience in defeating the aims of their successors.[68] One assembly complains that it can hardly succeed in wresting from the hands of the intendant the most necessary papers. Another is accused by the intendant of seeking to usurp powers which the edicts reserve to him. He appeals to the minister, who makes no answer, or answers doubtfully, being as new to the business as the others. Sometimes the assembly decides that the intendant has been guilty of maladminstration, that the roads he has made are in the wrong direction or in bad repair; he is accused of ruining the communities whose guardian he was. In their inexperience, everything is obscure to the assemblymen, and they often hesitate, send to distant assemblies for advice, keep couriers constantly on the road from one to another. The intendant of Auch pretends that he is entitled to oppose the assembly, which had authorized a *commune* to tax itself; the assembly replies that in this matter the intendant may offer advice, but nothing more, and sends to the assembly of Ile de France to ask what that body thinks on the point.

These recriminations and interchange of opinions often delay, and sometimes stop altogether, the transaction of public business. National life seems suspended. The Provincial Assembly of Lorraire – a mere echo of others – declares that 'the stagnation of public business is complete, and all good citizens are afflicted thereat'.

Others of these new administrations go wrong by excessive activity and self-reliance; they are full of a restless and disturbing zeal, which prompts them to want to change all the old methods with a stroke of the pen, and to correct the most deeply-rooted abuses in a day. Under the pretext that they are henceforth the guardians of cities, they assume the management of municipal affairs; in a word, their efforts to improve matters succeed in throwing everything into confusion.

Now consider the immense influence which the government had long exercised in France, the multitude of interests which it affected, the vast number of affairs which depended on it for support or aid; bear in mind that private individuals relied more on it than on themselves to secure the success of their own business, to develop their industry, to insure their means of subsistence, to make and mend their roads, to preserve the peace among them, and to guarantee their well-being; and then calculate how many individuals must have been personal sufferers by its disorder.

The vices of the new organization were more conspicuous in the villages than anywhere else; for there it not only disturbed the old divisions of authority, but changed suddenly the relative position of individuals, and drove the several orders into mutual hostility.

When Turgot, in 1775, proposed to the king to reform the administration of the rural districts, the greatest difficulty he met with, as he states himself, arose from the unequal distribution of taxes. For the chief parochial business was the distribution, levy, and appropriation of the taxes, and how was it possible to make people, on whom they pressed unequally, and some of whom were wholly exempt from them, deliberate and act in concert on their subject? Every parish contained some men of rank, or churchmen, who paid no taille, peasants who were partially or wholly exempt, others who paid an integral share. These formed three distinct parishes, each of which would have required a separate administration. The problem was insoluble.

Nowhere was the inequality of taxation so conspicuous as in the country; nowhere were people so divided into distinct and mutually hostile classes. Before attempting a collective administration and a free government in villages, the taxes should have been equalized, and distinctions of class and rank modified.

This was not the plan pursued when reform was attempted in 1787. Within the parish, the old distinctions of rank were maintained with the unequal taxation which marked them; yet the whole government was intrusted to elective bodies. This led directly to most singular results.

The curate and the seignior had no business to appear in the assembly which elected municipal officers; for they were respectively members of the orders of the clergy and the nobility, while the officials elected were the special representatives of the Third Estate.

But when the Municipal Council was chosen, the curate and the seignior were members *ex officio*, for it would not have been seemly to exclude from the government of the parish its two leading inhabitants. It was the seignior who presided over the municipal councillors, though he had not contributed to elect them, and could not take part in the bulk of their acts. Neither seignior nor curate, for instance, could vote on the distribution or levy of the taille, in consequence of their exemption. In return, the Council could not interfere with their capitation-tax, which continued to be regulated according to particular forms by the intendant.

Lest this president – so carefully isolated from the body which he was said to direct – should still exercise an indirect influence in opposition to the interest of the order to which he did not belong, it was proposed to disfranchise his tenants; and the Provincial Assemblies, to which the point was referred, considered the proposal proper, and in conformity with correct principle. Other men of rank, resident in the parish, were excluded from this municipal body, unless they were elected by the peasants; and then, as the regulation is careful to observe, they were representatives of the Third Estate alone.

The seignior then only appeared there to exhibit his subjection to his old subjects, who were now his masters, while he was more like their prisoner than their chief. Indeed, the principal object of the assemblage appeared to be less to bring the different ranks together than to show them how widely they differed, and how adverse their interests were.

Was the office of syndic still so discredited that it was never willingly accepted, or had it risen in importance side by side with the community whose chief agency it was? No one knew precisely.[69] I have seen a letter from a village bailiff of 1788, complaining indignantly that he has been elected syndic, 'which is in violation of the privileges of his office'. The comptroller-general replied that the ideas of this personage required to be rectified; 'that he must be made to understand that it was an honour to be elected by his fellow-citizens; and that, moreover, the new syndics would not resemble the functionaries hitherto known by the title, and might expect more consideration at the hands of government'.

On the other hand, the moment the peasantry became a power in the state, the leading citizens of the parishes and men of rank were suddenly attracted to their side. A seignior and high justiciary of a village near Paris complained that the edict prevented his taking part, even as a simple inhabitant of the parish, in the proceedings of the parochial assembly. Others 'consent' they said, 'to devote themselves for the public good, and accept the office of syndic'.

It came too late. In proportion to the advances of the wealthy classes, the people of the rural districts shrank back; when they tried to mingle with them, the people sheltered themselves in the isolation into which they had been driven. Some municipal assemblies declined to admit their seignior as a member; others made all sorts of objects to the reception of commoners who were rich. The Provincial Assembly of Lower Normandy states, 'We are informed that several municipal assemblies have refused to admit absentee landholders, who, as commoners, have an indisputable right to seats there. Other assemblies have declined to admit farmers who owned no land within their jurisdiction.'

Thus all was novelty, obscurity, conflict between the secondary laws, even before the chief laws which regulated the government of the state had been touched. Those which were still in force were shaken, and there was not a law or a regulation which the government had not announced its intention to abolish or modify.

Our Revolution, then, was preceded by a sudden and thorough remodeling of all administrative rules and habits. The event is barely remembered now, yet it was one of the greatest perturbations that ever marked the history of a great people. It was a first revolution, which exercised a prodigious influence over the second, and renderd it a very different affair from all former or subsequent revolutions.

The first English revolution, though it overthrew the political constitution of the country, and for a time abolished royalty itself, barely touched the secondary class of laws, and made no change in the prevailing customs and usages. Justice and government were administered in the old forms and in the beaten track. At the height of the civil war, it is said that the twelve judges of England continued their semi-annual circuits throughout the country to hold the assizes. The agitation was not universal. The effects of the revolution were circumscribed, and English society, though shaken at the top, was unmoved at the base.

We have ourselves seen in France, since 1789, several revolutions which have altered the whole edifice of government. Most of them have been very sudden, and have been achieved by violence, in open violation of existing laws. Yet none have given rise to long continued or general disorder; they have been scarcely felt, in some cases hardly noticed by the majority of the nation.

The reason is that, since 1789, the administrative system has always remained untouched in the midst of political convulsions. The person of the sovereign or the form of the central power has been altered, but the daily transaction of business has neither been disturbed nor interrupted. Each citizen has remained subject to the laws and usages which he understood, in the small matters which concerned him personally. He had to deal with secondary authorities, with which he had done business before, and which were rarely changed. For if each revolution struck off the head of the government, it left its body untouched and alive, so that the same functionaries continued to perform their functions, in the same spirit, and according to the same routine, under every different political system. They administered justice or managed public affairs in the name of the king, then in that of the republic, lastly in that of the emperor. Fortune's wheel turning on and on, the same individuals began again to administer and manage in the same way for the king, for the republic, for the emperor; what mattered the name of the master? It was their business to be good administrators and managers – not citizens. Thus, the first shock over, it seemed as though nothing had changed in the country.

At the outbreak of the Revolution, those branches of the government which, though subordinate, are most felt by individuals, and exercise the largest and most steady influence on their welfare, had just been overturned; the government had suddenly changed all its agents and all its principles. At first the state did not seem to have felt a severe shock from this sweeping reform; but every Frenchman had experienced a slight commotion. Not a man but was affected either in his rank, or in his habits, or in his business. Though great state affairs continued to be transacted in a sort of regular order, in those smaller transactions which consitute the routine of everyday life, no one knew whom to obey, where to apply, how to act.

Every part of the nation being thus thrown off the level, one final blow was enough to set the whole in motion, and produce the greatest convulsion and the most terrible disorders that were ever witnessed.

Chapter 20

How the Revolution sprang spontaneously out of the preceding Facts.

I desire, in conclusion, to put together some of the features which I have separately sketched, and, having drawn the portrait of the old regime, to watch the Revolution spring from it by its own unaided effort.

Let it be borne in mind that France was the only country in which the feudal system had preserved its injurious and irritating characteristics, while it had lost all those which were beneficial or useful; and it will seem less surprising that the Revolution which was to abolish the old constitution of Europe should have broken out there rather than elsewhere.

Let it also be borne in mind that France was the only feudal country in which the nobility had lost its old political rights, lost the right of administering government and leading the people, but had nevertheless retained and even largely increased its pecuniary indemnities and the individual privileges of its members; had, in its subordinate position, remained a close body, growing less and less of an aristocracy and more and more of a caste; and it will at once be understood why its privileges seemed so inexplicable and detestable to the French, and why their hearts were inflamed with a democratic envy that is not yet extinguished.

Let it be borne in mind, finally, that the nobility was separated from the middle classes, which it had eschewed, and from the people, whose affections it had lost; that it stood alone in the midst of the nation, seemingly the staff of an army, really a group of soldierless officers; and it will be easy to conceive how, after an existence of a thousand years, it was overthrown in a single night.

I have shown how the royal government abolished the provincial liberties, usurped the place of the local authorities in three-fourths of the kingdom, and monopolized public business, great and small; and I have also shown how Paris consequently became of necessity the master of the country instead of the capital, or rather, became itself the whole country. These two facts, which were peculiar to France, would alone suffice to show how a revolt could achieve the overthrow of a monarchy which had endured so violent shocks during so many centuries, and which, on the eve of its destruction, seemed immovable to its very assailants.

Political life had been so long and so thoroughly extinguished in France – individuals had so entirely lost the habit of mixing in public affairs, of judging for themselves, of studying popular movements, and even understanding the people at all, that the French quite naturally drifted into a terrible revolution without seeing it – the very parties who had most to fear from it taking the lead, and undertaking to smooth and widen the way for its approach.

In the absence of free institutions, and, consequently, of political classes, active political bodies, or organized parties, the duty of leading public opinion, when it revived, naturally fell to the lot of philosophers. Hence it might be expected that the Revolution would be conducted less in view of specific facts than in conformity with abstract principles and general theories. It might be conjectured that, instead of assailing specific laws, it would attack all laws together, and would assume to substitute for the old Constitution of France a new system of government which these writers had conceived.

The Church was mixed with all the old institutions that were to be destroyed. Hence it was plain that the Revolution would shake the religious while it overthrew the civil power; and this done, and men's minds set free from all the restraints which religion, custom, and law impose on reformers, it was impossible to say to what unheard-of lengths of boldness it might not go. Every careful student of the state of the country could perceive that there were no lengths of boldness that were too distant, no pitch of violence too frantic to be attempted.

'What!' cried Burke, in one of his eloquent pamphlets, 'one cannot find a man that can answer for the smallest district; not a man who can answer for his neighbour. People are arrested in their houses for royalism, for moderation, or anything else, and no one ever resists.' Burke had no idea of the state in which the monarchy he so deeply regretted had left us. The old government had deprived the French of the power and the desire to help each other. When the Revolution broke out, there were not ten men in the greater part of France who were in the habit of acting in concert, in a regular manner, and providing for their own defence; everything was left to the central power. And so, when that power made way for an irresponsible sovereign assembly, and exchanged its former mildness for ferocity, there was nothing to check or delay it for an instant. The same cause which had overthrown the monarchy had rendered everything possible after its fall.

At no former period had religious toleration, gentleness in the exercise of authority, humanity, and benevolence, been so generally advocated or so thoroughly accepted as sound doctrine as during the eighteenth century: the very spirit of war – last refuge of the spirit of violence – had been limited, and its rigors softened. Out of the bosom of this refined society how inhuman a revolution was about to spring! And yet the refinement was no mere pretence, for no sooner had the first fury of the Revolution been deadened than the spirit of the laws and political customs was softened and assuaged.

To comprehend the contrast between the benign theories and the violent acts of the Revolution, one must remember that it was prepared by the most civilized classes of the nation, and executed by the roughest and most unpolished. The former having no bond of mutual union, no common understanding among themselves, no hold on the people, the latter assumed the whole direction of affairs when the old authorities were abolished. Even where they did not govern they inspired the government; and a glance at the way they had lived under the old regime left no room for doubt as to what they would prove.

The very peculiarities of their condition endowed them with some rare virtues. They had long been free and landholders; they were temperate and proud in their independent isolation. They were hardened to toil, careless of the refinements of life, resigned to misfortune however great, firm in the face of danger. A simple, manly race, hereafter to constitute armies under which Europe shall bow the neck; but hence, also, a dangerous master. Crushed for centuries under the weight of abuses which no one shared with them, living alone, and brooding silently over their prejudices, their jealousies, and their hatreds, they were hardened by their hard experience, and were as ready to inflict as to bear suffering.

Such was the French people when it laid hands on the government, and undertook to complete the work of the Revolution. It found in books a theory which it assumed to put in practice, shaping the ideas of the writers to suit its passions.

The careful student of France during the eighteenth century must have noticed in the preceding pages the birth and development of two leading passions, which were not coeval, and not always similar in their tendencies.

One – the deepest and most solidly rooted – was a violent, unquenchable hatred of inequality. It took its rise and grew in the face of marked inequalities; drove the French with steady, irresistible force to seek to destroy utterly all the remains of the medieval institutions; and prompted the erection on their ruins of a society in which all men should be alike, and as equal in rank as humanity dictates.

The other – of more recent date, and less solidly rooted – prompted men to seek to be free as well as equal.

Toward the close of the old regime these two passions were equally sincere, and apparently equally active; they met at the opening of the Revolution, and, blending together into one, they took fire from contact, and inflamed the whole heart of France. No doubt 1789 was a period of inexperience, but it was also a period of generosity, of enthusiasm, of manliness, of greatness – a period of immortal memory, upon which men will look back with admiration and respect when all who witnessed it, and we who follow them, shall have long since passed away. The French were then proud enough of their cause and of themselves to believe that they could enjoy freedom and equality together. They planted, therefore, free institutions in the midst of democratic institutions. Not content with pulverizing the super-annuated laws which divided men into classes, castes, corporations, and endowed them with rights more unequal even than their ranks, they likewise annulled at a blow those other laws which were a later creation of the royal power, and which had stripped the nation of all control over itself, and set over every Frenchman a government to be his preceptor, his tutor, and, in case of need, his oppressor. Centralization fell with absolute monarchy.

But when the vigorous generation which began the Revolution perished or became enervated, as all generations must which undertake such enterprises; when, in the natural course of events of this character, the love of liberty had been discouraged and grown languid in the midst of anarchy and popular despotism, and the bewildered nation began to grope around for a master, immense facilities were offered for the restoration of absolute government; and it was easy for the genius of him who was destined both to continue and to destroy the Revolution to discover them.

The old regime contained, in fact, a large body of institutions of modern type which, not being hostile to equality, were susceptible of being used in the new order of things, and yet offered remarkable facilities for the establishment of despotism. They were sought for and found in the midst of the ruins. They had formerly given birth to habits, passions, and ideas which tended to keep men divided and obedient; they were restored and turned to account. Centralization was raised from its tomb and restored to its place; whence it happened that, all the checks which had formerly served to limit its power being destroyed, and not revived, there sprang out of the bosom of a nation which had just overthrown royalty a power more extensive, more detailed, more absolute than any of our monarchs had ever wielded. The enterprise seemed incredibly bold and unprecedentedly successful, because people only thought of what they saw before them, and forgot the past. The despot fell; but the most substantial portion of his work remained: his administrative system survived his government. And ever since, whenever an attempt has been made to overthrow an absolute government, the head of Liberty has been simply planted on the shoulders of a servile body.

During the period that has elapsed since the Revolution, the passion for liberty has frequently been extinguished again, and again revived. This will long be the case, for it is still inexperienced, ill regulated, easily discouraged, easily frightened away, easily overcome, superficial, and evanescent. Meanwhile, the passion for equality has retained its place at the bottom of the hearts it originally penetrated, and linked with their dearest sentiments. While the one is incessantly changing, now increasing, now diminishing, now gaining strength, now losing it, according to events, the other has remained uniformly the same, striving for its object with obstinate and often blind ardour, willing to sacrifice everything to gain it, and ready to repay its grant from government by cultivating such habits, ideas, and laws as a despotism may require.

The Revolution will ever remain in darkness to those who do not look beyond it; it can only be comprehended by the light of the ages which preceded it. Without a clear view of society in the olden time, of its laws, its faults, its prejudices, its suffering, its greatness, it is impossible to understand the conduct of the French during the sixty years which have followed its fall; and even that view will not suffice without some acquaintance with the natural history of our nation.

When I examine that nation in itself, I cannot help thinking it is more extraordinary than any of the events of its history. Did there ever appear on the earth another nation so fertile in contrasts, so extreme in its acts – more under the dominion of feeling, less ruled by principle; always better or worse than was anticipated – now below the level of humanity, now far above; a people so unchangeable in its leading features that it may be recognized by portraits drawn two or three thousand years ago, and yet so fickle in its daily opinions and tastes that it becomes at last a mystery to itself, and is as much astonished as strangers at the sight of what it has done; naturally fond of home and routine, yet, once driven forth and forced to adopt new customs, ready to carry principles to any lengths and to dare anything; indocile by disposition, but better pleased with the arbitrary and even violent rule of a sovereign than with a free and regular government under its chief citizens; now fixed in hostility to subjection of any kind, now so passionately wedded to servitude that nations made to serve cannot vie with it; led by a thread so long as no word of resistance is spoken, wholly ungovernable when the standard of revolt has been raised – thus always deceiving its masters, who fear it too much or too little; never so free that it cannot be subjugated, nor so kept down that it cannot break the yoke; qualified for every pursuit, but excelling in nothing but war; more prone to worship chance, force, success, eclat, noise, than real glory; endowed with more heroism than virtue, more genius than common sense; better adapted for the conception of grand designs than the accomplishment of great enterprises; the most brilliant and the most dangerous nation of Europe, and the one that is surest to inspire admiration, hatred, terror, or pity, but never indifference?

No nation but such a one as this could give birth to a revolution so sudden, so radical, so impetuous in its course, and yet so full of missteps, contradictory facts, and conflicting examples. The French could not have done it but for the reasons I have alleged; but, it must be admitted, even these reasons would not suffice to explain such a revolution in any country but France.

I have now reached the threshold of that memorable Revolution. I shall not cross it now. Soon, perhaps, I may be enabled to do so. I shall then pass over its causes to examine it in itself, and to judge the society to which it gave birth.

Appendix

Of the *pays d'etats*, and Languedoc in particular.

I t is not my intention to examine in detail, in this place, the condition of affairs in each of the *pays d'états*, as they stood before the Revolution.

I merely design to state how many there were; which of them were distinguished by local activity; on what footing they stood as regards the royal government; wherein they departed from the rules I have mentioned, and in what particulars they were governed by these rules; and lastly, to show, by the example of one of them, what they all might have become.

States had existed in most of the French provinces – that is to say, their government had been administered by members of the Three Estates (*gens des trois états*), as it was then the fashion to say; in other words, by an assembly composed of representatives of the clergy, the nobility, and the burghers. This provincial institution, like most of the political institutions of the Middle Ages, had flourished in a similar form throughout almost all civilized Europe, or, at all events, in every country into which German customs and ideas had made their way. In many German provinces States existed up to the French Revolution; in the others they did not disappear till the seventeenth or eighteenth century. For two centuries sovereigns had uniformly and steadily waged war against them, sometimes openly, sometimes secretly. No attempt had been anywhere made to adapt them to the improved condition of the times; but monarchs had never let slip an opportunity of destroying them or deforming them when this was the worst they could do.

In France there were but five provinces of any extent, and a few small, insignificant districts, in which States still existed in 1789. Provincial liberty, properly speaking, subsisted in two only, Bretagne and Languedoc; everywhere else the substantial features of the institution had been taken away, leaving only the semblance behind.

I shall examine Languedoc separately, and at some length.

It was the largest and most populous of the *pays d'états*. It

contained more than two thousand *communes*, or, as they were
then called, communities, and nearly two millions of inhabitants.
It was, moreover, the best ordered and prosperous, as well as the
largest of these provinces. We may therefore learn, from an
inquiry into its condition, what provincial liberty was under the
old regime, and to what extent, in those sections of the country
where it was most vigorous, it had been subordinated to the
royal power.

In Languedoc the Estates could not meet without an express
order from the king. Each member must have received individually a letter addressed to him inviting him to be present at
each session. Hence a malcontent of the time remarked: 'Of the
three bodies which compose our Estates, one, the clergy, is
appointed by the king, as all livings and bishoprics are in his gift;
and the two others are assumed to be in the same position, for
the king can prevent any member from being present by simply
withholding the invitation, though the member excluded has not
been exiled or even put on his trial.'

The period when the session of the Estates must end was
likewise fixed by the king. An Order in Council limited their
ordinary sessions to forty days. The king was represented in the
assembly by commissioners, who had seats whenever they chose
to demand them, and were the organ of the government. The
authority of the Estates was strictly limited. They could come to
no important decision, pass no appropriation bill, without an
Order in Council approving the measure: they could neither
impose a tax, nor effect a loan, nor institute an action at law
without the express permission of the king. All their rules,
including those which regulated their own sittings, were invalid
till the king had sanctioned them. Their receipts and expenditures, their budget, as we should say at present, was subject to
the same control.

The government exercised the same political rights in
Languedoc as elsewhere. Whatever laws it chose to promulgate,
whatever general rules it laid down, whatever measures it took,
applied to Languedoc as well as the *pays d'élection*. It performed
the natural functions of government, maintained the same
police, employed the same agents there as elsewhere, and

created, from time to time, a host of new functionaries, whose offices the province was obliged to buy up at very high rates.

Languedoc, like the other provinces, was governed by an intendant. In every district this intendant had sub-delegates, who were in relation with the heads of the communities, and directed them. The intendant was public guardian, precisely as in the *pays d'élection*. The smallest village, buried in the gorges of the Cevennes, could not make the least outlay without being authorized by an Order in Council from Paris. That branch of legal business which is now called the Department of Private Claims (*contentieux administratif*) was even more extensive there than elsewhere. The intendant had original jurisdiction over all questions of highways and roads, and generally over all disputes in which the government was, or chose to consider itself, interested. Nor were government agents less carefully protected there than elsewhere against prosecutions by citizens who were aggrieved by them.

Wherein, then, did Languedoc differ from the other provinces? How came it to be so envied by its neighbours? It differed from the rest of France in three respects:

1st. It possessed an assembly composed of substantial men, enjoying the confidence of the people and the respect of the general government. No government functionary, or, as they were called, king's officer, could be a member. The assembly discussed freely and seriously the affairs of the province every year. The proximity of this centre of intelligence obliged the government to exercise its privileges very cautiously and moderately: though its agents and its tendencies were the same there as elsewhere, they produced very different results.

2dly. Many public works were carried on in Languedoc at the cost of the king and directed by his agents; others were partly defrayed and substantially directed by the crown; but a still larger number were executed at the cost of the province. When the king had once approved the design and authorized the outlay necessary for the latter, they were prosecuted by officials chosen by the States, under the inspection of commissioners selected from the assembly.

3dly. The province was entitled to levy, in the way it liked best, a portion of the royal taxes, and all the taxes that were required for its own necessities.

We shall now see the use which Languedoc made of these privileges. It is a matter which deserves close attention.

A most striking feature in the *pays d'élection* was the rarity of local taxes. The general taxes were often burdensome, but the province spent little or nothing on itself. In Languedoc, on the contrary, enormous sums were spent by the province for public works; in 1780 the annual appropriation exceeded 7,000,000 *livres*.

The central government was occasionally shocked at such extravagance. It began to fear that such appropriations would exhaust the province, and incapacitate it from paying the royal taxes. It reproached the States with a want of moderation. I have read a memorial in which the assembly replied to these criticisms. A few extracts from that document will depict the spirit which animated that little government better than anything I could say.

The memorial admits that the province has certainly undertaken and is prosecuting immense works; but, instead of apologizing therefore, it declares that, if the king has no objection, this policy will be still farther carried out. The province has already improved and facilitated the navigation of the chief rivers which cross its territory, and is now engaged in prolonging the Burgundy Canal – which was constructed under Louis XIV, and is now inadequate – through Lower Languedoc, by Cette and Agde to the Rhone. It has adapted the port of Cette to commercial purposes, and keeps it in repair at great expense. These outlays, it is observed, are for national rather than provincial objects, but the province has made them, as it will be the chief gainer by the works. It is further engaged in draining and reclaiming the marsh of Aigues-Mortes. But its chief outlays have been for roads. It has either opened or repaired all the high roads which traverse its surface and lead into neighbouring provinces. It has mended all the roads between the different cities and bourgs of Languedoc. All these roads are excellent even in winter, and compare very favourably with the hard, rough, ill-kept roads which are met with in most of the neighbouring provinces, such as Dauphiné, Quercy, and

Bordeaux (which, it is observed, are *pays d'élection*). On this head the memorial refers to the judgment of travellers and merchants; nor without reason, for Arthur Young, who travelled through the country a year afterward, notes, 'Languedoc, *pays d'état* – good roads, made without *corvées*.'

If the king will grant permission, continues the memorial, the Estates will do more yet; they will undertake to improve the parish roads, which affect as many interests as the others. 'For if produce,' continued the memorial, 'cannot find its way from the producer's barn to the market, it is of very little use to provide for its exportation to a distance.' 'The principle of the States with regard to public works,' the memorial adds, 'has always been to look at their usefulness, not at their cost.' Rivers, canals, roads, give value to all products of the soil and of industry, by facilitating their conveyance at all seasons and at small expense to a market, and spreading commercial activity throughout the province; they are always worth more than they cost. Moreover, works of this character, if undertaken moderately, and spread uniformly over the territory of the province, sustain the value of labour, and give employment to the poor. 'The king,' adds the memorial, proudly, 'need be at no expense for the establishment of work-houses in Languedoc, as he has been obliged to do in the rest of France. We seek no favours of the kind: the works of public utility which we undertake ourselves stand us in the stead of work-houses, and furnish a remunerative demand for all our labour.'

The more I study the regulations which the king permitted the States of Languedoc to establish in those branches of administration which were left under their control, the more I admire the wisdom, the equity, the mildness which characterize them, and the more satisfied am I of the superiority of the policy of the local government over that which obtained in the provinces administered by the king.

The province was divided into communities, towns, or villages – into administrative districts, which were called dioceses; and, lastly, into three great departments, called *sénéchaussées*. Each of these divisions was separately represented in the Assembly; each had its own separate government, which acted under the direction of the States or the king. Public works for the benefit of any particular divison were only undertaken when that division expressed a desire for them. If the work demanded by the community would be beneficial to the diocese, the latter was bound to bear a proportionate share of the expense. If the sénéchaussée was interested, it paid a share. But diocese, sénéchaussée, and province were all bound to contribute to works which the interests of a community required, if they were necessary, and beyond the means of the body directly concerned; for, as the States frequently observed, 'The fundamental principle of our constitution is that all the divisions of the province are jointly and severally liable to each other, and bound to contribute to each other's progress.'

Works undertaken by the province were required to have been planned deliberately, and to have received the assent of all the secondary bodies concerned. All labour consumed was paid for in cash; *corvées* were unknown. I have stated that in *pays d'élection* land taken for objects of public utility was always tardily and inadequately paid for, and that occasionally the owner was not paid at all. This was one of the leading grievances of the Provincial Assemblies when they met in 1787. Some even complained that it was impossible to estimate the debts that had been thus incurred, as the property taken had been destroyed or transformed before it had been valued. In Languedoc, every foot of land taken from its owner was carefully valued before it was touched, and *the value paid before the expiration of a year from the time the works were begun.*

This system of the States of Languedoc with regard to public works appeared so excellent to the central government, that, without imitating, it admired it. The Royal Council, after having authorized its establishment, had it printed at the royal printing-office, and sent it to the intendants as a useful document to consult.

All that I have said with regard to public works is applicable, even in a greater degree, to that other and equally important branch of the provincial administration, the collection of the taxes. When one examines this department, first in the kingdom, then in the province, it seems impossible to believe that both are parts of the same empire.

I had occasion some time since to mention that the system used in Languedoc for the distribution and collection of the taille was substantially the same as the one now employed for the collection of our modern imposts. I shall not again revert to the subject, but will add simply that the province was so well convinced of the superiority of its method that, whenever the king established new taxes, the States paid heavily for the right of levying them in their own way, and by the hands of their own agents.

Notwithstanding all the outlays I have enumerated, the financial condition of Languedoc was so prosperous, and her credit so well established, that the central government often applied to it for endorsements, and borrowed in the name of the province at lower rates than would have been charged to the crown. I find that Languedoc borrowed in its own name, but for the use of the king, in the later years of the monarchy, 73,200,000 *livres*.

Yet the government watched these provincial liberties with a very jealous eye. Richelieu first mutilated, then abolished them. The weak and slothful Louis XIII, who loved nothing, detested them; he had such a dislike for provincial privileges, according to Boulainvilliers, that he would fly into a rage at the mere mention of the subject. Weak minds always find energy enough to hate things which oblige them to exert themselves; their whole vigour is concentrated upon that one point, and, weak as they are everywhere else, they contrive to hate with some force. Good fortune happily restored the Constitution of Languedoc during the infancy of Louis XIV; and that monarch, regarding it as his work, respected it. Louis XV suspended it for a couple of years, but suffered its restoration afterward.

The creation of municipal offices involved great indirect dangers for the province. This detestable institution tended not only to destroy the constitution of cities, but to disfigure that of provinces. I am not aware whether the deputies of the Third Estate in the Provincial Assemblies had ever been chosen in view of the business they had to perform; certain it is that for a long period of time they had not been so elected. The only legitimate representatives of the middle classes and the people were the municipal officers of cities.

So long as the cities chose their magistrates freely by universal suffrage, and generally for a short period of time, but little inconvenience was occasioned by the fact that these deputies had not been specially appointed to represent the people, and defend their interest at that particular moment. Perhaps the mayor, council, or syndic was as faithful an exponent of the popular will as if he had been expressly chosen to represent the people in the assembly. But it will at once be understood that this ceased to be the case when the official had acquired his office for money. In this case he represented no one but himself, or, at best, only the small interests and petty passions of his coterie. Yet the powers of the magistrate by purchase were the same as those of the elected magistrate had been. Hence a total change in the character of the institution. Instead of a firm body of popular representatives, the nobility and the clergy had to contend in the Provincial Assembly with no one but a few isolated, timid, and powerless burghers; the Third Estate became more and more insignificant in the government as it grew more and more powerful in society. This was not the case in Languedoc, as the province always took care to buy up the offices which the king established from time to time. For this object a loan of more than four millions of livres was effected in the year 1773 alone.

Other causes, more potent still, had operated to imbue these old institutions with a modern spirit, and imparted to the States of Languedoc an indisputable superiority over all others.

In that province, as in a large portion of the South, the taille was a tax on the realty, not on the person. It was regulated by the value of the property, not the fortune of the owner. True, certain lands enjoyed a privilege of exemption. These lands had formerly all belonged to the nobility; but, in the course of events and the progress of industry, part of them had fallen into the hands of commoners, while, on the other hand, noblemen had in many cases become proprietors of land subject to the taille. The absurdity of privileges was enhanced, no doubt, by their transfer from persons to property; but their burden was diminished, because, inconvenient as they were, they involved no humiliation. They were no longer inseparably bound up with class ideas; they created no class interests hostile to those of the public; they threw no obstacle in the way of a general administration of the public business by all classes. Nor was there, in fact, any part of France in which all classes mixed so freely, or on so decided a footing of equality as in Languedoc.

In Bretagne, all men of rank were entitled to be present in person at the States; hence these latter bore some resemblance to Polish Diets. In Languedoc, the nobility was represented in the States by twenty-three deputies; the clergy was represented by twenty-three bishops. It is worthy of remark, that the cities had as many members as the other two orders combined.

There was but one assembly, and votes were taken by heads, not by orders; hence the Third Estate naturally became the preponderating body, and gradually imbued the whole assembly with its peculiar spirit. The three magistrates, known as syndics-general, who were intrusted with the general management of business before the States, were always lawyers, that is to say, commoners. The nobility was strong enough to maintain its ranks, but not to rule. The clergy, on the other hand, though counting many men of rank among its members, always maintained a good understanding with the Third Estate. It took an ardent interest in many of the schemes proposed by the burghers, laboured in concert with them to augment the material property of citizens, and extend commerce and industry, and often placed at their service its extensive knowledge of men, and its peculiar skill in the management of affairs. It was almost always an ecclesiastic who was sent to Versailles to discuss with ministers questions that were in dispute between the States and the crown. It may be said that during the whole of the last century the government of Languedoc was administered by burghers, under the control of noblemen, and with the aid of bishops.

Thanks to the peculiar constitution of the province, the spirit of the new era penetrated Languedoc easily, and made many modifications in its old system without destroying anything.

This might have been the case everywhere. A portion of the perseverance and energy that were employed by the kings in abolishing or crippling the Provincial States would have sufficed for their improvement and adaptation to the necessities of modern civilization, had those monarchs ever sought anything beyond extending and maintaining their own power.

Notes

Influence of the Roman law in Germany – how it had replaced the Germanic law.

At the close of the Middle Ages the Roman law became the chief and almost the only study of the Germany lawyers, most of whom, at this time, were educated abroad at the Italian universities. These lawyers exercised no political power, but it devolved on them to expound and apply the laws. They were unable to abolish the Germanic law, but they did their best to distort it so as to fit the Roman mould. To every German institution that seemed to bear the most distant analogy to Justinian's legislation they applied Roman law. Hence a new spirit and new customs gradually invaded the national legislation, until its original shape was lost, and by the seventeenth century it was almost forgotten. Its place had been usurped by a medley that was Germanic in name, but Roman in fact.

I have reason to believe that this innovation of the lawyers had a tendency to aggravate the condition of more than one class of Germans, the peasantry especially. Persons who had up to that time succeeded in preserving the whole or a part of their liberty or their property, were ingeniously assimilated to the slaves or emphyteutic tenants of the Roman law, and lost rights and possessions together.

This gradual transformation of the national law, and the efforts which were made to prevent its accomplishment, were plainly seen in the history of Wurtemberg.

From the rise of the county of this name in 1250 to the creation of the duchy in 1495, the whole legislation of Wurtemberg was indigenous in character. It consisted of customs, local city laws, ordinances of seigniorial courts, or statutes of the States. Ecclesiastical affairs alone were regulated by foreign, that is to say, by canon law.

But from the year 1495 a change took place. Roman law began to penetrate the legislation of the duchy. The *doctors*, as they were called – that is to say, the individuals who had studied at foreign schools – connected themselves with the government, and took the management of the high courts. From the commencement to the middle of the fifteenth century, a struggle between them and the politicians of the day was carried on, similar in character, though different in result from the struggle that took place in England at the very same time. At the Diet of Tubingen in 1514 and the following Diets, the lawyers were attacked violently by the representatives of feudal institutions and the city deputies; they were loudly charged with invading all the courts of justice, and altering the spirit or the letter of all the laws and customs. At first, victory seemed to rest with the assailants. They obtained of government a promise that honourable and enlightened persons, chosen from the nobility and the States of the duchy – not doctors – should be set over the higher courts, and that a commission, consisting of government agents and representatives of the States, should be appointed to draft a bill for a Code to have force throughout the country. Useless effort! The Roman law soon expelled the national law from a large section of the legislative sphere, and even planted its roots in the section where the latter was allowed to subsist.

German historians ascribe this triumph of foreign over domestic law to two causes: 1st. The attraction exercised over the public mind by ancient literature, which necessarily led to a contempt for the intellectual products of the national genius; and, 2dly. The idea – with which the Germans of the Middle Ages, and even their laws, were imbued – that the Holy Empire was a continuation of the Roman Empire, and hence that the legislation of the latter was an heirloom of the former.

These causes do not suffice to explain the simultaneous introduction of Roman law into every Continental country. I think that the singular availability of the Roman law – which was a slave-law – for the purposes of monarchs, who were just then establishing their absolute power upon the ruins of the old liberties of Europe, was the true cause of the phenomenon.

The Roman law carried civil society to perfection, but it invariably degraded political society, because it was the work of a highly civilized and thoroughly enslaved people. Kings naturally embraced it with enthusiasm, and established it wherever they could throughout Europe; its interpreters became their ministers or their chief agents. Lawyers furnished them at need with legal warrant for violating the law. They have often done so since. Monarchs who have trampled the laws have almost always found a lawyer ready to prove the lawfulness of their acts – to establish learnedly that violence was just, and that the oppressed were in the wrong.

NOTE 2
Transition from feudal to democratic monarchy.

As all European monarchies became absolute about the same time, it is not probable that the constitutional change was due to accidental circumstances which occurred simultaneously in every country. The natural supposition is that the general change was the fruit of a general cause operating on every country at the same moment.

That general cause was the transition from one social state to another, from feudal inequality to democratic equality. The nobility was prostrate; the people had not yet risen up; the one was too low, the other not high enough to embarrass the movements of the supreme power. For a period of a hundred and fifty years kings enjoyed a golden age. They were all-powerful, and their thrones were stable, advantages usually inconsistent with each other. They were as sacred as the hereditary chiefs of a feudal monarchy, and as absolute as the masters of a democracy.

NOTE 3
Decline of free German cities. – imperial cities
(Reichstadten).

According to the German historians, these cities reached their highest point of prosperity during the fourteenth and fifteenth centuries. They were then the refuge of the wealth, of the arts, of the learning of Europe, the mistress of commerce, and the centre of civilization. They ended, especially in northern and southern Germany, by forming, with the surrounding nobility, independent confederations, as the Swiss cities had done with the peasantry.

They were still prosperous in the sixteenth century; but their decline had begun. The Thirty Years' War hastened their downfall; they were nearly all destroyed or ruined during that period.

The Treaty of Westphalia, however, made special mention of them, and maintained their condition as 'immediate states', that is to say, communities independent of all control but the emperor. But neighbouring monarchs on one side, and on the other the emperor himself, whose power, after the Thirty Years' War, was nearly confined in its exercise to these small vassals of the empire, constantly encroached on their sovereignty. They still numbered fifty-one in the eighteenth century. They occupied two benches at the Diet, and had a separate vote. But, practically, their influence over the direction of public affairs was gone.

At home they were overloaded with debts, chiefly arising from the fact that they were still taxed in proportion to their past splendour, and also, in some degree, from their defective administration. It is not a little remarkable that this maladministration appeared to flow from some secret disease that was common to all of them, whatever their constitution happened to be. Aristocratic and democratic forms of government provoked equal discontent. Aristocracies were said to be mere family coteries, in which favour and private interest controlled the government. Democracies were said to be under the sway of intrigue and corruption. Both forms of government were accused of dishonesty and profligacy. The Emperor was constantly obliged to interfere in their affairs to restore order. Their population was falling off, their wealth vanishing. They were no longer the centres of German civilization; the arts had fled from them to take refuge in new cities created by kings, and representing the modern era. Trade had deserted them. Their former energy, their patriotic vigour, had disappeared. Hamburg alone continued to be a great centre of wealth and learning; but this flowed from causes peculiar to itself.

NOTE 4
Date of the abolition of serfdom in Germany.

It will be seen from the following table that serfdom has only been very recently abolished in the greater part of Germany. Serfdom was abolished,

1. In Baden not till 1783.
2. In Hohenzollern in 1789.
3. Schleswig and Holstein in 1804.
4. Nassau in 1808.
5. Prussia. Frederick William I abolished serfdom in his domains in 1717. The code of Frederick the Great, as has been observed, pretended to abolish it throughout the kingdom, but in reality it only abolished its hardest form, *leibeigenschaft*; it preserved the milder form, called *erbuntertahnigkeit*. It did not cease entirely till 1809.
6. In Bavaria serfdom disappeared in 1808.
7. A decree of Napoleon's, dated Madrid, 1808, abolished it in the Grand-duchy of Berg, and in several small territories, such as Erfurth, Baireuth, &c.
8. In the kingdom of Westphalia its destruction dates from 1808 and 1809.
9. In the principality of Lippe-Detmold from 1809.
10. In Schomberg-Lippe from 1810.
11. In Swedish Pomerania from 1810.
12. In Hesse-Darmstadt from 1809 and 1811.
13. In Wurtemberg from 1817.
14. In Mecklenburg from 1820.
15. In Oldenburg from 1814.
16. In Saxony for Lusatia from 1832.
17. In Hohenzollern-Sigmaringen from 1833 only.
18. In Austria from 1811. In 1782, Joseph II had abolished the *leibeigenschaft*; but serfdom in its mild form – *erbuntertahnigkeit* – lasted till 1811.

NOTE 5

A portion of Germany, such as Brandenburg, old Prussia, and Silesia, was originally peopled by the Slavic race, and was conquered and partly occupied by Germans. In those countries serfdom was always much harsher than in the rest of Germany, and left much plainer traces at the close of the eighteenth century.

NOTE 6
Code of Frederick the Great.

Of all the works of Frederick the Great, the least known, even in his own country, and the least striking, is the Code drawn up by his orders, and promulgated by his successor. Yet I doubt whether any of his other works throws as much light on the mind of the man or on the times in which he lived, or shows as plainly the influence which they exercised one upon the other.

This Code was a real constitution in the ordinary sense of the word. It regulated not only the mutual relations of citizens, but also their relations to the state. It was a civil code, a criminal code, and a charter all in one.

It rests, or appears to rest, on a certain number of general principles, expressed in a highly philosophical and abstract form, and which bear a strong resemblance in many respects to those which are embodied in the Declaration of the Rights of Man in the Constitution of 1791.

It proclaims that the welfare of the commonwealth and of its inhabitants is the aim of society and the limit of law; that laws can not restrain the freedom and the rights of the citizen save for public utility; that every member of the commonwealth ought to labour for the public good in proportion to his position and his means; that the rights of individuals ought to give way to those of the public.

It makes no allusion to any hereditary rights of the sovereign, nor to his family, nor even to any particular right as distinguished from that of the state. The royal power was already designated by no other name than that of the state.

On the other hand, it alludes to the rights of man, which are founded on the natural right of everyone to pursue his own happiness without treading on the rights of others. All acts not forbidden by natural law, or a positive state law, are allowable. Every citizen is entitled to claim the protection of the state for himself and his property, and may defend himself by using force if the state does not come to his defence.

These great principles established, the legislator, instead of evolving from them, as the constitution of 1791 did, the doctrine of popular sovereignty, and the organization of a democratic government in a free society, turns sharp round and arrives at another conclusion, democratic enough, but not liberal. He considers the sovereign the sole representative of the state, and invests him with all the rights which he has stated belong to society. The sovereign does not figure in the Code as the representative of God; he is the representative, the agent, the servant of society, as Frederick stated at full length in his works; but he is its sole representative, he wields its whole authority alone. The head of the state, on whom the duty of securing the public welfare – which is the sole object of society – devolves, is authorized to direct and regulate all the actions of individuals in this view.

Among the chief duties of this all-powerful agent of society, I find such as these mentioned: maintaining order and public safety at home, so that every citizen shall be guaranteed against violence; making peace and war; establishing all laws and police regulations; granting pardons; annulling criminal prosecutions.

Every association in the country, and every public establishment, is subject to his inspection and superintendence in the interest of the general peace and security. In order that the head of the state may be able to perform his duties, he must have certain revenues and lucrative rights; hence he is allowed to tax private fortunes, persons, professions, commerce, industry, articles of consumption. Public functionaries acting in his name must be obeyed as he is in all matters within the scope of their duties.

Under this very modern head we shall now see a thoroughly Gothic body placed. Frederick has taken away nothing but what might impede the action of his own power, and the whole will form a monstrous being, which looks like a compromise between two creations. In this strange production Frederick evinces as much contempt for logic as care for his own power, and anxiety not to create useless difficulties in attacking what was still capable of defence.

With the exception of a few districts and certain localities, the inhabitants of the rural districts are placed in a state of hereditary serfdom; not only is the land clogged with *corvées* and inherent services, but, as has been seen already, similar burdens attach to the persons of the peasants.

Most of the privileges of landholders are recognized anew by the Code – or, it might be said, in contradiction to the Code; for it is expressly stated that, wherever the new legislation clashes with local customs, the latter must prevail. It is formally declared that the state can not abolish any of these privileges except by purchase, according to the legal forms.

True, the Code states that serfdom, properly so called (*leibeigenschaft*), is abolished in so far as it interferes with personal liberty; but the hereditary subjection which takes its place (*erbuntertahnigkeit*) is, after all, a species of serfdom, as the text shows.

According to the Code, the burgher remains wholly distinct from the peasant. Between the noble and the burgher, an intermediate class, consisting of high functionaries who are not noble, ecclesiastics, professors of learned schools, gymnasia, and universities, is placed.

Superior to the burghers, these personages were not to be confounded with the nobility, to whom they were clearly understood to be inferior. They could not purchase equestrian estates, or fill the highest posts in the civil service. Nor were they *hoffähig*; that is to say, they could but rarely appear at court, and never with their families. As was the case in France, these distinctions became more insulting in proportion to the increasing knowledge and influence of this class, which, though excluded from the most brilliant posts, filled all those where business of importance was transacted. The privileges of the nobility necessarily gave birth to irritation, which mainly contributed to cause the revolution here, and make it popular in Germany. The principal author of the Code was a burgher, but no doubt he merely obeyed the instructions of his master.

The old constitution of Europe is not in such ruin in this part of Germany that Frederick thinks it safe to allow his contempt for it to lead him to destroy its relics. Generally speaking, he deprives the nobility of the right of assemblage and corporate action; leaving to each nobleman his privileges, he limits and regulates their use. Hence it happens that this Code, drawn up by the orders of a disciple of one of our philosophers, and put in force after the outbreak of the French Revolution, is the most authentic and latest legislative document which gives a legal warrant for the feudal inequalities which the Revolution was about to abolish throughout Europe.

The nobility is declared to be the first body in the state. Men of rank, it states, are to be preferred to all others for posts of honour, if they are capable of filling them. None but they are to possess noble estates, create substitutions, enjoy rights of chase, justiciary rights inherent to noble estates, and rights of presentation to clerical livings; none but they can assume the name of their estates. Burghers, specially authorized to acquire noble estates, can only enjoy the rights and honours attached to such possessions within these limits. A burgher owning a noble estate cannot leave it to an heir burgher unless he be heir in the first degree. When there are no such heirs and no heirs noble, the property must be sold at auction.

One of the most characteristic portions of the Code of Frederick the Great is its criminal provision for political offences.

Frederick's successor, Frederick William II, who, notwithstanding the feudal and absolutist provisions above noted, fancied he detected revolutionary tendencies in this work of his uncle's, and refrained from promulgating it till 1794, was only reconciled to it by the excellent penal provisions which served to counteract its bad principles. Nor has there ever been anything since devised more complete of the kind. Not only are revolts and conspiracies punished with the greatest rigor, but disrespectful criticisms of government are repressed with equal severity. It is forbidden to purchase or to distribute dangerous writings; printer, publisher, and vender are all responsible for the act of the author. Public balls and masquerades are declared to be public meetings, which can not take place without the authority of the police. Similar rules govern dinners in public places. Liberty of the press and of speech are under close and arbitrary supervision. It is forbidden to carry fire-arms.

By the side of this work, which was more than half borrowed from the Middle Ages, are provisions whose spirit borders on socialism. Thus it is declared that it devolves on the state to provide food, work, and wages for all who cannot support themselves, and have no claim for support on the seignior or the *commune*; they must be provided with work suited to their strength and capacity. The state is bound to provide establishments for relieving the poor. It is authorized to abolish establishments which tend to encourage idleness, and to distribute personally to the poor the money by which these establishments were supported.

Boldness and novelty in point of theory, and timidity in practice characterize every portion of this work of Frederick the Great. On the one side, that great principle of modern society – that all are equally subject to taxes – is loudly proclaimed; on another, provincial laws containing exemptions to this rule are allowed to subsist. It is affirmed that all lawsuits between the sovereign and the state must be tried in the same forms and according to the same rules as all other cases; but, in fact, this rule was never carried into effect when the interests or passions of the king were opposed to it. The mill of Saint Souci was ostentatiously shown to the people, and justice was quietly made subject to royal convenience in other cases.

What proves that this Code, which assumed to be such a novelty, really made but few changes, and is therefore a curious study of German society in this section of country at the close of the eighteenth century, is that the Prussian nation hardly noticed its publication. Lawyers were the only persons who studied it; and even in our time there are many enlightened men who have never read it.

NOTE 7
Property of the German peasants.

Many families among the peasantry were not only free and landholders, their property constituted a species of perpetual *majorat*. Their estate was indivisible, and passed by descent to one of the sons – usually the youngest – as was the case in some English customs. He was expected to endow his brothers and sisters.

The *erbgütter* of the peasantry were spread more or less over the whole of Germany, for the land was nowhere absorbed by the feudal tenures. Even in Silesia, where the nobility owned immense estates comprising most of the villages, other villages were possessed by the inhabitants and were wholly free. In certain parts of Germany, such as the Tyrol and Frise, the rule was that the peasantry owned the land by *erbgütter*.

But in the greater part of the German countries this kind of property was an exception, sometimes rarely met with. In the villages where it occurred, landholders of this kind constituted a sort of aristocracy among the peasantry.

NOTE 8
Position of the nobility and division of land along the Rhine.

From information obtained on the spot, and from persons who lived under the old regime, it appears that in the Electorate of Cologne, for instance, there were a great number of villages without seigniors, and governed by agents of the king; that in the places where the nobility lived, their administrative powers were very limited; that their position (individually at all events) was rather brilliant than powerful; that they possessed honours and offices, but no direct control over the people. I also ascertained that in the same electorate property was much divided, and that many of the peasants owned the land they occupied. The fact was ascribed to the poverty that had long oppressed many of the noble families, and obliged them to sell their estates to the peasants for an annual rent or a sum of money. I have had in my hands a schedule of the population and estates within the Bishopric of Cologne at the beginning of the eighteenth century: it indicated that, at that time, one third of the soil belonged to the peasantry. From this fact arose sentiments and ideas which predisposed these people to a far greater extent than the inhabitants of other parts of Germany to welcome a revolution.

NOTE 9
How the usury laws favoured subdivision of land.

At the close of the eighteenth century it was still illegal to lend money on interest, whatever was the rate charged. Turgot says that this law was observed in many places as late as 1769. These laws are still in force, says he, but they are often violated. Consular judges allow interest on loans, while the ordinary courts condemn the practice. Dishonest debtors still prosecute their creditors criminally for having lent money without alienating the capital.

Independently of the effects which such laws as these must have had on commerce, industry, and the morals of business men, they affected the division and tenure of lands to a very great extent. They caused an immense increase of perpetual rents, as well ground-rents (*foncières*) as others. They compelled the old landowners, instead of borrowing in times of need, to sell small portions of their domains partly for a given sum, partly for a rent; hence leading, first, to the infinite subdivision of estates, and, secondly, to the creation of a multitude of perpetual rents on their little properties.

NOTE 10a
Example of the irritation caused by tithes ten years before the Revolution.

In 1779, a petty lawyer of Lucé complains in a bitter and revolutionary tone that curates and other large titheholders are selling at exorbitant prices to farmers the straw which has been paid them by way of tithes; and which the farmers absolutely need for manure.

NOTE 10b
Example of the manner in which the privileges of the clergy alienated the affection of the people from them.

In 1780, the prior and canons of the Priory of Laval complain of being made to pay duty on articles of consumption, and on the materials required for the repair of their buildings. They argue that the duty is an accessory of the taille, and that, being exempt from the one, they ought not to be liable for the other. The minister tells them to apply to the *election*, with recourse to the Court of Aides.

NOTE 11
Feudal rights exercised by priests – one example out of a thousand.

The Abbey of Cherbourg, in 1753, possessed seigniorial rents, payable in money or produce, in almost all the villages in the neighbourhood of Cherbourg: one village alone paid 306 bushels of wheat. It owned the barony of Sainte Geneviève, the barony and seigniorial mill of Bas du Roule, and the barony of Neuville au Plein, at least ten leagues distant. It received, moreover, tithes from twelve parishes on the peninsula, some of which were at a great distance from the abbey.

*Irritation among the peasantry proceeding from the
feudal rights, especially those of the church.*

Letter written shortly before the Revolution by a peasant to the intendant. It is no authority for the facts it states, but it indicates admirably the state of feeling in the class to which the writer belonged:

'Though we have but few nobles in this part of the country,' it says, 'it must not be supposed that real estate is free from rents; on the contrary, nearly all the fiefs belong to the Cathedral, or the archbishopric, or the collegiate church of Saint Martin, or the Benedictines of Noirmontiers, of Saint Julien, or some other ecclesiastics, against whom no prescription runs, and who are constantly bringing to light old musty parchments whose date God only knows!

'The whole country is infected with rents. Most of the farmlands pay every year a seventh of a bushel of wheat per acre, others wine; one pays the seignior a fourth of all fruits, another a fifth, another a twelfth, another a thirteenth – the tithes being always paid on the gross. These rights are so singular that they vary from a fourth part of the produce to a fortieth.

'What must be thought of these rents in kind – in vegetables, money, poultry, labour, wood, fruit, candles? I am acquainted with rents which are paid in bread, in wax, in eggs, in headless pigs, in rose shoulder-knots, in bouquets of violets, in golden spurs, &c; and there are a host of seigniorial dues besides these. Why has France not been freed from all these extravagant rents? Men's eyes are at last being opened; one may hope everything from the wisdom of the present government. It will stretch a kindly hand to the poor victims of the exactions of the old fiscal system, called seigniorial rights, which could not be alienated or sold.

'What must be thought of this tyranny of mutation fines? A purchaser exhausts his means in acquiring a property, and is obliged to pay besides in expenses to secure his title, contracts, actual entry, *procès-verbaux*, stamp, registry, *centième denier*, eight *sous* per *livre*; after which he must exhibit his title to his seignior, who will exact the mutation fine on the gross price of his purchase, now a twelfth, and now a tenth. Some claim a fifth, others a fifth and a twenty-fifth besides. All rates are demanded; I know some who charge a third of the price paid. No, the most ferocious and the most barbarous nations of the known world have never invented such or so many exactions as our tyrants heaped on the heads of our forefathers.' (This literary and philosophical tirade is sadly defective in orthography.)

'What! the late king permitted the commutation of ground-rents on city property, but excluded those on farms! He should have begun with the latter. Why not permit poor farmers to break their chains, to pay off and get rid of the hosts of seigniorial dues and ground-rents, which are such an injury to the vassal and so small a gain to the seignior? No distinction should have been made between city and country, seigniors and private individuals.

'The stewards of the owners of ecclesiastical estates rob and plunder the farmers at every mutation. We have seen a recent example of the practice. The steward of our new archbishop gave notice to quit to all the farmers holding under leases from M. de Fleury, his predecessor, declared all their leases null and void, and turned out every man who refused to submit to his rent being doubled, and to pay a large bonus besides, though they had already paid a bonus to M. de Fleury's steward. They have thus been deprived of seven or eight years' holding, though their leases were executed in due form, and have been driven out upon the world on Christmas eve, the most critical period of the year, owing to the difficulty of feeding cattle. The King of Prussia could have done nothing worse.'

It appears, in fact, that, with regard to Church property, leases granted by one titulary did not bind his successor. The writer of the letter states what is true when he says that feudal rents were redeemable in cities, but not in the country; a new proof of the neglect in which the peasantry lived, and of the manner in which all who were placed above them contrived to provide for their own interest.

NOTE 13

Every institution that has long been dominant, after establishing itself in its natural sphere, extends itelf, and ends by exercising a large influence over those branches of legislation which it does not govern. The feudal system, though essentially political, had transformed the civil law, and greatly modified the condition of persons and property in all the relations of private life. It had operated upon successions by creating unequal divisions of property – a principle carried out in certain provinces even among the middle classes (as witness Normandy). It had affected all real estate, for there were but few tracts of land that were wholly freed from its effects, or whose possessors felt none of the consequences of its laws. It affected the property of *communes* as well as that of individuals. It affected labour by the impositions it laid upon it. It affected incomes by the inequality of taxation, and, in general, the pecuniary interest of every man in every business: landowners, by dues, rents, *corvées;* farmers in a thousand ways, among others by rights of banality, ground-rents, mutation-fines, &c; traders, by market dues; merchants, by tolls, &c. In striking it down, the Revolution made itself perceived and felt at the same time at all points by every private interest.

NOTE 14a
Public charities granted by the state – favouritism.

In 1748 – a year of great famine and misery, such as often occurred in the eighteenth century – the king granted 20,000 pounds of rice. The Archbishop of Tours claimed that he alone had obtained the gift, and that it ought to be distributed by him alone, and in his diocese. The intendant argued that the gift was made to the whole province, and should be distributed by him to all the parishes. After a long contest, the king, to settle the quarrel, doubled the quantity of rice given to the province, so that the archbishop and the intendant might each distribute half. Both agreed that it ought to be distributed by the curates. No one thought of the seigniors or the syndics. It appears from the correspondence between the intendant and the comptroller-general that the former accused the archbishop of wishing to give the rice to his favourites, and especially to the parishes which belonged to the Duchess of Rochechouart. The collection also contains letters from noblemen which demand aid for their parishes in particular, and letters from the comptroller-general which make reference to the parishes of certain individuals.

Public charities are always liable to abuses under every system; but when distributed from a distance, without publicity, by the central government, they are actually futile.

NOTE 14b
Example of the manner in which these public charities
were distributed.

A report, made in 1780 to the Provincial Assembly of Upper Guienne, states 'Out of the sum of 385,000 livres which his majesty has granted to this province from the year 1773, when workhouses were established, to the year 1779 inclusive, the *election* of Montauban, capital and place of residence of the intendant, has alone had more than 240,000 livres, most of which has been spent in the *commune* of Montauban.'

NOTE 15
Powers of the intendant for the regulation of
manufactures.

The archives of the intendants' offices are full of papers which refer to the regulation of industrial enterprises by the intendants.

Not only is labour subject to the inconvenience of trade-companies, guilds, &c, it is liable to be affected by every whim of government, that is to say, of the Council in great matters, of the intendants in small ones. The latter are constantly giving directions about the length of woofs, the kind of thread to use, the pattern to prefer, errors to avoid.

Independently of the sub-delegates, they have local inspectors of manufactures under their orders. In this particular centralization had gone farther than it now does; it was more capricious, more arbitrary; it created a swarm of public functionaries, and gave rise to general habits of submission and dependence.

Note also that these habits were imparted to the middle classes, merchants, and traders, which were about to triumph, to a far greater extent than to the classes that were on the point of defeat. Hence, instead of destroying, the Revolution tended to confirm and spread them.

The preceding remarks have been suggested by the perusal of a quantity of correspondence and documents taken from the intendant's office of the Ile de France, and indorsed, 'Manufactures and Fabrics,' 'Drapery', 'Drugs'. I have found in the same place reports from the inspectors to the intendant giving full and detailed accounts of their visits of inspection to factories; moreover, various Orders in Council, passed on reports of the intendant, prohibiting or permitting manufactures of certain stuffs, or in certain places, or in certain methods.

The dominant idea in the intercourse of these inspectors with the manufacturer – who, by the way, is treated very cavalierly – seems to be that their duty and the rights of the state compel them to see that the manufacturer not only acts fairly toward the public, but looks after his own interest. They consequently feel bound to make him adopt the best methods, and admonish him on the most trifling details of his business, larding the whole with a profusion of penalties and heavy fines.

NOTE 16

Spirit of the government of Louis XI.

Nothing indicates more clearly the spirit of the government of Louis XI than the constitutions he gave to cities. I have had occasion to study very closely those which he gave to most of the cities of Anjou, Maine, and Touraine.

All these constitutions are framed on the same plan, and all reveal the same designs. Louis XI appears in a new light in these charters. He is generally regarded as the enemy of the nobility, but the sincere though somewhat brutal friend of the people. They reveal him as a hater alike of the political rights of the people and those of the nobility. He uses the middle classes to lower the nobility and keep down the people: he is both anti-aristocratic and anti-democratic – the model of the burgher king. He loads city notables with privileges in the view of increasing their importance, grants them titles of nobility in order to cheapen rank, and thus destroys the popular and democractic city governments, and places the whole authority in the hands of a few families, attached to his policy, and pledged to his support by every tie of gratitude.

A city government in the eighteenth century.

I select from the Inquiry into City Governments, made in 1764, the papers which relate to Angers; they contain an analysis, attacks upon, and defences of the constitution of this city, emanating from the presidial, the city corporation, the sub-delegate, and the intendant. As the same facts occurred in many other places, the picture must not be regarded as a solitary example.

Memorial of the presidial on the present state of the municipal constitution of Angers, and on the reforms that it needs.

'The Corporation of Angers never consults the people at large even on the most important occasions unless, it is compelled to do so; hence its policy is unknown to everyone but its own members. Even the movable aldermen have only a superficial acquaintance with its mode of proceeding.'

(The tendency of all these little burgher oligarchies was, in truth, to consult the people at large as little as possible.)

The corporation is composed of twenty-one officers, in virtue of a decree of 29 March 1681, to wit:

A mayor, who becomes noble *ex officio*, and whose term is four years;

Four movable aldermen, who hold office for two years;

Twelve consulting aldermen, who are elected and hold office for life;

Two city counsel;

One counsel holding the reversion of the office;

A clerk.

They enjoy many privileges: among others, their capitation-tax is fixed at a moderate sum; they are exempt from lodging soldiers, arms, or baggage; they are exempt from dues *de cloison double et triple*, from the old and new excise, from the accessory dues on articles of consumption, even from benevolences, 'from which latter they have asserted their own freedom', says the presidial. They enjoy, moreover, allowances in the shape of lights, and in some cases salaries and lodgings.

We see from this that a post of perpetual alderman of Angers was not to be despised in those days. Note here, as everywhere else, the contrivances to secure exemptions from taxes for the rich. The memorial goes on to say that 'these offices are eagerly sought by the richest citizens, who desire them in order to reduce their capitation-tax, and increase that of their fellow-citizens in proportion. There are at this moment several municipal officers who pay 30 livres of capitation, and ought to pay 250 to 300 livres; one, among others, ought, in proportion to his fortune, to pay 1000 livres at least.' In another part of the memorial it is said that among the richest inhabitants of the place are more than forty officers, or widows of officers (office-holders), whose rank exempts them from the heavy capitation-tax paid by the city. The tax consequently falls upon an infinite number of poor mechanics, who, believing themselves overtaxed, constantly complain of the amount of their tax – unjustly so, for there are no inequalities in the division of the burden laid upon the city.

The General Assembly is composed of seventy-six persons:

The mayor;
Two deputies of the chapter;
A syndic of the clerks;
Two deputies of the presidial;
A deputy of the university;
A lieutenant-general of police;
Four aldermen;
Twelve consulting aldermen;
A king's attorney near the presidial;
A city counsel;
Two deputies of the woods and forests;
Two of the *election*;
Two of the salt warehouse;
Two of the *traites*;
Two of the mint;
Two of the advocates and attorneys;
Two of the consular judges;
Two of the notaries;
Two of the shop-keepers;
And, lastly, two deputies from each of the sixteen parishes.

These latter are understood to be the special representatives of the people; they are, in fact, the representatives of industrial corporations, and the council is so arranged, as the reader has seen, that they are sure to be in a minority.

When posts in the corporation become vacant, the General Assembly chooses three candidates for each vacancy.

Most of the posts in the city government are free to persons of all professions; the Assembly is not – as others which I have noticed – obliged to choose a magistrate or a lawyer to fill a vacancy. To this the presidial objects strongly.

According to the same presidial, which seems terribly jealous of the city corporation, and whose main objection to the constitution was, I suspect, that it did not confer privileges enough on the presidial, 'the

General Assembly is too numerous, and composed of persons too devoid of intelligence to be consulted on any matters but sales of the city property, the negotiation of loans, the establishment of town dues, and the election of municipal officers. All other business should be transacted by a small body, wholly composed of *notables*. No one should be a member of this assembly but the lieutenant-general of the *sénéchaussée*, the king's attorney, and twelve other notables chosen out of the six bodies, the clergy, the magistracy, the nobility, the university, the merchants, and the burghers, and others who do not belong to any of these six classes. The first choice of notables should be made by the Assembly, and future elections by the assembly of notables or the body from which each notable is chosen.'

A resemblance existed between these public functionaries, who thus became members of municipal bodies as office-holders or notables, and the functionaries of the same title and character in our day. But their position was very different from that of modern office-holders – a fact which cannot be safely overlooked; for nearly all these old functionaries were city notables before they obtained office, or only sought office in order to become notables. They had no notion of either resigning their rank or being promoted; this alone creates a vast difference between them and their successors in office.

Memorial of the municipal officers.

This document shows that the city corporation was created in 1474 by Louis XI, upon the ruins of the old democratic constitution of the city, and that its principle was of the nature explained above; that is to say, nearly all political power was vested in the middle classes; the people were kept at a distance, or weakened; a vast number of municipal officers were created in order to muster partisans for the scheme; hereditary titles of nobility were granted in profusion, and all sorts of privileges were secured to the burgher administrators.

The same paper also contains letters patent from successors of Louis XI, which recognize this new constitution and curtail still further the power of the people. It mentions that in 1485 the letters patent granted with this view by Charles VIII were assailed by the people of Angers before the Parliament, just as, in England, disputes relative to the charter of a city would have been carried before the courts. In 1601 a decree of Parliament again fixed the political rights which were authorized by the royal charter. From thenceforth, no other controlling authority appears but the Royal Council.

It appears from the same memorial that mayors, like all other city officers, were selected by the king out of a list of three names presented by the General Assembly; this was in virtue of an Order in Council of

22 June 1708. It also appears that, in virtue of Orders in Council of 1733 and 1741, the small traders were entitled to one alderman (perpetual) or councillor. Finally, the memorial shows that at that time the corporation was intrusted with the distribution of the tax levied for the capitation, equipment, lodgings, provisions of the poor, of the troops, of the revenue service, of foundlings.

Then follows an enumeration of the great labours which devolve upon municipal officers. They fully justify, in the opinion of the memorialists, the privileges and the permanent rank which they enjoy, and which, it is plain, they are much afraid of losing. Many of the reasons which they assign for the severity of their office-labours are curious, such as the following: 'Their financial duties have been much increased by the extensions which are constantly being made to the aid dues, the gabel, the stamp and registry dues, and the unlawful exactions of registry dues and freehold duties. They have been involved, on the city's behalf, in perpetual lawsuits with the financial companies in reference to these taxes; they have had to go from court to court, from the Parliament to the Council, in order to resist the oppression under which they are groaning. An experience and a public service of thirty years enable them to state that the life of man is hardly long enough to defend one's self against the stratagems and the traps which the agents of the revenue-farmers are constantly laying for the citizen, in order to preserve their commissions.'

Curiously enough, it is to the comptroller-general that these things are said, and said with the view of winning his support for the privileges of the class that expresses these views. So deeply rooted was the habit of viewing the companies which farmed the taxes as an adversary that might be abused on all sides without objection from anyone. This habit steadily spread and gained strength; men learned to view the treasury as an odious tyrant, hateful to all; the common enemy instead of the common agent.

'All offices were first united with the corporation,' adds the same memorial, 'by an Order in Council of the 4 September 1694, in consideration of a sum of 22,000 livres;' that is to say, the offices were redeemed that year for that sum. By an order of 26 April 1723, the offices created by the edict of 24 May 1722 were also united to the corporation, or, in other words, the city was permitted to redeem them. By another order of 21 May 1723 the city was authorized to borrow 120,000 livres for the acquisition of the said offices. Another, of 26 July 1728, authorized it to borrow 50,000 livres to redeem the office of clerk-secretary of the City Hall. 'The city', says the memorial, 'has paid its money to preserve the freedom of its elections, and to secure to the officers it elects for one or two years, or for life, the various prerogatives attached to their offices.' Some of the municipal offices were re-established by the edict of

November 1733; an order was subsequently obtained at the instance of
the mayor and aldermen, allowing the city to purchase an extension of
its rights, for a term of fifteen years for a sum of 170,000 livres.

This is a fair criterion of the policy of the government of the old
regime, as regards cities. It compelled them to contract debts, then
authorized them to establish extraordinary taxes to liquidate them. And
to this it must be added that afterward many of these taxes, which were
naturally temporary, were made perpetual, and then the government
got its share.

The memorial continues: 'The municipal officers were never deprived
of their judicial functions till the establishment of royal courts. Until
1669, they had sole cognizance of disputes between masters and servants.
The accounts of the town dues are rendered before the intendant, in
obedience to the decrees establishing or continuing the said dues.'

The memorial makes it plain that the representatives of the sixteen
parishes, who, as above mentioned, had seats in the General Assembly,
were chosen by companies, corporate bodies, or communities, and were
the mere organs of these bodies. They were bound by their instructions
on all points.

In fine, this memorial shows that, at Angers as elsewhere, no expenses
could be incurred by the city without the concurrence of the intendant
and the Council. And it must be acknowledged that, when the
government of a city is intrusted to certain men to be used as their
private property, and when these men receive no salary, but enjoy in lieu
thereof privileges which exonerate them from all responsibility to their
fellow-citizens for maladministration, the guardianship of the state may
seem a necessity.

The whole of this memorial, which is clumsily drawn up, indicates a
state of great alarm on the part of these officials lest the existing state of
things should be changed. All kinds of reasons, good and bad, are
accumulated together, and pressed into the service of the *statu quo*.

Memorial of the sub-delegate.

The intendant, having received these two contradictory memorials, asks
for the opinion of his sub-delegate. He gives it:

'The memorial of the municipal councillors,' says he, 'does not
deserve attention; its only aim is to subserve their own privileges. That
of the presidial may be beneficially consulted, but there is no reason for
granting them all the prerogatives they desire.'

He admits that the constitution of the civic body has long needed
reform. Besides the immunities already mentioned, which were enjoyed
by all the municipal officers of Angers, he states that the mayor, during
his term of service, was lodged at a cost of at least 600 francs; that he

received 50 francs salary, and 100 francs for expenses of his office, besides the *jetons*. The attorney-syndic was also lodged, and so was the clerk. In order to escape aid and town dues, the municipal officers had fixed upon a presumed amount of consumption by each of them; and by accounting for this, they could introduce into the city as many casks of wine or other merchandise as they pleased.

The sub-delegate does not propose to deprive the councillors of their exemption from taxes; but he thinks their capitation-tax, which is now fixed at a very low figure, should be settled every year by the intendant. He also advises that these officials should be made to contribute with everyone else to the *don gratuit*, their exemption from which is without authority or precedent.

The municipal officers, says the memorial, are intrusted with the preparation of the capitation-rolls for the people. They perform this duty carelessly and arbitrarily, whence the intendant is regularly overwhelmed every year with petitions and reclamations. It would be desirable that this tax should be distributed hereafter, in the interest of each community or company, by its members, in a general and stable manner; and that municipal officers should in future fix the capitation of burghers only, and of persons belonging to no public body, such as certain workmen and the servants of privileged persons.

The memorial of the sub-delegate confirms what the municipal officers have already stated in regard to the redemption, in 1735, of the municipal offices, for the sum of 170,000 livres.

Letter from the intendant to the comptroller-general.

Armed with these various documents, the intendant writes to the minister: 'The public interest and that of the citizens,' he says, 'require a reduction in the number of municipal officers, whose privileges have become a heavy burden on the public.'

'I am struck,' he adds, 'with the enormous amount of money that has been repeatedly paid for the redemption of municipal offices at Angers. A similar sum, employed usefully, would have done the city much good; as it is, it has only made people feel the weight of the authority and of the privileges of these officials.

'The internal abuses of this government fully deserve the attention of the Council. Independently of *jetons* and candle, which consume the annual appropriation of 2127 livres (this was the sum set apart for this class of expenditures in the normal budget, which was occasionally imposed on cities by the king), the public money is squandered and employed for clandestine purposes by these officers. The king's attorney, who has held his office for thirty or forty years, has obtained such a mastery over the administration, of which he alone understands the details, that the citizens have been unable to obtain the least information with regard to the employment of their money.' In consequence, the intendant proposes to the minister to reduce the corporation to a mayor serving for four years, six aldermen serving for six years, one king's attorney serving for eight, and a perpetual clerk and receiver.

In other respects the Constitution which he proposes for Angers is precisely the same as the one he elsewhere proposed for Tours. In his opinion,

1st. The government should preserve the General Assembly, but merely as an electoral body for the election of municipal officers.

2nd. It should create an extraordinary Council of Notables, whose functions should be those with which the edict of 1764 appeared to invest the General Assembly. This council to be composed of twelve persons, holding office for six years, and elected, not by the General Assembly, but by the twelve bodies esteemed notable, each body electing one. He designates as notable bodies,

The presidial,
The university,
The *election*,
The office of woods and forests,
The salt warehouse,
The office of the *traites*,
The mint,
The advocates and attorneys,
The consular judges,
The notaries,
The traders (*marchands*),
The burghers (*bourgeois*).

As will be remarked, nearly all these notables were public functionaries, and all the public functionaries were notables. From this, as from a thousand other papers in these collections, it may be inferred that the middle classes were then as great place-hunters and as destitute of independent ambition as they are now. The only difference is, as I remarked in the text, that formerly the petty importance afforded by these places was bought, whereas now candidates beg the government to grant them the charity of a place for nothing.

It is here seen that the whole real power in the municipality is vested in the extraordinary council, and the administration of the city is thus further confined to a small circle of burghers. The only assembly in which the people continue to exercise the least interference is now confined to the electing of municipal officers whom it can not instruct. It is to be remarked also, that the intendant is more unbending and antipopular in his principles than the king, who seemed in his edict to have transferred most of the public authority to the General Assembly, and again, that the intendant is far more liberal and democratic than the burghers. This last inference is at all events a fair one from the memorial I have quoted in the text, from which it appears that the notables of another city were desirous of excluding the people from the election of municipal officers in opposition to the views of the intendant and the king.

It may be noticed that the intendant recognises two distinct classes of notables under the names of *bourgeois* and *marchands*. It may not be useless to give an exact definition of these words, in order to show into how many small fragments the *bourgeoisie* was divided, and by how many petty vanities it was actuated.

The word *bourgeois* had a general and also a particular meaning; it meant the members of the middle classes at large, and it also meant a certain number of men within those classes. '*Bourgeois*' says a memorial filed at the inquiry of 1764, 'are individuals whose birth and fortune enable them to live without engaging in lucrative pursuits.' Other portions of the memorial show that the word *bourgeois* does not apply to persons who belong to companies or industrial corporations; it is not so easy to say to whom it does apply. 'For,' as the same memorial says, 'many persons assume the title of *bourgeois* whose only claim to it is their idleness, who have no fortune, and lead a rude, obscure life. *Bourgeois* should, on the contrary, always be distinguished by their fortune, their birth, their talents, manners, and mode of life. Mechanics composing trade-companies have never been classed in the rank of notables.' *

Traders (*marchands*) were another class of individuals who, like the *bourgeois*, belonged to no company or corporation: but where were the limits of this little class? 'Must we', says the same memorial, 'confound small, low-born dealers with wholesale merchants?' To overcome the difficulty, the memorial proposes to have the aldermen draw up every year a table of notable traders (*marchands*), to be handed to their chief or syndic, who shall invite to the deliberations at the city hall none but those who are thereon inscribed. Care will be taken to inscribe on this table no traders who may have been domestics, porters, wagoners, or followers of other low trades.

* In the text the words *bourgeois* and *bourgeoisie* are translated 'burghers' or 'the middle classes', according to the context. The exact meaning of the French word is often doubtful, and the search for an exact English equivalent almost always hopeless. — TRANS.

NOTE 18

One of the most striking features of the administration of cities in the eighteenth century is, not the absence of all representation and intervention of the public in city business, but the extreme variability of the rules governing such adminstration. Civic rights were constantly bestowed, taken away, restored, increased, diminished, modified in a thousand ways, and unceasingly. No better indication of the contempt into which all local liberties had fallen can be found than these eternal changes of laws which no one seemed to notice. This mobility would alone have sufficed to destroy all initiative or recuperative energy, and all local patriotism in the institution which is best adapted to it. It helped to prepare the great work of destruction which was to be effected by the Revolution.

NOTE 19
A village government in the eighteenth century (taken from the papers of the intendant's office in the Ile de France).

The affair which I am about to relate is one instance out of a thousand which illustrates the forms and the dilatory methods used by parochial governments, and shows what a general parochial assembly really was in the eighteenth century.

The parsonage-house and steeple of a rural parish – that of Ivry, Ile de France – required repair. To whom was application to be made to make the repairs? Who was to pay for them? How was the money to be procured?

1st. Petition from the curate to the intendant, setting forth that the parsonage-house and steeple need immediate repairs; that his predecessor had caused useless buildings to be erected adjoining the parsonage-house and had thus altered and deformed the character of the spot; and that the inhabitants, having permitted him to do this, ought to bear the expense of all needful repairs, having their recourse on the late curate's heirs for the expense.

2nd. Ordinance of monseigneur the intendant (29 August 1747), ordering the syndic diligently to convene an assembly to deliberate on the necessity of the repairs.

3rd. Deliberation of the inhabitants, by which they declare that they do not object to the parsonage-house being repaired, but as for the steeple, they hold that, as it is built on the choir, which the curate, as a large tithe-holder, is bound to repair, he must pay for any repairs it may need. [An Order in Council of April 1695 had, in fact, imposed the duty of keeping the choir in repair upon the tithe-holder, leaving the tithe-payers to look after the nave.]

4th. New ordinance of the intendant, which, in view of the conflict of statements, orders an architect, the *Sieur* Cordier, to visit and examine the parsonage-house and steeple, hear evidence, and make estimates of the works.

5th. Authentic report of all these proceedings, testifying that a certain number of landholders of Ivry, apparently men of rank, burghers, and peasants, appeared before the intendant's commissioner, and gave evidence for or against the pretensions of the curate.

6th. New ordinance of the intendant, directing that the estimates prepared by his architect be laid before the landholders and inhabitants in a general assembly convoked with due diligence by the syndic for the purpose.

7th. New parochial assembly in pursuance of the ordinance, in which the people declare that they adhere to their expressed opinions.

8th. Ordinance of the intendant, directing, first, that in presence of his sub-delegate at Corbeil, the curate, syndic, and principal inhabitants of the parish being also present, the contracts for the work according to the estimates shall be given out; and, secondly, that, whereas the want of repairs involves absolute danger, the whole cost shall be levied upon the inhabitants, without prejudice to the legal rights of those who conceive that the cost of repairing the steeple should be borne by the curate as tithe-holder.

9th. Notice to all parties to be present at the office of the sub-delegate at Corbeil, where the contracts are to be given out.

10th. Petition of the curate and several inhabitants, praying that the costs of the preliminary proceedings be not charged, as usual, against the contractor, lest they should deter bidders from coming forward.

11th. Ordinance of the intendant, directing that all expenses incurred in order to bring the affair to issue be settled by the sub-delegate, added to the contract, and included in the imposition.

12th. Authority from several notables of the parish to the Sieur X to be present on their behalf at the execution of the contract, and confirm it according to the architect's estimates.

13th. Certificate of the syndic, stating that the usual notices and advertisements have been made.

14th. Official report of the contract:

Expenses of repairs	487*l*.
Legal expenses pertaining thereto	237*l*. 18*s*. 6*d*.
	724 18 6

15th. Lastly, Order in Council (23 July 1748), authorizing an impost to raise this sum.

It may have been noticed that frequent allusions are here made to the parochial assembly. The following report of one of these assemblies will show how matters were usually managed on these occasions.

Notarial act. – 'This day, at the close of the parochial mass, at the usual and customary place, was present at the assembly held by the inhabitants of the said parish before X, notary at Corbeil under-signed, and the witnesses hereinafter mentioned, the Sieur Michaud, vine-dresser, syndic of the said parish, who presented the ordinance of the intendant authorizing the assembly, read the same, and applied for an official certificate of his due diligence in the premises:

'And then and there appeared an inhabitant of the said parish, who stated that the steeple was upon the choir, and, consequently, that its repairs should be charged to the curate; did furthermore appear – (here follow the names of various parishioners, who, on the contrary, consent to the request of the curate); and thereafter appeared fifteen peasants, mechanics, masons, and vine-dressers, who declare themselves of the same mind as the preceding persons. Did also appear the Sieur Raimbaud, vine-dresser, who declared that he would agree to whatever monseigneur the intendant decided in the premises. Did also appear the Sieur X, doctor of the Sorbonne, curate, who persists in the allegations and conclusions of his request.

'Whereof the said parties have required of us official certificate.

'Done and passed at the said place of Ivry, in front of the burial-ground of the said parish, before the undersigned; and the meeting aforesaid lasted from eleven o'clock in the morning till two.'

It will be noticed that this parish assembly was a mere administrative inquiry, in the same form and as costly as judicial inquiries; that it never led to a vote or other clear expression of the will of the parish; that it was merely an expression of individual opinions, and constituted no check upon government. Many other documents indicate that the only object of parish assemblies was to afford information to the intendant, and not to influence his decision even in cases where no other interest but that of the parish was concerned.

It may be remarked, also, that this affair gives rise to three separate inquiries; one before the notary, another before the architect, and a third before two notaries, to ascertain whether the people have not changed their minds.

The impost of 724 *liv.* 18 *s.*, authorized by the Order of 23 July 1748, bears upon all landholders, whether privileged or not. This was generally the case in affairs of this kind; but the share of the various rate-payers was not fixed on uniform principles. Persons who paid the taille were taxed in proportion to their taille. Privileged individuals, on the other hand, were taxed in proportion to their assumed fortunes, which gave them a great advantage over the former class.

It appears, finally, that in this matter the distribution of the impost was made by two collectors, inhabitants of the village; not elected, nor serving in their turn, as was usually the custom, but chosen and appointed by the intendant's sub-delegate.

NOTE 20

The pretext which Louis XIV put forward for destroying the municipal liberty of towns was the maladministration of their finances; yet the evil, according to Turgot, continued to exist, and even assumed larger proportions after the reform of this monarch. He adds that most cities are heavily in debt at the present time, partly for moneys lent to government, and partly for expenses or decorations which municipal officers – who dispose of other people's money, who render no account, and receive no instructions – are constantly incurring, in order to increase the splendour or the profit of their position.

NOTE 21
The state was guardian of convents as well as communes; instance thereof.

The comptroller-general, authorizing the intendant to pay over 15,000 livres to the Convent of Carmelites, to which certain indemnities were due, desires the intendant to satisfy himself that the money, which represents a capital, is properly invested. Similar instances abound.

NOTE 22
How the administrative centralization of the old regime can be best judged in Canada.

The physiognomy of governments can be best detected in their colonies, for there their features are magnified, and rendered more conspicuous. When I want to discover the spirit and vices of the government of Louis XIV I must go to Canada. Its deformities are seen there as through a microscope.

A number of obstacles, created by previous occurrences or old social forms, which hindered the development of the true tendencies of government at home, did not exist in Canada. There was no nobility, or, at least, none had taken deep root. The Church was not dominant. Feudal traditions were lost or obscured. The power of the judiciary was not interwoven with old institutions or popular customs. There was, therefore, no hindrance to the free play of the central power. It could shape all laws according to its views. And in Canada, therefore, there was not a shadow of municipal or provincial institutions; and no collective or individual action was tolerated. An intendant far more powerful than his colleagues in France; a government managing far more matters than it did at home, and desiring to manage everything from Paris, notwithstanding the intervening 1800 leagues; never adopting the great principles which can render a colony populous and prosperous, but, instead, employing all sorts of petty, artificial methods, and small devices of tyranny to increase and spread population; forced cultivation of lands; all lawsuits growing out of the concession of land removed from the jurisdiction of the courts and referred to the local administration; compulsory regulations respecting farming and the selection of land – such was the system devised for Canada under Louis XIV: it was Colbert who signed the edicts. One might fancy one's self in the midst of modern centralization and in Algeria. Canada is, in fact, the true model of what has always been seen there. In both places the government numbers as many heads as the people; it preponderates, acts, regulates, controls, undertakes everything, provides for everything, knows far more about the subjects business than he does himself – is, in short, incessantly active and sterile.

In the United States, on the contrary, the English anti-centralization system was carried to an extreme. Parishes became independent municipalities, almost democratic republics. The republican element, which forms, so to say, the foundation of the English constitution and English habits, shows itself and develops without hindrance. Government proper does little in England, and individuals do a great deal; in America, government never interferes, so to speak, and individuals do everything. The absence of an upper class, which renders the Canadian more defenceless against the government than his equals were in France, renders the citizen of the English colonies still more independent of the home power.

In both colonies society ultimately resolved itself into a democratic form. But in Canada, so long as it was a French possession at least, equality was an accessory of absolutism; in the British colonies it was the companion of liberty. And, so far as the material consequences of the two colonial systems are concerned, it is well known that in 1763, at the conquest, the population of Canada was 60,000 souls, that of the English provinces 3,000,000.

NOTE 23

An example chosen at haphazard, of the general regulations which the council of state was in the habit of making for the whole of France, and by which it created special misdemeanours of which the government courts had sole cognizance.

I take the first which I happen to find. Order in Council of 29 April 1779, which enacts that thereafter throughout the kingdom all sheep-growers and sheep-dealers shall mark their sheep in a peculiar manner, under penalty of 300 *livres* fine. 'His majesty orders the intendant to see this order obeyed,' it says, whence it follows that it devolved upon the intendant to pronounce penalties incurred. Another instance: An Order in Council of 21 December 1778 forbids express companies and wagoners to warehouse the goods they have in charge, under pain of 300 *livres* fine. 'His majesty enjoins upon his lieutenant general of police and his intendants to see to it.'

NOTE 24

The Provincial Assembly of Guienne cries aloud for new brigades of horse-police, just as in our day the council-general of the department of Aveyron or Lot no doubt demands new brigades of *gendarmerie*. Always the same idea – *gendarmerie* constitute order, and order cannot be had with the gendarme except through government. The report adds: 'Complaint is daily made that there is no police in the country.' (How could there be? Noblemen take no concern for any thing, burghers live in town; and the community is represented by a rude peasant, and has no power at all.) 'It must be admitted that, except in some *cantons* in which benevolent and just seigniors use their influence over their vassals to prevent those appeals to violence to which the country people are prone, in consequence of the rudeness of their manners and the roughness of their character, there exists hardly anywhere any means of controlling these ignorant, rough, and hot-headed men.'

Such was the manner in which the nobles of the Provincial Assembly allowed themselves to be spoken of, and in which the Third Estate, comprising half the assembly, spoke of the people in public documents.

NOTE 25

Tobacco licences were as eagerly sought after under the old regime as at present. The most distinguished people begged them for their dependents. Some, I find, were granted at the request of noble ladies, some to please archbishops.

NOTE 26

Local life was more thoroughly extinguished than almost seems credible. One of the roads leading from Maine into Normandy had become impassable. Who calls for its repair? The district of Touraine, which it crosses? The province of Normandy, or that of Maine, both vitally interested in the cattle-trade of which it is the outlet? Some canton particularly injured by the bad condition of the road? Neither district, nor province, nor canton utter a word. The duty of attracting the attention of government to the road is left to the traders who use it, and whose wagons stick in the mud. They write to Paris to the comptroller-general, and beg him to come to their rescue.

NOTE 27
Varying value of seigniorial rents and dues according to provinces.

Turgot says in his works: 'I must remark that the importance of these dues is very different in most of the rich provinces, such as Normandy, Picardy, and the vicinity of Paris. In the latter, riches usually consist in the produce of land; the farms are large, close together, and bring high rents. The seigniorial rents of large farms form a very small portion of the income from them, and are regarded rather as honorary than lucrative. In poorer and worse-farmed provinces, seigniors and men of rank possess but little land of their own; farms, which are much subdivided, are burdened with heavy rents in produce, and all the co-tenants are jointly responsible for their payment. These rents eat up the clearest portion of the income of the land, and constitute the bulk of the seignior's revenue.'

NOTE 28a
Discussion of public affairs antagonistic to the establishment of castes.

The unimportant labours of the agricultural societies of the eighteenth century show how the general discussion of public affairs militated against castes. Though these assemblages took place thirty years prior to the Revolution, in the midst of the old regime, the mere fact that they discussed questions in which all classes were interested, and that all classes mingled in the discussion, drew men together and effected a sort of fusion. Ideas of reasonable reform suggested themselves to the minds even of the privileged classes, and yet they were mere conversations about agriculture.

I am satisfied that no government but one which relied wholly on its own strength, and invariably dealt with individuals singly, as that of the old regime did, could have maintained the ridiculous and insane inequality which existed at the time of the Revolution. The least touch of self-government would have soon altered or destroyed it.

NOTE 28b

Provincial liberties may survive national liberty for a time, when they are of old standing, and interwoven with manners, customs, and recollections, and the despotism is new. But it is unreasonable to suppose that local liberties can be created at will, or maintained for any length of time, when general liberty is extinct.

NOTE 29

Turgot gives a statement of the extent of the privileges of the nobility, in the matter of taxation, in a memorial to the king. It appears to me to be quite correct.

1st. Privileged persons may claim exemption from taxes for a farm which consumes the labour of four plows. Such a farm in the neighbourhood of Paris would usually pay 2000 francs of taxes.

2dly. The same privileged persons pay nothing for woods, meadows, rivers, ponds, or inclosed lands near their chateau, whatever be their extent. Some cantons are almost wholly laid out in meadow or vineyard; in these, seigniors who have their lands managed by a steward pay no impost whatever. All the taxes fall on the taille-payers. The advantage of this is immense.

NOTE 30a
Indirect privilege in respect of taxes. – difference in the manner of collection when the tax is levied on all alike.

Turgot draws a picture of this, which I have reason to believe is correct.

'The indirect advantages of the privileged classes with regard to the capitation-tax are very great. The capitation-tax is naturally an arbitrary impost; it is impossible to divide it among the citizens at large otherwise than blindly. It was found convenient to take the taille rolls, which were already made, as a basis. A special roll was made for the privileged classes; but, as the latter made objections, and the taille-payers had no one to speak for them, it came about that the capitation of the privileged classes was gradually reduced in the provinces to a very small sum, while the taille-payers paid as much for capitation as the principal of the taille.'

NOTE 30b
Another example of inequality in the collection of a uniform tax.

It is known that local imposts were levied on all classes equally; 'which sums,' say the Orders in Council authorizing these expenditures, 'shall be levied on all persons without distinction, whether privileged or not, jointly with the capitation-tax, or in proportion thereto.'

Note that, as the capitation-tax of taille-payers, which was assimilated to the taille, was always heavier than the capitation of privileged persons, the very plan which seemed to favour uniformity kept up the inequality between the two.

NOTE 30c
Same subject.

I find in a bill of 1764, which designed to render the taxes uniform, all sorts of provisions that were intended to preserve a distinction in favour of the privileged classes in respect to the tax levy. For instance, no property of theirs could be appraised for taxation except in their presence or in the presence of their attorney.

NOTE 31

How the government admitted that, even in the case of
taxes weighing alike on all classes, the tax ought to
be collected differently from the privileged and
unprivileged classes.

'I see,' said the minister in 1766 that the most difficult taxes to collect are
those which are due by nobles and privileged persons, in consequence of
the consideration which the tax-collectors feel bound to pay to these
persons. It has resulted from this that they are heavily in arrears on their
capitation-tax and twentieths (the taxes which they paid in common
with the people).

NOTE 32

Arthur Young, in his Journey in 1789, draws a picture in which the
condition of the two societies is so agreeably sketched and so skilfully
set that I cannot resist giving it here.

In travelling through France during the emotion caused by the
capture of the Bastille, Young was arrested in a village by a mob, who,
seeing no *cocarde* on his hat, were about to drag him to jail. To get out
of the scrape, Young improvises the following little speech:

'"Gentlemen, it has just been said that the taxes are to be paid just as
before. The taxes must be paid, certainly, but not as before. They must
be paid as they are in England. We have many more taxes than you; but
the Third Estate, the people, pays none of them; they fall upon the rich.
In my country, windows pay a tax; but a man who has only six in his
house pays nothing. A seignior pays his twentieths and the taille, but the
owner of a small garden escapes scot free. Rich men pay for their horses,
their carriages, their servants, for the right of shooting their own
partridges; but small landholders know nothing of these taxes. More
than this: we have, in England, a tax that is levied on the rich for the
maintenance of the poor. If, then, taxes are still to be paid, they must be
paid on a new plan. The English plan is the best."'

'As my bad French,' adds Young, 'suited their patois well enough,
they understood what I said. They applauded every word of this speech,
and concluded that I might be a good fellow – an impression which I
confirmed by crying *Vive le Tiers*! They then let me pass with a hurrah.'

NOTE 33

The church of X, election of Chollet, was falling into ruin. Measures
were being taken to repair it, according to the plan indicated by the
Order of 16 December 1684, that is to say, by a tax on all the citizens.
When the collectors proceed to levy the tax, the Marquis of X, seignior

of the parish, declares that, as he undertakes to repair the choir without assistance, he cannot be expected to contribute to the tax. The other inhabitants reply very reasonably that, as seignior and large tithe-holder (he possessed, no doubt, the tithes enfeoffed), he was bound to repair the choir, and that he was by no means, on that account, relieved from his obligation to contribute to the other repairs. On reference to the intendant, he decides against the marquis and in favour of the collectors. The records of the affair contain more then ten letters of the marquis, each more pressing than the last, begging that the other people of the parish be made to pay in his stead, and condescending to call the intendant 'monseigneur', and even to 'supplicate him'.

NOTE 34

*Example of the manner in which the government of the
old regime respected acquired rights, formal contracts,
and city or associate liberties.*

Royal declaration 'suspending, in time of war, repayment of all loans made to the crown by cities, bourgs, colleges, communities, hospitals, poor-houses, corporations of artisans and tradesmen, and others, for the payment of which town or other dues were pledged; interest to accrue on the same'.

This was not only suspending payment at the time fixed, but laying hands on the security pledged for the payment of the loan. Similar measures were common under the government of the old regime; they could never have occurred in a country where a free press or free assemblies existed. Compare these proceedings with those which have taken place in England and America in the like circumstances. Here the contempt for right was not less flagrant than the contempt for local liberties.

NOTE 35

The case cited in the text is not the only one in which the privileged classes perceived that they were affected by the feudal dues which weighed upon the peasantry. An agricultural society, composed wholly of privileged persons, said, thirty years before the Revolution,

'Irredeemable rents, whether ground-rents or feudal rents attaching upon land, become so onerous to the debtor when they are consider-able, that they ruin him and the land too. He is forced to neglect his farm, for he cannot effect loans on a property so burdened, nor can he find a purchaser for it. If the rent were redeemable, he would soon find a lender to advance money to pay it off, or a purchaser to extinguish it. One is always glad to improve a property of which one believes one's self peaceable owner. It would be of infinite service to agriculture if a means could be found of rendering these rents redeemable. Many feudal seigniors are convinced of this, and would gladly concur in any arrangement for the purpose. It would therefore be desirable to indicate a plan for redeeming all these ground-rents.'

NOTE 36

All public functionaries, including the agent of the tax-farmers, enjoyed exemptions from taxes. The privilege was granted them by the ordinance of 1681. An intendant says, in a letter addressed to the minister in 1782, 'The most numerous class of privileged persons consists of clerks of the gabel, of *traites*, of the domain, of the post, of aids, and other excise of all kinds. One or more of these are to be found in every parish.'

The object was to prevent the ministers from proposing to the Council a measure to extend the exemption from taxes to the clerks and servants of these privileged agents. The farmers-general, says the intendant, are always asking for extensions of the privilege, in order to obtain clerks without paying them a salary.

NOTE 37

Venal offices were not wholly unknown abroad. In Germany some small sovereigns had introduced the system; but they had applied it to but few offices, and these subordinate ones. The system was carried out on a grand scale in France only.

NOTE 38

One must not be surprised – though it certainly seems surprising – to see functionaries of the old government, closely connected with the administration, go to law before the Parliament about the limits of their respective powers. The fact is easily explained: the questions at issue were questions of public administration, but they were also questions of private property. What here appears to be an encroachment of the judiciary was, in fact, nothing but a consequence of the fault which the government committed in selling offices. All places being bought, and their incumbents being paid by fees, it was impossible to alter the functions of an office without injuring individual rights which had been purchased for a valuable consideration. One example out of a thousand: the lieutenant general of police of Mans institutes an action against the financial department of that city to claim the right of paving the streets, and obtaining fees thereon, that being, he says, part of the police of the streets, which devolves upon him. The department replies that the very title of its commission intrusts it with the paving of the streets. This time it is not the king's council which decides between them; as the point involved is chiefly the interest of the capital invested by the lieutenant in the purchase of his office, the case goes before the Parliament. Instead of being a government question, it is a civil suit.

NOTE 39

Analysis of the cahiers of the nobility in 1789.

The French Revolution is the only one, I believe, at the beginning of which the different classes of society were enabled to present an authentic account of the ideas they had conceived, and express the feelings which animated them, before the Revolution had distorted or modified those ideas and feelings. This authentic account was recorded, as is known, in the *cahiers* which the three orders drew up in 1789. These *cahiers* or *memoires* were drawn up in perfect freedom, in the midst of the widest publicity, by each of the three orders; they were the fruit of long discussion by the parties in interest, and ripe deliberation by their authors; for in those days, when the government spoke to the nation, it did not undertake to answer its own questions. At the time the cahiers were composed, the principal parts of them were collected and published in three volumes, which are to be found in all libraries. The originals are deposited in the national archives, and with them the reports of the assemblies which drew them up, and a portion of the correspondence between M. Necker and his agents in reference to the subject. This collection forms a long series of folio volumes, and is the most precious document we have on the subject of ancient France. All who desire to become acquainted with the spirit of our forefathers at the time of the Revolution should consult it without delay.

I had imagined that perhaps the printed extract, in three volumes, which I have mentioned above, was a one-sided performance, and an unfaithful reflection of this immense collection; but I find, on comparing the two, that the smaller work is a correct miniature of the greater.

The following extract from the cahiers of the nobility shows the spirit which animated the majority of that body. It shows which of their old privileges the nobility desired at all hazards to keep, which they were half inclined to abandon, and which they proposed of their own accord to sacrifice. It discloses especially the views which pervaded the whole body on the subject of political liberty. Curious and melancholy spectacle!

Individual Rights – The nobility demand, in the first place, that an explicit declaration of the rights of man be made, and that declaration bear witness to the liberty and secure the safety of all men.

Personal Liberty – They desire that the serfdom of the glebe be abolished wherever it may still exist, and that means be sought for the extinction of the slave-trade and negro slavery; that all be free to travel withersoever they will, and to reside where they please, within or without the kingdom, without being liable to arbitrary arrest; that the police regulations be amended, and that the police be under control of the magistracy, even in case of riot; that no one be arrested and judged except by his natural judges; that, in consequence, state prisons and other illegal places of detention be suppressed. Some demand the destruction of the Bastille. The nobility of Paris insist warmly on this point.

All letters of *cachet* should be prohibited. If the danger of the state requires the arrest of a citizen who cannot be handed over directly to the ordinary courts of justice, measures must be taken to prevent injustice, either by notifying the Council of State, or in some other way.

The nobility desire that all special commissions, irregular courts, privileges of *committimus*, reprieves, be abolished; that the most severe penalties be laid upon all who execute or order the execution of an arbitrary command; that the ordinary courts – which alone should be preserved – take all necessary measures to secure individual liberty, especially in criminal matters; that justice be administered gratuitously, and useless jurisdictions abolished. One cahier says, 'Magistrates were made for the people, not the people for magistrates.' They demand that an honorary counsel and advocates for the poor be established in every bailiwick; that all examinations be public, and prisoners be allowed to defend themselves; that in criminal matters the prisoner be provided with a counsel, and the judge assisted by a number of citizens of the same order as the prisoner, who shall decide upon the fact of the crime or misdemeanor charged (reference is here made to the constitution of England); that penalties be proportioned to offences, and uniform; that capital punishment be employed more rarely, and all corporal punishments, torture, &c., be abolished; that the condition of prisoners be improved, especially those who are confined before their trial.

The cahiers demand that an effort be made to respect individual liberty in the recruiting service both of soldiers and sailors. It should be allowable to avoid military service by paying a sum of money. No lots should be drawn save in the presence of deputies of the three orders. Finally, an attempt should be made to reconcile military discipline and subordination with the rights of the citizen and the freeman. Blows with the flat of the sword should be forbidden.

Liberty and Inviolability of Property. – Property should be inviolable, and should never be molested save for the necessities of the public weal. In such cases the government should pay a high price, and that promptly. Confiscations should be abolished.

Liberty of Trade, Labour, and Industry. – Freedom of labour and trade should be secured. In consequence, all monopolies should be taken from trade-companies, as well as other privileges of the kind. No custom-houses should exist except on the frontier.

Liberty of Religion. – The Catholic faith shall be the only dominant religion in France, but all other religions shall be tolerated, and persons who are not Catholics shall be reinstated in their properties and civil rights.

Liberty of the Press, Inviolability of Letters in the Post-office. – The liberty of the press shall be secured, and a law shall fix beforehand the restrictions that may be established in the interest of the public. No works but such as treat of religious doctrine shall be liable to ecclesiastical censorship; in the case of all others, it shall be sufficient that the names of the author and printer are known. Many demand that charges against the press be tried before jury.

All the cahiers insist energetically on the inviolability of secrets confided to the post, so that private letters may never be brought in accusation against individuals. The opening of letters, say they, bluntly, is the most odious form of espionage, as it violates the public faith.

Education. – The cahiers of the nobility confine themselves to recommending that all proper means be taken to spread education, both in cities and in the country, and that each boy be taught with a view to his future vocation. They insist on the necessity of teaching children the political rights and duties of the citizen, and suggest that a catechism on the principal points of the Constitution be used in schools. They do not, however, point out any means to be used to facilitate and spread education. They merely demand educational establishments for the children of the poor nobility.

Care to be taken of the People. – Many of the cahiers demand that the people be treated with more consideration. They exclaim against the police regulations, in virtue of which they say hosts of mechanics and useful citizens are daily thrust into prisons and jails without any regular commitment, and often on mere suspicions, a manifest violation of natural liberty. All cahiers demand that *corvées* be definitely abolished. A majority of bailiwicks desire that rights of banality and toll be made redeemable. Many demand that the collection of various feudal dues be rendered less oppressive, and that the freehold duty be abolished. One cahier observes that the government is interested in facilitating the purchase and sale of lands. This is precisely the reason that will soon be urged for abolishing at a blow all seigniorial rights, and throwing all mainmortable lands into the market. Many cahiers ask that the right of pigeon-houses be rendered less prejudicial to agriculture. As for the establishments for the preservation of the king's game, known by the name of captainries, they demand their immediate abolition, as being subversive of the rights of property. They desire to see, in lieu of the present taxes, new ones established which shall be less onerous to the people.

The nobility demand that an effort be made to disseminate plenty and comfort throughout the rural districts; that looms and factories of coarse stuffs be established in the villages, so as to occupy the country-people during the idle season; that in each bailiwick public store-houses be founded, under the inspection of the provincial governments, to provide for seasons of famine, and sustain the regularity of prices; that attempts be made to improve agriculture and better the condition of the country parts; that more public works be undertaken, and especially that marshes be drained, and means taken to guard against inundations, &c; finally, that special encouragements be offered to agriculture and trade in all the provinces.

The cahiers suggest that, instead of the present hospitals, small establishments of the kind be founded in every district; that the poor-houses be abolished, and replaced by work-houses; that a charitable fund be placed at the disposal of the Provincial States; that surgeons, physicians, and midwives be appointed for every county to tend the poor gratuitously, and paid by the province; that the Courts of Justice should always be open to the poor, free of charge; that thought be taken for the establishment of blind, deaf and dumb asylums, foundling-hospitals, &c.

In all these matters the nobility express their general views as to what reforms are needed; they do not enter into details. It is easy to see that they have been less frequently brought into contact with the poor than the lower order of clergy, and that, having seen less of their sufferings, they have reflected less on the subject of a remedy.

Of Eligibility to Office, of the Hierarchy of Ranks, and of the honorary Privileges of the Nobility. – It is chiefly, or, rather, it is only when they come to deal with distinctions of rank and class divisions that the nobles turn their backs on the prevailing spirit of reform. They make important concessions, but, on the whole, they adhere to the spirit of the old regime. They feel that they are fighting for life. Their cahiers thus demand energetically that the nobility and the clergy be maintained as distinct orders. They even desire that a method be devised for preserving the purity of the order of the nobility; that, for instance, the practice of selling titles or coupling them with certain offices be prohibited, and that rank be the reward of long and meritorious services rendered to the state. They wish that all the false nobles could be found out and prosecuted. All the cahiers, in short, demand that the nobility be maintained in all its honours. Some think it would be well for men of rank to wear a distinctive badge.

Nothing could be more characteristic than such a demand; nothing could indicate more plainly the similarity between the noble and the commoner. Generally speaking, the nobility, while abandoning many of their beneficial rights, cling with anxiety and warmth to those which are purely honorary. They want not only to preserve those which they possess, but also to invent new ones. So conscious were they that they were being dragged into the vortex of democracy: so terribly did they dread perishing there. Singular fact! Their instinct warned them of the danger, but they never perceived it.

As to the distribution of office, the nobility demand that posts in the magistracy be no longer sold, but that any citizen of suitable age and capacity be eligible as a candidate to be presented by the nation to the king. In respect to military rank, a majority of the cahiers are against excluding the Third Estate, and conceive that a man who has deserved well of his country ought to be able to attain the highest rank. Several cahiers say, 'The order of the nobility disapproves all laws which close the door of military preferment to the order of the Third Estate.' Some few, however, suggest that noblemen alone should have the right of entering the army as officers without passing through the inferior grades. Nearly all the cahiers demand that uniform rules be established with regard to promotion, that advancement be not wholly obtained by favour, and that, with the exception of the highest posts, promotion proceed by seniority.

As for clerical functions, they demand that elections be re-established for the distribution of livings, or, at all events, that the king appoint a committee to guide him in distributing ecclesiastical preferment.

They say that henceforth pensions must be granted with more discrimination, and not accumulated in certain families; that no citizen must receive two pensions, or draw pay for two offices at once; that survivorships must be abolished.

Church and Clergy. – When they have done with their own rights and peculiar constitution, and turn to the privileges and constitution of the Church, the nobility are not so timid; they have a very sharp eye for abuses.

They demand that the clergy be deprived of all exemptions from taxes; that they pay their debts, and do not call upon the nation to pay them; that the monastic orders be thoroughly reformed. Most of the cahiers declare that these institutions have departed from the spirit of their founders.

Most of the bailiwicks desire that tithes be rendered less injurious to agriculture; several demand their entire abolition. One cahier says that 'tithes are for the most part exacted by those curates who give themselves the least trouble to supply their flocks with spiritual food'. The first Order, as is seen, handled the second unceremoniously. Nor was it more respectful in dealing with the Church itself. Many bailiwicks formally assert the right of the States-General to suppress certain religious orders, and apply their property to other uses. Seventeen bailiwicks declare that the States-General may regulate ecclesiastical discipline. Many say that there are too many fête-days; that they injure agriculture, and favour drunkenness; that, in consequence, a great number of them must be suppressed, and Sundays kept instead.

Political Rights. – As to these, the cahiers recognize the right of all Frenchmen to take part directly or indirectly in the government, that is to say, to be electors and eligible. But this right is restricted by the distinction of ranks; that is to say, no one can be elected but by and for his Order. This principle laid out, representation should be so devised as to secure to each Order an active share in the public affairs.

Opinions are divided as to the way of taking votes in the assembly of the States-General: a majority advocate voting by Order, others think this rule ought not to apply to questions of taxation, and others, again, object to it altogether. These latter say, 'Each member shall have a vote, and all questions shall be decided by a majority of votes. This is the only rational plan, and the only one that can extinguish that *esprit de corps* which has been the only source of our misfortunes, draw men together, and lead them to the result which the nation is entitled to expect of an assembly in which patriotism and the virtues are enlightened by learning.' Still, as this innovation might be fraught with danger if hastily introduced in the present state of the public mind, many are for postponing its adoption to subsequent assemblies of the States-General. In any event, the nobility demand that each order preserve the dignity that is meet in Frenchmen; that, consequently, the old humiliating forms which were imposed on the Third Estate – such as bending the knee – be abolished. One cahier says that the 'sight of one man on his knees before another is offensive to the dignity of man, and indicates an unnatural inequality among men whose essential rights are the same'.

Of the form of Government and its Constitutional Principles. – As to the form of government, the nobility demand the maintenance of royalty, the preservation of legislative, judicial, and executive powers in the hands of the king, but, at the same time, the establishment of fundamental laws for the purpose of guarding the rights of the nation against the exercise of arbitrary power.

Consequently, all the cahiers proclaim that the nation is entitled to be represented in the States-General, which body must be numerous enough to secure its independence. They desire that these States meet at periodical intervals, and at every change of monarch without special summons. Many bailiwicks express a wish to see this assembly permanent. If the States-General are not convened at the time appointed, it ought to be lawful to refuse to pay taxes. Some cahiers propose that during the interval between the sessions of the States a small committee be intrusted with the duty of watching the administration; but the bulk oppose this scheme flatly, on the ground that such a committee would be unconstitutional. The reason they allege is curious. They say there would be reason to fear that so small a body could easily be seduced by government.

The nobility deny to ministers the right of dissolving the assembly, and propose that they be prosecuted before the courts when they disturb it with their intrigues; they desire that no official, or person in any way dependent on government, shall be a deputy; that the persons of deputies shall be inviolable, and that they shall not be liable to account for opinions expressed in debate; finally, that all sittings of the assembly shall be public, and that the nation be made a spectator by printing the debates.

The nobility unanimously demand that the principles which must govern the state administration be applied to the administration of every portion of he national territory; hence, that in every province, district, and parish, assemblies be established composed of members freely elected for a limited period.

Many cahiers think that the offices of intendant and receiver-general should be abolished; all are of opinion that thenceforth the business of distributing taxes, and managing provincial business, should be left to the provincial assemblies. They advise that a similar plan be adopted with regard to county and parochial assemblies, which henceforth should be under the control of the Provincial States.

Division of Powers: Legislative Power. – In dividing power between the assembled nation and the king, the nobility ask that no law shall take effect until it has been sanctioned by the States-General and the king, and recorded in the registers of the courts appointed to enforce it; that the business of establishing and fixing the quotas of taxes shall belong exclusively to the States-General; that subsidies voted shall only be considered as having been appropriated for the interval between one session of the States and another; that all taxes, established or levied without the consent of the States, shall be deemed illegal, and that all ministers and collectors who shall have ordered or levied such taxes shall be prosecuted for extortion; that, on the same principle, no loan shall be contracted without the consent of the States-General, but that a limited credit shall be opened by the States, to be used by government in case of war or sudden calamity, until a new session of the States can be called; that all the national treasuries shall be under the supervision of the States; that the expenses of each department shall be fixed by them, and that the most careful precautions shall be taken to prevent any appropriation being exceeded.

Most of the cahiers demand the suppression of those vexatious imposts known by the names of insinuation dues, *centième denier*, ratification dues, and comprised under the title of *régie* of the king's domains (one cahier says: 'The word *régie* would alone suffice to condemn them, since it implies that property which actually belongs to citizens is owned by the king'); that all the public domains which are not sold shall be placed under the government of the Provincial States, and that no ordinance or edict for raising extraordinary taxes shall be issued, except with the consent of the three orders of the nation.

The idea of the nobility obviously was to transfer the whole administration of the finances, including loans, taxes, and this class of imposts, to the nation as represented by the general and provincial assemblies.

Judicial Power. – In the same way, the organization of the judiciary tends to make the power of the judges largely dependent upon the assembled nation. Thus several cahiers declare:

'That magistrates shall be responsible for their acts to the assembled nation'; that they shall only be dismissed with the consent of the States-General; that no court shall, on any pretext whatever, be disturbed in the exercise of its functions without the consent of these States; that delinquencies of the Court of Cassation and of the Parliaments shall be judged by these States. Most of the cahiers recommend that no judges but such as the people present for office be appointed by the king.

Executive Power. – This is wholly reserved to the king, but it is limited in order to prevent abuses.

Thus, as to the administration, the cahiers demand that the accounts of the various departments be printed and made public, and that the ministers be responsible to the nation assembled; and in like manner, that the king be bound to communicate his intentions to the States-General before he can employ the troops on foreign service. At home, the troops shall not be used against the people without a requisition from the States-General. The standing army shall be limited; and in ordinary seasons, two thirds only shall be kept in effective service. As to the foreign troops which the king may have in his service, they must be kept away from the heart of the kingdom, and stationed on the frontier.

The most striking feature of the cahiers of the nobility – a feature which no extract can reproduce – is the perfect harmony which exists between these noblemen and their age. They are imbued with its spirit and speak its language. They speak of 'the inalienable rights of man', 'principles inherent to the social compact'. In treating of individuals, they speak of their rights; in alluding to society, they talk of its duties. Political principles seem to them 'as absolute as moral truths, both the one and the other having reason for their basis'. When they want to abolish the remains of serfdom, they say the must 'efface the last traces of human degradation'. They sometimes call Louis XVI a 'citizen king', and constantly allude to the crime of 'high-treason against the nation', with which they are so soon themselves to be charged. In their eyes, as in those of everyone else, public education seems the grand panacea, and its director must be the state. One cahier says that 'the States-General will give their attention to forming the national character by modifying the education of children'. Like their contemporaries, they are fond of uniformity in legislative measures, always excepting everything that concerns the existence of the Orders. They seek a uniform administration, uniform laws, &c., as ardently as the Third Estate. They call for all kinds of reforms, and those radical enough. They are for abolishing or transforming all the taxes without exception, and the whole judicial system, with the exception of the seigniorial courts, which only need improvement. Like all other Frenchmen, they regard France as a trial-field – a sort of political model-farm – in which everything should be tried, everything turned upside down, except the little spot in which their particular privileges grow. To their honour, it may even be said that they did not wholly spare that spot. In a word, it is seen from these cahiers that the only thing the nobles lacked to effect the Revolution was the rank of commoners.

NOTE 40
Example of the religious government of an ecclesiastical province in the middle of the eighteenth century.

1. The archbishop.
2. Seven vicars general.
3. Two ecclesiastical courts called officialities: the one, known as the 'metropolitan officiality', having cognizance of all sentences of the suffragans; the other, known as the 'diocesan officiality', having cognizance, first, of all personal affairs among the clergy, and, secondly, of all disputes regarding the validity of marriages, in reference to the sacrament. This last tribunal is composed of two judges: there are attorneys and notaries attached to it.
4. Two fiscal courts: one, styled the diocesan office, has original jurisdiction over all disputes which may arise respecting the taxes of the clergy in the diocese (the clergy, as is known, imposed their own taxes). This tribunal consisted of the archbishop, presiding, and six other priests. The other court hears appeals from the other diocesan offices of the ecclesiastical province. All these courts admit lawyers, and hear cases pleaded in due form.

NOTE 41
Spirit of the clergy in the provincial states and assemblies.

What I say in the text of the States of Languedoc applies equally to the Provincial States which assembled in 1779 and 1787, especially those of Haute Guienne. The members of the clergy are distinguished in this assembly for their learning, their activity, their liberality. The proposition to make the reports of the assembly public comes from the Bishop of Rodez.

NOTE 42

This liberal tendency of the clergy in political matters, which was evidenced in 1789, was not the fruit of the excitement of the moment; it was of old standing. It was witnessed in Berri in 1779, when the clergy offered 68,000 *livres* as a free gift if the provincial administration were allowed to subsist.

NOTE 43

Note that political society was disjointed, but that civil society still held together. In the heart of the different classes individuals were linked together; there even subsisted some trace of the old bond of union between seigniors and people. These peculiarities of civil society had their influence on politics; men thus united formed irregular and ill-organized masses, but bodies that were certain to be found refractory by government. The Revolution burst these ties, and substituted no political bonds in their stead; it thus paved the way for both equality and servitude.

NOTE 44
Example of the tone in which the courts spoke of certain arbitrary measures.

It appears from a memorial laid before the comptroller-general by the intendant of the district of Paris, that it was the custom of that district that each parish should have two syndics, one elected by the people in an assembly over which the sub-delegate presided, the other appointed by the intendant, and directed to superintend his colleague. A quarrel took place between the two syndics of the parish of Rueil, the one who was elected refusing to obey his colleague. The intendant induced M. de Breteuil to imprison the refractory syndic for a fortnight in the prison of La Force; on his liberation he was discharged, and a new syndic appointed in his stead. Thereupon the syndic appealed to the Parliament. I have not been able to find the conclusions of the proceedings, but the Parliament took occasion to declare that the imprisonment of the syndic and the nullification of his election could not but be considered 'arbitrary and despotic acts'. The courts were sometimes badly muzzled in those days.

NOTE 45a

The educated and wealthy classes, the burghers included, were far from being oppressed or enslaved under the old regime. On the contrary, they had generally too much freedom; for the crown could not prevent them from securing their own position at the sacrifice of the people's, and, indeed, almost always felt bound to purchase their good-will or soothe their animosity by abandoning the people to their mercy. It may be said that a Frenchman belonging to this class in the eighteenth century was better able to resist government and protect himself than an Englishman of the same period would have been in the like case. The crown felt bound to use more tenderness and deal more gently with him than the English government would have done to a man of the same standing. So wrong it is to confound independence with liberty. No one is less independent than a citizen of a free state.

NOTE 45b
A reason which often compelled the government of the old regime to use moderation.

In ordinary times, the most perilous acts for governments are the augmentation of old or the creation of new taxes. In olden times, when a king had expensive tastes, when he rushed into wild political schemes, when he let his finances fall into disorder, or when he needed large sums of money to sustain himself by gaining over his opponents, by paying heavy salaries that were not earned, by keeping numerous armies on foot, by undertaking extensive works, &c, he was obliged to have recourse to taxation, and this at once aroused all classes, especially that one which achieves violent revolutions – the people. Nowadays, in the same circumstances, loans are effected, which are not immediately felt, and whose burden falls on the next generation.

NOTE 46a

One of the many examples of this is to be found in the *election* of Mayence. The chief domains of that *election* were farmed out to farmers-general, who hired as sub-farmers small wretched peasants, who had nothing in the world, and to whom the most necessary farm-tools had to be furnished. It is easy to understand how creditors of this stamp would deal harshly with the farmers or debtors of the feudal seignior whom they represented, and would render the feudal tenure more oppressive than it had been in the Middle Ages.

NOTE 46b
Another example.

The inhabitants of Montbazon had entered on the taille-roll the stewards of a duchy owned by the Prince of Rohan, in whose name it was worked. The prince, who was no doubt very rich, not only has 'this abuse', as he calls it, corrected, but recovers a sum of 5344 *livres* 15 *sous*, which he had been wrongfully made to pay, and has the same charged to the inhabitants.

NOTE 47
Example of the effect of the pecuniary rights of the clergy in alienating the affections of those whose isolation should have made them friends of the church.

The curate of Noisai declares that the people are bound to repair his barn and wine-press, and proposes that a local tax be imposed for the purpose. The intendant replies that the people are only bound to repair the parson's house; the curate, who seems more attentive to his farm than to his flock, must himself repair his barn and wine-press. (1767.)

NOTE 48

The following passage is taken from a clear and moderate memorial presented in 1788 by the peasantry to a provincial assembly: 'To the other grievances incident to the collection of the taille must be added that of the bailiff's followers. They usually appear five times during the levy. They are, in general, invalid soldiers or Swiss. At each visit they remain four or five days in the parish, and for each of them 36 sous a day are added to the tax-levy. As for the distribution of the tax, we will not expose the well-known abuses of authority, or the bad effects of a distribution made by persons who are often incapable, and almost invariably partial and vindictive. These causes have, however, been a source of trouble and strife. They have led to lawsuits which have been very costly to litigants, and very advantageous to the places where the courts sit.'

NOTE 49
Superiority of the methods used in the pays d'états admitted by officials of the central government itself.

In a confidential letter dated 3 June 1772, and addressed by the Director of Taxes to the intendant, it is stated, 'In the *pays d'états* the imposition is a fixed percentage, which is exacted and really paid by the taxable. This percentage is raised in the levy in proportion to the increase in the total required by the king (a million, for instance, instead of 900,000 *livres*). This is a very simple matter. In our districts, on the contrary, the tax is personal, and, to a certain degree, arbitrary. Some pay what they owe, others only half, others a third, others a quarter, and some nothing at all. How is it possible to increase such a tax one ninth, for instance?'

Arbitrary imprisonment for corvées.

Example. – It is stated in a letter of the high provost in 1768, 'I ordered three men to be arrested yesterday on the requisition of M. C., the assistant engineer, for not having performed their *corvée*. The affair made quite a stir among the women of the village, who cried, "Nobody thinks of the poor people when the *corvée* is in question; nobody cares how they live – do you see?"'

Of the manner in which the privileged classes originally understood the progress of civilization in reference to roads.

The Count of K., in a letter to the intendant, complains of the want of zeal with which a road that is to pass near his place is prosecuted. He says it is the fault of the sub-delegate, who is not energetic enough, and does not force the peasantry to perform their *corvées*.

There were two means of making roads. One was by *corvées* for all heavy work requiring mere manual labour; the other – and the least valuable resource – was by imposing a general tax, whose proceeds were placed at the disposal of the Department of Bridges and Roads for the construction of scientific works. The privileged classes, that is to say, the principal landholders, who were of course the parties most interested in the roads, had nothing to do with *corvées*; and as the general tax in favour of the Bridge and Road Department was always joined with the *taille*, and levied on those who paid it, they escaped that too.

Instance of corvées for the removal of convicts.

A letter dated 1761, and addressed to the intendant by the commissioner of the chain-service, states that the peasants were forced to transport the convicts in carts; that they did so very reluctantly; that they were often maltreated by the keepers of the convicts, 'who,' says the letter, 'are coarse, brutal men, while the peasants, who dislike this duty, are often insolent'.

Turgot's sketches of the inconveniences and annoyances of *corvées* for the transportation of military baggage do not seem to me exaggerated now that I have read the documents bearing on the subject. He says, among other things, that the first inconvenience of the system is the extreme inequality with which this heavy burden is borne. It falls wholly on a small number of parishes, who are exposed to it by the misfortune of their position. The distance to be traversed is often five, six, and sometimes ten or fifteen leagues; three days are consumed in the journey and the return. The sum allowed is not one fifth the value of the labour. These *corvées* are almost invariably required in summer during harvest-time. The oxen are almost always overdriven, and often come home sick, so that many farmers prefer paying 15 or 20 *livres* to furnishing a cart and four oxen. The work is done in a most disorderly manner; the peasantry are constantly in prey to the violence of the soldiery. Officers almost always exact more than the law allows: they sometimes compel the farmers to yoke saddle-horses to carts, whereby the animals are often lamed. Soldiers will insist on riding on carts that are already heavily laden; in their impatience at the slow gait of the oxen, they will prick them with their swords, and if the farmer objects he is very roughly handled.

NOTE 55
Example of the application of corvées to everything.

The marine intendant of Rochefort complains that the peasants are indisposed to perform their *corvées* by carting the timber that has been purchased by the naval purveyors in the various provinces. (This correspondence shows that the peasants were, in fact, still – 1775 – bound to *corvées* of this kind, for which the intendant fixed their remuneration.) The Minister of Marine sends the letter to the intendant of Tours, and says that the carts required must be supplied. The intendant, M. Ducluzel, refuses to sanction *corvées* of this nature. The Minister of Marine writes him a threatening letter, in which he notifies him that he will apprize the king of his resistance. The intendant replies directly (11 December 1775), and states firmly, that during the whole ten years of his service as intendant at Tours, he has always refused to authorize these *corvées*, in consequence of the abuses they involve – abuses which the rates of wages do not compensate; 'for,' says he, 'the cattle are often lamed by drawing heavy logs over roads as bad as the weather in which this service is usually required of them'. The secret of this intendant's firmness seems to have been a letter of M. Turgot's, filed with the correspondence, and dated 30 July 1774, when Turgot entered the ministry; the letter states that Turgot never sanctioned these *corvées* at Limoges, and approves M. Ducluzel for refusing to sanction them at Tours.

Other portions of this correspondence show that purveyors of timber frequently exacted these *corvées* without being authorized to do so by a bargain with the state. They saved at least a third in freight. A sub-delegate gives the following instance of this profit: 'Distance to draw the logs from the place where they are cut to the river, over roads almost impassable, six leagues; time consumed, two days. The *corvéables* are paid at the rate of six *liards* a league per cubic foot; they will thus receive 13 *frs.* 10 *s.* for the journey, which will barely cover the expenses of the farmer, his assistant, and the cattle yoked to his cart. He loses his own time, his trouble, and the labour of his cattle.'

On 17 May 1776, a positive order of the king to insist on this *corvée* is intimated to the intendant by the minister. M. Ducluzel having died, his successor, M. L'Escalopier, hastens to obey, and to promulgate an ordinance stating that 'the sub-delegate is empowered to distribute the duty among the parishes; and all persons liable to *corvées* in the said parishes are hereby ordered to be present, at the hour directed by the syndics, at the place where the timber lies, and to cart it at the rate that shall be fixed by the sub-delegate'.

NOTE 56
Instance of the manner in which the peasantry were often treated.

1768. The king remits 2000 francs of the taille to the parish of Chapelle Blanche, near Saumur. The curate claims a portion of this sum to build a steeple, and so rid himself of the noise of the bells which incommodes him in his parsonage. The inhabitants object and resist. The sub-delegate takes the side of the curate, and has three of the principal inhabitants arrested at night, and locked up in jail.

Another example: Order of the king to imprison for two days a woman who has insulted two troopers of the horse-police. Another to imprison for a fortnight a stocking-maker who has spoken ill of the horse-police. In this case the intendant replies that he has already had the fellow arrested, for which he is warmly praised by the minister. The police, it seems had been insulted in consequence of the arrests of beggars, which had shocked people. When the intendant arrested the stocking-maker, he gave out that any persons thereafter insulting the police would be still more severely punished.

The correspondence between intendant and sub-delegates (1760-1770) shows that the former ordered the arrest of mischievous persons, not to bring them to trial, but to get them out of the way. The sub-delegate asks permission to keep two dangerous beggars he has arrested in perpetual confinement. A father protests against the imprisonment of his son, who has been arrested as a vagabond because he travelled without papers. A landowner of X demands that a neighbour of his, who has lately come to settle in his parish, whom he aided, but who is conducting himself badly towards him and annoying him, be forthwith arrested. The intendant of Paris begs his colleague of Rouen to oblige him thus far, as the petitioner is his friend.

To someone who desired to have some beggars set at liberty, the intendant replied 'that poor-houses must not be considered prisons, but mere establishments intended for the detention of beggars and vagabonds by way of *administrative correction*'. This idea found its way into the Penal Code. So well preserved have been the notions of the old regime in this matter.

NOTE 57

It has been said that the character of the philosophy of the eighteenth century was a sort of adoration of human intellect, an unlimited confidence in its power to transform at will laws, institutions, customs. To be accurate, it must be said that the human intellect which some of these philosophers adored was simply their own. They showed, in fact, an uncommon want of faith in the wisdom of the masses. I could mention several who despised the public almost as heartily as they despised the Deity. Toward the latter they evinced the pride of rivals – the former they treated with the pride of parvenus. They were as far from real and respectful submission to the will of the majority as from submission to the will of God. Nearly all subsequent revolutionaries have borne the same character. Very different from this is the respect shown by Englishmen and Americans for the sentiments of the majority of their fellow-citizens. Their intellect is proud and self-reliant, but never insolent; and it has led to liberty, while ours has done little but invent new forms of servitude.

NOTE 58

Frederick the Great says in his Memoirs, 'The Fontenelles, the Voltaires, the Hobbeses, the Collinses, the Shaftesburys, the Bolingbrokes – all these great men dealt a deadly blow to religion. Men began to examine what they had stupidly adored. Intellect overthrew superstition. Fables that had long been believed fell into disgust. Deism made many converts. If Epicureanism was fatal to the idolatrous worship of the pagans, Deism was equally fatal to the Judaical visions of our ancestry. The liberty of thought which reigned in England was very favourable to the progress of philosophy.'

It may be here seen that Frederick the Great, at the time he wrote these lines, that is to say, the middle of the eighteenth century, regarded

England as the centre of irreligious doctrines. A still more striking fact is the total ignorance displayed by one of the most enlightened and experienced sovereigns of history, of the political utility of religion. The faults of his masters had injured the natural qualities of his mind.

NOTE 59

A similar spirit of progress manifested itself at the same time in Germany, and there, as in France, was accompanied by a desire for a change of institutions. See the picture which a German historian draws of the state of his country at that time:

'During the second half of the eighteenth century,' says he, 'the new spirit of the age has been introduced even into ecclesiastical territory, on which reforms are commenced. Industry and tolerance penetrate into every corner of it; it is reached by the enlightened absolutism which has already mastered the greater states. And it must be acknowledged that at no period during the century has the territory of the Church been ruled by sovereigns as worthy of esteem and respect as those who figured during the ten years which preceded the French Revolution.'

Note how this sketch resembles France, where progress and reform took a start at the same moment, and the men who were most worthy of governing appeared just when the Revolution was about to devour them all.

Note, also, how visibly this part of Germany was drawn into the French movement of civilization and politics.

NOTE 60
How the organization of the English courts proves that institutions may have made secondary faults without failing in their original object.

Nations have a faculty of prospering in spite of imperfections in the secondary parts of their institutions, so long as the general principles and spirit of these institutions are imbued with vitality. This phenomenon is well illustrated by the judicial organization of England during the last century, as we find it in Blackstone.

Two anomalies at once meet the eye: 1st. The laws differ; 2nd. They are carried into effect by different tribunals.

1st. As to the laws:

1. One set of laws is in force for England proper, another for Scotland, another for Ireland, another for certain European possessions of Great Britain, such as the Isle of Man and the Channel Islands, others for the colonies.

2. In England alone four systems of law are in use: customary law, statute law, Roman law, equity. Customary law, again, is subdivided into general customs which apply to the whole kingdom, customs which

apply to certain seigniories or towns, and customs which apply to certain classes – such, for instance, as the custom of merchants. Some of these customs differ widely from the others, as, for instance, those which, in opposition to the general spirit of the English laws, direct the equal division of property among children (gavelkind), and those more singular customs still which award a right of primogeniture to the youngest child.

2nd. As to the courts:

The law, says Blackstone, has established an infinite variety of courts. Some idea may be formed of their number from the following very brief analysis:

1. One meets first with the courts established out of England proper, such as the courts of Scotland and Ireland, which were not subordinate to the superior courts of England, though they were all, I fancy, subject to appeal to the House of Lords.

2. As to England proper, if my memory serves me, Blackstone counts, 1st. eleven kinds of courts existing at common law, of which four seem, indeed, to have fallen into disuse in his time. 2nd. Three kinds of courts exercising jurisdiction over certain cases throughout the country. 3rd. Ten kinds of special courts: one of these is local courts, created by special acts of Parliament or existing by custom, either at London or in the towns or boroughs of the provinces. These are so numerous and so varied in their systems and rules that Blackstone abandons the attempt to describe them in detail.

Thus, in England proper, if Blackstone is to be believed, there existed at the time he wrote, that is to say, during the second half of the eighteenth century, twenty-four kinds of courts, of which several were subdivided into various species, each having a particular physiognomy. Setting aside those which seem to have fallen into disuse, there yet remain eighteen or twenty.

Now the least examination of this judicial system brings to light ever so many imperfections.

Notwithstanding the immense number of courts, there are none, it seems, close at hand, which can hear petty cases promptly and at small expense, and hence the administration of justice is embarrassing and costly. Several courts exercise jurisdiction over the same class of cases, whence troublesome doubts are thrown upon the validity of judgments. Nearly all the courts of appeal exercise original jurisdiction of one kind or another, either at common law or as equity courts. There are a variety of courts of appeal. The only point where all business centres is the House of Lords. Suits against the crown are not distinguished from other suits, which would seem a great deformity in the eyes of most of our lawyers. Finally, all these courts judge according to four different systems of laws, one of which consists wholly of precedents, and another – equity – has no settled basis, being designed, for the most part, to contradict the customs or statutes, and to correct the obsolete or over-harsh provisions of these by giving play to the discretion of the judge.

Here are astounding defects. Compare this old-fashioned and monstrous machine with our modern judiciary system, and the contrast between the simplicity, the coherence, and the logical organization of the one will place in still bolder relief the complicated and incoherent plan of the other. Yet there does not exist a country in which, even in Blackstone's time, the great ends of justice were more fully attained than in England; not one where every man, of whatever rank, and whether his suit was against a private individual or the sovereign, was more certain of being heard, and more assured of finding in the court ample guarantees for the defence of his fortune, his liberty, and his life.

This does not indicate that the faults of the judiciary system of England served the ends of justice. It only shows that there may exist in every judiciary system secondary faults which are but a slight impediment to the proper transaction of business, while there are radical faults which, though they coexist with many secondary excellences, may not only interfere with, but absolutely defeat the ends of justice. The former are the easiest to detect; they are instantly noticed by common minds. One can see them at a glance. The others are more difficult to discover, and lawyers are not always the people who perceive or point them out.

Note, also, that the same qualities may be secondary or principal, according to the times and the political organization of society. In aristocratic times, all inequalities, or other contrivances to diminish the privileges of certain individuals before the courts, to guarantee the protection of the weak against the strong, or to give predominance to the action of the government, which naturally views disputes between its subjects wth impartiality, are leading and important features. They lose their importance when society and political institutions point toward democracy.

Studying the judiciary system of England by the light of this principle, it will be discovered that, while defects were allowed to exist which rendered the administration of justice among our neighbours obscure, complicated, slow, costly, and inconvenient, infinite pains had been taken to protect the weak against the strong, the subject against the monarch; and the closer the details of the system are examined, the better will it be seen that every citizen had been amply provided with arms for his defence, and that matters had been so arranged as to give to everyone the greatest possible number of guarantees against the partiality and venality of the courts, and, above all, against that form of venality which is both the commonest and the most dangerous in democratic times – subserviency to the supreme power.

In all these points of view, the English system, notwithstanding its secondary faults, appears to me superior to our own. Ours has none of its vices, it is true, but it is not endowed with the same excellences. It is admirable in respect of the guarantees it offers to the citizen in suits against his neighbour, but it fails in the particular that is most essential in a democratic society like ours, namely, the guarantees of the individual against the state.

NOTE 61
Advantages enjoyed by the district of Paris.

This district (généralité) enjoyed as large advantages in respect of government charities as of taxes. For example, the comptroller-general writes, on 22 May 1787, to the intendant of the district of Paris, to say that the king has fixed the sum to be spent in charitable works, in the district of Paris, during the year, at 172,800 livres. Besides this, 100,000 livres are to be spent in cows to be given to farmers. This letter shows that this sum of 172,800 livres was to be distributed by the intendant alone, in conformity with the general rules laid down by the government, and subject to the general approval of the comptroller-general.

NOTE 62

The administration of the old regime comprised a multitude of different powers, which had been created – rather to help the treasury than the government – at various times, and often intrusted with the same sphere of action. Confusion and conflicts of authority could only be avoided on condition that each power should agree to do little or nothing. The moment they shook off inertia, they clashed and incommoded each other. Hence it happened that complaints of the complications of the administrative system and of the confusion of powers were much more pressing just before the Revolution than they had been thirty or forty years previous. Political institutions had grown better, not worse; but political life was more active.

NOTE 63
Arbitrary increase of the taxes.

What the king here says of the taille might have been said with equal truth of the twentieths, as is shown by the following correspondence. In 1772, Comptroller-general Terray had decided upon a considerable increase – 100,000 livres – in the twentieths in the district of Tours. M. Ducluzel, an able administrator and a good man, shows all the grief and annoyance he feels at the step in a confidential letter, in which he says, 'It is the facility with which the 250,000 livres were obtained by the last increase which has doubtless suggested the cruel step, and the letter of the month of June.'

In a very confidential letter from the director of taxes to the intendant, in reference to the same matter, he says, 'If you still think the increase as aggravating and revolting, in view of the public distress, as you were good enough to say it was, it would be desirable that you should contrive to spare the province – which has no other defender or protector but yourself – the supplementary rolls, which, being retro-active in their effect, are always odious.'

This correspondence likewise shows how sadly some standard rule of action was needed, and how arbitrarily matters were managed even with honest views. Intendant and minister both throw the surplus tax sometimes on agriculture rather than labour, sometimes on one branch of agriculture (vines, for instance) rather than another, according to their own ideas as to which interest requires gentle treatment.

NOTE 64
Style in which Turgot speaks of the people of the country parts in the preamble of a royal declaration.

'The country communities,' says he, in most parts of the kingdom, are composed of poor, ignorant, and brutal peasants, incapable of self-government.'

NOTE 65
How revolutionary ideas were spontaneously germinating in men's minds under the old regime.

In 1779 a lawyer begs the Council to pass an order establishing a maximum price for straw throughout the kingdom.

NOTE 66

The chief engineer wrote to the intendant, in 1781, on the subject of a demand for increased indemnity: 'The applicant forgets that these indemnities are a special favour granted to the district of Tours, and that he is fortunate in obtaining partial repayment for his loss. If all the parties in interest were reimbursed on the scale he proposes, four millions would not suffice.'

NOTE 67

This prosperity did not cause the Revolution; but the spirit which was to cause it – that active, restless, intelligent, innovating, ambitious, democratic spirit, which imbued the new society, was giving life to every thing, and stirring up and developing every social element before it overthrew the whole.

NOTE 68
Conflict of the several administrative powers in 1787.

Example – The intermediate commission of the provincial assembly of Ile de France claims the administration of the poorhouse. The intendant insists on retaining control of it, as 'it is not kept up out of the provincial funds'. During the discussion, the commission applies to the intermediate commissions of other provinces for their opinion. That of Champagne, among others, replies that the same difficulty has been raised there, and that it has, in like manner, resisted the pretensions of the intendant.

NOTE 69

I find in the reports of the first provincial assembly of Ile de France this assertion, made by the reporter of a committee: 'Hitherto the functions of syndic have been more onerous than honorable, and persons who possessed both means and information suitable to their rank were thus deterred from accepting the office.'

Note referring to various passages in this volume

Feudal rights existing at the time of the revolution, according to the feudal lawyers of the day.

I do not design to write a treatise on feudal rights, or to inquire into their origin. My object is merely to state which of them were still exercised in the eighteenth century. They have played so important a part in subsequent history, and filled so large a place in the imagination of those who have been freed from them, that I have thought it would be curious to ascertain what they really were at the time the Revolution destroyed them. With this view I have studied, first, the *terriers*, or registers of a large number of seigniories, choosing those which were most recent in date in preference to the older ones. Finding that this plan led to no satisfactory results, as the feudal rights, though regulated by the same general system of laws throughout Europe, varied infinitely in matters of detail in the different provinces and cantons, I resolved to pursue a different method, which was this. The feudal rights gave rise to countless lawsuits. These suits involved such questions as, How were these rights acquired? how were they lost? in what did they consist? which of them required to be based on a royal patent? which on a private contract? which on the local custom or long-established practice? how were they valued in case of sale? what sum of money was each class supposed to represent in proportion to the others? All these had been and still were litigated questions, and a school of lawyers had devoted their whole attention to their study. Of these, several wrote during the second half of the eighteenth century, some shortly before the Revolution. They were not jurisconsults, properly so called; they were legal practitioners, whose sole aim was to furnish the profession with rules of practice for a special and unattractive branch of the law. A careful study of these writers throws light on the intricate and confused details of the subject. I subjoin the most succinct analysis that I have been able to make of my work. It is mainly derived from the work of Edme de Freminville, who wrote about 1750, and that of Renauldon, written in 1765, and entitled *Traité Historique et Pratique des Droits Seigneuriaux*.

The *cens* (that is to say, the perpetual rent, in money or produce, which the feudal laws impose on certain possessions) still continues, in the eighteenth century, to modify the condition of many landholders. It is still indivisible; that is to say, when the property which owes the *cens* has been divided, it may be exacted from any one of the owners. It is not subject to prescription. According to some customs, the owner of a property burdened with *cens* cannot sell it without exposing himself to the *retrait censuel*; that is to say, the creditor of the *cens* may take the property by paying the same price as the other purchaser. The custom of Paris ignores this right.

Lods et ventes (mutation-fine). – The general rule, in those parts of France where customary law obtains, is that a mutation-fine is due on every sale of land subject to *cens*: it is a due on the sale which accrues to the seignior. These dues differ in different customs, but they are considerable in all. They exist also in those parts of the country where written law obtains; there they amount to a sixth of the price, and are called *lods*; but the seignior, in these districts, must prove his right. Throughout the country the *cens* creates a privilege for the seignior, in virtue of which he is preferred to all other creditors.

Terrage or *champart, agrier, tasque*. – These are dues in produce which the debtor of the *cens* pays to the seignior; the quantity varies according to custom and private agreement. These dues were often met with during the eighteenth century. I believe that, even where customary law obtained, *terrage* required to be founded on a contract. It was either seigniorial, or connected with the land (*foncier*). It would be superfluous to explain here the signs by which these two kinds were distinguished; suffice it to say that the latter, like ground-rents, was subject to a prescription of thirty years, while the former could never be lost by prescription. Land subject to *terrage* could not be hypothecated without the consent of the seignior.

Bordelage. – This was a due which existed only in Nivernais and Bourbonnais, and consisted in an annual rent payable by all land subject to *cens*, in the shape of money, grain, and poultry. This due entailed very rigorous consequences: the non-payment of it for three years involved the *commise*, or confiscation of the property to the seignior. The rights of property of debtors of *bordelage* were, moreover, inchoate: in certain cases the seignior was entitled to their inheritance, to the exclusion of the rightful heirs. This was the most rigorous of all the dues of the feudal tenure, and its exercise had gradually been restricted to the rural districts; for, as the author says, 'peasants are mules ready to carry any load'.

Marciage was a peculiar right, only exercised in certain places. It consisted in a certain return which was paid by the possessors of property liable to *cens* on the natural death of the seignior.

Enfeoffed tithes. – A large portion of the tithes were still enfeoffed during the eighteenth century. In general, they could only be claimed in virtue of a contract, and did not result from the mere fact of the land being seigniorial.

Parcières were dues levied on the harvest. They bore some resemblance to the *champart* and enfeoffed tithes, and were chiefly in use in Bourbonnais and Auvergne.

Carpot, a due peculiar to Bourbonnais, was to vines what *champart* was to arable land – a right to a portion of the produce. It was one quarter of the vintage.

Serfdom. – Those customs which retain traces of serfdom are called serf customs; they are few in number. In the provinces where they obtain, no lands, or very few indeed, are wholly free from traces of serfdom. (This was written in 1765.) Serfdom, or, as the author terms it, servitude, was either personal or real.

Personal servitude was inherent in the person, and clung to him wherever he went. Wherever he removed his household, the seignior could pursue and seize him. The authors contain several judgments of the courts based on this right. Among them, one, dated 17 June 1760, rejects the claim of a seignior of Nivernais upon the succession of one Pierre Truchet. Truchet was the son of a serf under the custom of Nivernais, who had married a free woman of Paris, and died there. The court rejected the seignior's demand on the ground that Paris was a place of refuge from which serfs could not be recovered. The ground of this judgment shows that the seigniors were entitled to claim the property of their serfs when they died in the seigniory.

Real servitude flowed from the possession of certain land, and could not be got rid of except by removing from the land and residing elsewhere.

Corvées were a right by which the seignior employed his vassals or their cattle for so many days for his benefit. *Corvées* at will, that is to say, at the discretion of the seignior, are wholly abolished. They were long since reduced to so many days' work in the year.

Corvées were either personal or real. Personal *corvées* were due by every labourer living on the seigniory, each working at his own trade. Real *corvées* were attached to the possession of certain lands. Noblemen, ecclesiastics, clergymen, officers of justice, advocates, physicians, notaries, bankers, notables, were exempt from *corvées*. The author quotes a judgment of 13 August 1735, rendered in favour of a notary whose seignior wished to compel him to work for three days in the year in drawing up deeds for the seignior. Also another judgment of 1750, decided that when the *corvée* is to be paid either in money or in labour, the choice rests with the debtor. *Corvées* must be substantiated by a written document. Seigniorial *corvées* had become very rare in the eighteenth century.

Banality. – There are no banal rights in the provinces of Artois, Flanders, and Hainault. The custom of Paris strictly forbids the exercise of this right when it is not founded on a proper title. All who are domiciled in the seigniory are subject to it – men of rank and ecclesiastics even oftener than others.

Independently of the banality of mills and ovens, there are many others:

1st. *Banality of Factory-mills*, such as cloth-mills, cork-mills, hemp-mills. Several customs, among others those of Anjou, Maine, and Touraine, establish this banality.

2nd. *Banality of Wine-presses.* – Very few customs speak of it. That of Lorraine establishes it, as also does that of Maine.

3rd. *Banal Bull.* – No custom alludes to it, but it is established by certain deeds. The same is true of banal butcheries.

Generally speaking, this second class of banalities are rarer and less favourably viewed than the others. They can only be established in virtue of a clear provision of the custom, or, in default of this, by special agreement.

Ban of the Vintage. – This was a police authority, which high justiciary seigniors exercised, without special title, throughout the kingdom during the eighteenth century. It was binding on everyone. The custom of Burgundy gave to the seignior the right of gathering his crop of grapes one day before any other vine-grower.

Right of Banvin. – This right, which, according to the authors, a host of seigniors exercised either in virtue of the custom or under private contracts, entitled them to sell the wine made on their own estates a certain time – usually a month or forty days – before any other vine-grower could send his wine to market. Of the greater customs, those of Tours, Anjou, Maine, and Marche are the only ones which recognize and regulate this right. A judgment of the Court of Aides, bearing date 28 August 1751, permits innkeepers to sell wine during the *banvin*; but this was an exceptional case; they were only allowed to sell to strangers, and the wine sold must have come from the seignior's vineyard. The customs which mention and regulate the right of *banvin* usually require that it be founded on written titles.

Right of Blairie. – This is the right in virtue of which high justiciary seigniors grant permission to the inhabitants of the seigniory to pasture their cattle upon the lands within their jurisdiction, or waste lands. This right does not exist in those districts which are governed by written law; but it is well known within the limits of the various customs. It is found under different names in Bourbonnais, Nivernais, Auvergne, and Burgundy. It rests on the assumption that the property of all the land was originally in the seignior, and that, after having distributed the best portions in feuds, copyholds (*censives*), and other concessions, for specific rents, he is still at liberty to grant the temporary use of those lands which are only fit for pasture. *Blairie* is established by several customs; but no one can claim it but a high justiciary, and he must be able to show either a positive title to it, or old acknowledgments of its existence, fortified by long usage.

Tolls. – Originally, say the authors, there existed a vast number of seigniorial tolls on bridges, rivers, and roads. Louis XIV abolished many of them. In 1724, a commission appointed to inquire into the subject abolished twelve hundred of them; and in 1765 they were still being reduced. The first principle in this matter, says Renauldon, is that a toll, being a tax, must not only be established in virtue of a title, but that title must emanate from the crown. The toll is mentioned as being *de par le roi*. One of the conditions of tolls is that there must be attached to them a tariff of the rates which all merchandise must pay. This tariff must always be approved by an Order in Council. The title, says the author, must be confirmed by uninterrupted possession. Notwithstanding the precautions taken by the legislator, the value of some tolls has largely increased of late years. I know a toll, he adds, which was farmed out for 100 *livres* a century since, and which now brings in 1400; another, farmed out for 39,000 *livres*, now produces 90,000. The chief ordinances and edicts regulating tolls are the 29th title of the ordinance of 1669, and the edicts of 1683, 1693, 1724, and 1775.

The authors whom I quote, though rather prepossessed, in general, in favour of feudal rights, acknowledge that great abuses are practised in the collection of tolls.

Ferries. – The right of ferry differs sensibly from the right of tolls. The latter is levied on merchandise only; the former on persons, cattle, and vehicles. This right cannot be exercised without the king's sanction, and the tariff of rates charged must be included in the Order in Council authorizing or establishing the ferry.

The Right of Leyde (its name varies in different places) is an impost on merchandise sent to fairs or markets. The lawyers I am quoting say that many seigniors erroneously consider this a right appurtenant to high justice, and purely seigniorial; whereas it is a tax which requires the sanction of the king. At any rate, the right can only be exercised by a high justiciary, who receives the fines levied in virtue thereof. And it appears that though theoretically the right of *leyde* could not be exercised except by grant from the king, it was often in part exercised in virtue of a feudal title and long usage.

It is certain that fairs could only be established by authorization of the king.

Seigniors need no specific title or royal grant to regulate the weights and measures that are to be used in the seigniory. It suffices that the right is founded on the custom or long continued usage. The authors say that all the attempts that have been made by the kings to introduce a uniform standard of weights and measures have been failures. No progress has been made in this matter since the customs were drawn up.

Roads. – Rights exercised by the seigniors over the roads.

The highways, which are called the king's roads, belong wholly to the crown. Their establishment, their repairs, crimes committed upon them, are not within the jurisdiction of the seigniors or their judges; but all private roads within the limits of a seigniory belong, without doubt, to the high justiciary. They have entire control over them, and all crimes committed thereon, except cases reserved to the king, are within the jurisdiction of the seigniorial judges. Formerly the seigniors were expected to keep in repair the high roads which traversed their seigniory, and rights of toll, boundary, and *traverse* were granted them by way of indemnity; but the king has since taken the direction of all highways.

Rivers. – All rivers navigable for boats or rafts belong to the king, though they traverse seigniories, any title to the contrary notwithstanding (ordinance of 1669). Any rights which the seigniors may exercise on these rivers – rights of fishing, establishing mills or bridges, or levying tolls – must have been acquired by grant from the king. Some seigniors claim civil or police jurisdiction over these rivers; but any such rights have been usurped or obtained by fraudulent grants.

Small rivers undoubtedly belong to the seigniors whose domain they traverse. They have the same rights of property, jurisdiction, and police, as the king has over navigable rivers. All high justiciaries are universal seigniors of non-navigable rivers flowing through their territory. They need no better title to establish their right of property than the fact of their existence as high justiciaries. Some customs, such as that of Berri, authorize individuals to erect mills on seigniorial rivers flowing through their property without permission from the seignior. The custom of Bretagne granted this right to noblemen. Generally, the law restricts to the high justiciary the right of granting permission to build mills within his jurisdiction. Even traverses cannot be made upon a seigniorial river, for the protection of a farm, without permission from the seigniorial judges.

Fountains, Pumps, Retting-tanks, Ponds. – Rain falling upon the highway belongs exclusively to the high justiciary, who alone can make use of it. He can make a pond in any part of his jurisdiction, even on the property of his tenants, by paying them for the land that is submerged. This rule is distinctly laid down by several customs; among others, by those of Troyes and Nivernais. Private individuals can only have ponds on their own land; and even for this, according to several customs, they must obtain leave from the seignior. The customs which require leave to be asked of the seignior forbid his selling permission.

Fishery. – The right of fishery in rivers navigable for boats or rafts belongs to the king. He alone can grant it. His judges have sole cognizance of infractions of the fishery laws. Many seigniors, however, enjoy rights of fishery on these rivers, but they have either usurped them or hold them by special grant from the king. As for non-navigable rivers, it is forbidden to fish therein, even with line, without the leave of the high justiciary in whose domain they flow. A judgment of 30 April

1749, condemned a fisherman on this rule. Seigniors themselves must obey the general regulations regarding fisheries in fishing in these rivers. The high justiciary may grant the right of fishing in his river, either as a feud, or for a yearly *cens*.

Hunting. – The right of hunting cannot be farmed out like the right of fishery. It is a personal right. It is held to be a royal right, which even men of rank cannot exercise within their own jurisdiction, or on their own feud, without the king's permission. This doctrine is laid down in the 30th title of the ordinance of 1669. The seigniorial judges are competent to sit in all cases relative to hunting, except those which refer to the chase of *red* beasts (these are, I imagine, large game, such as stags and deer), which must be left to the royal courts.

The right of hunting is, of all seigniorial rights, the one most carefully withheld from commoners; even the *franc-aleu roturier* does not carry it. The king does not grant it in his pleasures. So strict is the principle, that a seignior cannot grant leave to hunt. That is the law. But in practice seigniors constantly grant permission to hunt, not only to men of rank but to commoners. High justiciaries may hunt throughout the limits of their jurisdiction, but they must be alone. Within these limits they are entitled to make all regulations, prohibitions, and ordinances regulating hunting. All feudal seigniors, even without justiciary rights, may hunt within their feud. Men of rank, who have neither feud nor justiciary rights, may hunt upon the lands adjoining their residences. It has been held that a commoner who owns a park within the limits of a high justice must keep it open for the pleasures of the seignior; but the judgment is old; it dates from 1668.

Warrens. – None can now be established without a title. Commoners can establish warrens as well as noblemen, but none but men of rank can have forests.

Pigeon-houses. – Certain customs restrict the right of having pigeon-houses to high justiciaries; others grant it to all owners of feuds. In Dauphiné, Brittany, and Normandy, no commoner can own a pigeon-house; no one but a noble can keep pigeons. Most severe punishments, often corporal, were inflicted on those who killed pigeons.

Such are, according to the authors quoted, the chief feudal rights exacted during the latter half of the eighteenth century. They add that 'these rights are generally established. There are a host of others, less known and less extended, which exist only in certain customs or in certain seigniories in virtue of special titles'. These rare or restricted rights which the authors enumerate number ninety-nine. Most of them weigh upon agriculture, being dues to the seignior on harvests, or on the sale or transport of produce. The authors say that many of these rights were disused in their time. I fancy, however, that several of them must have been enforced in some places as late as 1789.

Having ascertained from the feudal lawyers of the eighteenth century what feudal rights were still enforced, I wished to ascertain what pecuniary value was set upon them by the men of that day.

One of the authors I have quoted, Renauldon, furnishes the requisite information. He gives a set of rules for legal functionaries to follow in appraising in inventories the various feudal rights which existed in 1765, that is to say, twenty-four years before the Revolution. They are as follows:

Rights of Jurisdiction. – He says, 'Some of our customs value the right of jurisdiction, high, low, and middle (*justice haute, basse, et moyenne*), at one tenth of the revenue of the land. Seigniorial jurisdictions were then highly important. Edme de Treminville thinks that, in our day, jurisdiction should not be valued higher than a twentieth of the income of the land. I think even this valuation too high.'

Honorary Rights. – Though these rights are not easily appreciated in money, our author, who is a practical man, and not easily imposed upon by appearances, advises the appraisers to value them at a very small sum.

Seigniorial Corvées. – The author supplies rules for the valuation of *corvées*, which shows that they were still occasionally enforced. He values the day's work of an ox at 20 *sous*, and that of a man at 5 *sous*, besides his food. This is a fair indication of the wages paid at the time.

Tolls. – With regard to the valuation of tolls, the author says: 'No seigniorial rights should be valued at a lower rate than these tolls. They are very fluctuating; and now that the king and the provinces have taken charge of the roads and bridges which are of most use to trade, many tolls have become useless, and they are being abolished daily.'

Right of Fishing and Hunting. – The right of fishery may be farmed out and regularly appraised. The right of hunting cannot be farmed out, being a personal right. It is, therefore an honorary, not a productive right, and cannot be estimated in money.

The author then proceeds to speak of the rights of banality, *banvin, leyde, blairie*, and the space he devotes to them shows that they were the most frequently exercised and the most important of the surviving feudal rights. He adds: 'There are, besides, a number of other seigniorial rights, which are met with from time to time, but it would be tedious and even impossible to enumerate them here. In the examples we have given, appraisers will find rules to guide them in estimating the rights which we have not specially valued.'

Valuation of the Cens. – Most of the customs say that the *cens* must be valued at rather more than 3³/₁₀ per cent. This high valuation is due to the fact that the *cens* carries with it various casual benefits, such as mutation-fines.

Enfeoffed Tithes, Terrage. – Enfeoffed tithes cannot be valued at less than four per cent., as they involve no care, labour, or expense. When the *terrage* or *champart* carries with it mutation-fines to the seignior, this casualty must settle the value at 3³/₁₀ per cent., otherwise it must be valued like the tithes.

Ground-rents, bearing no mutation-fines or right of redemption – that is to say, which are not seigniorial – must be valued at five per cent.

Estimate of the various tenures in use in France before the Revolution.

We only know in France, says the author, three kinds of real estate:
1st. The *franc-aleu*, which is a freehold, exempt from all burdens, and subject to no seigniorial dues or rights, either beneficial or honorary.

Francs-aleux are either noble or common (*roturiers*). Noble *francs-aleux* carry with them a right of jurisdiction, or they have feuds or lands held by *cens* depending on them. They are divided according to feudal law. Common *Francs-aleux* have no jurisdiction, or feuds, or lands held by *cens*. They are divided according to the ordinary rules (*roturière-ment*). The author considers that the holders of *francs-aleux* are the only landholders who enjoy a complete right of property.

The *franc-aleu* was valued higher than any other kind of tenure. The customs of Auvergne and Burgundy valued it 2½ per cent. The author thinks that 3⅓ per cent. would be a better valuation.

It must be noticed that common *francs-aleux*, existing within the limits of a seigniorial jurisdiction, were dependent thereon. It was not a sign of subjection to the seignior, but an acknowledgment of the jurisdiction of courts which took the place of the royal tribunals.

2nd. Lands held by feudal tenure (*à fief*).

3rd. Lands paying *cens*, or, as they are here called in law, *rotures*.

The valuation of lands held by feudal tenure was the lower in proportion to the feudal burdens laid upon them. In some customs, and in that part of the country which was governed by written law, feuds paid nothing but '*la bouche et les mains*', that is to say, feudal homage. In other customs, such as Burgundy, feuds not only owed homage, but were what was called *de danger*; that is to say, they were liable to *commise*, or feudal confiscation, when the owner took possession of them without having rendered 'fealty and homage'. Other customs, such as that of Paris, for instance, and many more, declared feuds subject not only to fealty and homage, but likewise to re-emption, *quint* and *requint*. Others again, such as that of Poitou and some others, burdened them with a fine on the oath of fealty (*chambellage*), and service on horseback, etc.

The first class of feuds must be valued higher than the others. The custom of Paris set them down at five per cent., which the author thinks very reasonable.

To arrive at a valuation of lands held *en roture* and those subject to *cens*, they must be divided into three clases:

1st. Lands paying the mere *cens*.

2nd. Lands liable not only to *cens*, but to other burdens.

3rd. Lands mainmortable, subject to real taille, to *bordelage*.

The first two classes of lands *en roture* were common enough in the eighteenth century. The third was rare. The first, says the author, must be valued higher than the second, the second than the third. Indeed, landholders of the third class can hardly be called owners, in the strict sense of the word, as they cannot alienate their property without leave from the seignior.

Terriers. – The feudal lawyers I have quoted furnish the following rules for drawing up or renewing the seigniorial registers called *terriers*, which I have mentioned in the text. The *terrier*, as is known, was a great register, in which all the deeds establishing right belonging to the seigniory, whether beneficial or honorary, real, personal, or mixed, were entered at length. It contained all the declarations of the copyholders, the customs of the seigniory, quit-rent leases, etc. In the custom of Paris, the authors say that seigniors may renew their *terriers* every thirty years at the expense of the copyholders. They add, however, that 'one is fortunate to find a fresh one every century'. The *terrier* could not be renewed (it was a troublesome formality for all those who held under the seignior) without obtaining an authorization which was called *lettres à terrier*. When the seigniory was within the jurisdiction of several Parliaments, this was obtained from the high chancellor; in other cases it was procured from the Parliament. The court named the notary, before whom all vassals, noblemen and commoners, copyholders, emphyteutic lessees, and persons amenable to the seigniorial jurisdiction, were bound to appear. A plan of the seigniory was required to be attached to the *terrier*.

Besides the *terriers*, there were kept in each seigniory other registers called *lièves*, in which the seigniors or their stewards entered the sums they had received from their copyholders, with their names, and the dates of the payments.